VBA for Microsoft
Office 2013

BRIEF

SERIES

(ex•ploring)

1. Investigating in a systematic way: examining. 2. Searching into or ranging over for the purpose of discovery.

VBA for Microsoft Office 2013

BRIEF

Mary Anne Poatsy

Keith Mulbery and Jason Davidson

Series Created by Dr. Robert T. Grauer

PEARSON

Boston   Columbus   Indianapolis   New York   San Francisco   Hoboken
Amsterdam   Cape Town   Dubai   London   Madrid   Milan   Munich   Paris   Montréal   Toronto
Delhi   Mexico City   São Paulo   Sydney   Hong Kong   Seoul   Singapore   Taipei   Tokyo

Vice President of Career Skills: Andrew Gilfillan
Senior Editor: Samantha McAfee Lewis
Team Lead, Project Management: Laura Burgess
Project Manager: Laura Karahalis
Program Manager: Natacha Moore
Development Editor: Nancy Lamm
Editorial Assistant: Victoria Lasavath
Director of Product Marketing: Maggie Waples
Director of Field Marketing: Leigh Ann Sims
Product Marketing Manager: Kaylee Carlson
Field Marketing Managers: Brad Forrester & Joanna Sabella

Marketing Coordinator: Susan Osterlitz
Senior Operations Specialist: Maura Zaldivar
Senior Art Director: Diane Ernsberger
Interior and Cover Design: Diane Ernsberger
Cover Photo: Courtesy of Shutterstock® Images
Associate Director of Design: Blair Brown
Digital Media Editor: Eric Hakanson
Director of Media Development: Taylor Ragan
Media Project Manager, Production: John Cassar
Full-Service Project Management: Jenna Vittorioso, Lumina Datamatics, Inc.
Composition: Lumina Datamatics, Inc.

Credits and acknowledgments borrowed from other sources and reproduced, with permission, in this textbook appear on the appropriate page within text.

Many of the designations by manufacturers and sellers to distinguish their products are claimed as trademarks. Where those designations appear in this book, and the publisher was aware of a trademark claim, the designations have been printed in initial caps or all caps.

Library of Congress Control Number: 2014943830

10 9 8 7 6 5 4 3 2 1

ISBN-10:   0-13-342816-8
ISBN-13: 978-0-13-342816-2

Dedications

I dedicate this book in memory to Grandpa Herman Hort, who dedicated his life to his family and to the education field as a teacher and administrator. He inspired a daughter and several grandchildren to become passionate educators and provide quality curriculum to students.

Keith Mulbery

I dedicate this book to my mother, Valerie Davidson. A loving, resilient, charismatic force of nature. I couldn't have asked for a better parent. I never could have made it without you. Thank you for your unyielding faith in me! I will always strive to make you proud.

Jason Davidson

For my husband Ted, who unselfishly continues to take on more than his share to support me throughout the process; and for my children, Laura, Carolyn, and Teddy, whose encouragement and love have been inspiring.

Mary Anne Poatsy

About the Authors

Dr. Keith Mulbery

Dr. Keith Mulbery is the Department Chair and a Professor in the Information Systems and Technology Department at Utah Valley University (UVU), where he currently teaches systems analysis and design, and global and ethical issues in information systems and technology. He has also taught computer applications, C# programming, and management information systems. Keith served as Interim Associate Dean, School of Computing, in the College of Technology and Computing at UVU.

Keith received the Utah Valley State College Board of Trustees Award of Excellence in 2001, School of Technology and Computing Scholar Award in 2007, School of Technology and Computing Teaching Award in 2008, and the College of Technology and Computing Faculty Excellence Award in 2013. In addition, Keith received the Utah Business Education Association Distinguished Post-Secondary CTE Business Teacher of the Year Award for 2013–2014. He has authored more than 17 textbooks, served as Series Editor for the Exploring Office 2007 series, and served as developmental editor on two textbooks for the Essentials Office 2000 series. He is frequently asked to give presentations and workshops on Microsoft Office Excel at various education conferences.

Keith earned his B.S. and M.Ed. in Business Education from Southwestern Oklahoma State University and earned his Ph.D. in Education with an emphasis in Business Information Systems at Utah State University. His dissertation topic was computer-assisted instruction using Prentice Hall's Train and Assess IT program (the predecessor to MyITLab) to supplement traditional instruction in basic computer proficiency courses.

Jason Davidson

Jason Davidson is a faculty member in the College of Business at Butler University, where he teaches Advanced Web Design, Data Networks, Data Analysis and Business Modeling, and introductory MIS courses. He is the co-author of Exploring Microsoft Excel 2013 Comprehensive, Exploring Microsoft Office 2013, Volume 2, and Exploring Microsoft Office 2013, Plus.

With a background in media development, prior to joining the faculty at Butler, he worked in the technical publishing industry. Along with teaching, he currently serves as an IT consultant for regional businesses in the Indianapolis area. He holds a B.A. in Telecommunication Arts from Butler University and an M.B.A. from Morehead State University. He lives in Indianapolis, Indiana, and in his free time, enjoys road biking, photography, and spending time with his family.

Mary Anne Poatsy, Series Editor

Mary Anne is a senior faculty member at Montgomery County Community College, teaching various computer applications and concepts courses in face-to-face and online environments. She holds a B.A. in psychology and education from Mount Holyoke College and an M.B.A. in finance from Northwestern University's Kellogg Graduate School of Management.

Mary Anne has more than 12 years of educational experience. She is currently adjunct faculty at Gwynedd-Mercy College and Montgomery County Community College. She has also taught at Bucks County Community College and Muhlenberg College, as well as conducted personal training. Before teaching, she was vice president at Shearson Lehman in the Municipal Bond Investment Banking Department.

Dr. Robert T. Grauer, Creator of the Exploring Series

Bob Grauer is an associate professor in the Department of Computer Information Systems at the University of Miami, where he is a multiple winner of the Outstanding Teaching Award in the School of Business, most recently in 2009. He has written numerous COBOL texts and is the vision behind the Exploring Office series, with more than three million books in print. His work has been translated into three foreign languages and is used in all aspects of higher education at both national and international levels. Bob Grauer has consulted for several major corporations including IBM and American Express. He received his Ph.D. in Operations Research in 1972 from the Polytechnic Institute of Brooklyn.

Contents

VBA for Microsoft Office 2013, brief

Acknowledgments

The Exploring team would like to acknowledge and thank all the reviewers who helped us throughout the years by providing us with their invaluable comments, suggestions, and constructive criticism.

We'd like to especially thank our Focus Group attendees and User Diary Reviewers for this edition:

Stephen Z. Jourdan
Auburn University at Montgomery

Ann Rovetto
Horry-Georgetown Technical College

Jacqueline D. Lawson
Henry Ford Community College

Diane L. Smith
Henry Ford Community College

Sven Aelterman
Troy University

Suzanne M. Jeska
County College of Morris

Susan N. Dozier
Tidewater Community College

Robert G. Phipps Jr.
West Virginia University

Mike Michaelson
Palomar College

Mary Beth Tarver
Northwestern State University

Alexandre C. Probst
Colorado Christian University

Phil Nielson
Salt Lake Community College

Carolyn Barren
Macomb Community College

Sue A. McCrory
Missouri State University

Lucy Parakhovnik
California State University, Northridge

Jakie Brown Jr.
Stevenson University

Craig J. Peterson
American InterContinental University

Terry Ray Rigsby
Hill College

Biswadip Ghosh
Metropolitan State University of Denver

Cheryl Sypniewski
Macomb Community College

Lynn Keane
University of South Carolina

Sheila Gionfriddo
Luzerne College

Dick Hewer
Ferris State College

Carolyn Borne
Louisiana State University

Sumathy Chandrashekar
Salisbury University

Laura Marcoulides
Fullerton College

Don Riggs
SUNY Schenectady County Community College

Gary McFall
Purdue University

James Powers
University of Southern Indiana

James Brown
Central Washington University

Brian Powell
West Virginia University

Sherry Lenhart
Terra Community College

Chen Zhang
Bryant University

Nikia Robinson
Indian River State University

Jill Young
Southeast Missouri State University

Debra Hoffman
Southeast Missouri State University

Tommy Lu
Delaware Technical Community College

Mimi Spain
Southern Maine Community College

We'd like to thank everyone who has been involved in reviewing and providing their feedback, including for our previous editions:

Adriana Lumpkin
Midland College

Alan S. Abrahams
Virginia Tech

Ali Berrached
University of Houston–Downtown

Allen Alexander
Delaware Technical & Community College

Andrea Marchese
Maritime College, State University of New York

Andrew Blitz
Broward College; Edison State College

Angel Norman
University of Tennessee, Knoxville

Angela Clark
University of South Alabama

Ann Rovetto
Horry-Georgetown Technical College

Astrid Todd
Guilford Technical Community College

Audrey Gillant
Maritime College, State University of New York

Barbara Stover
Marion Technical College

Barbara Tollinger
Sinclair Community College

Ben Brahim Taha
Auburn University

Beverly Amer
Northern Arizona University

Beverly Fite
Amarillo College

Bonita Volker
Tidewater Community College

Bonnie Homan
San Francisco State University

Brad West
Sinclair Community College

Brian Powell
West Virginia University

Carol Buser
Owens Community College

Carol Roberts
University of Maine

Carolyn Barren
Macomb Community College

Cathy Poyner
Truman State University

Charles Hodgson
Delgado Community College

Cheri Higgins
Illinois State University

Cheryl Hinds
Norfolk State University

Chris Robinson
Northwest State Community College

Cindy Herbert
Metropolitan Community College–Longview

Dana Hooper
University of Alabama

Dana Johnson
North Dakota State University

Daniela Marghitu
Auburn University

David Noel
University of Central Oklahoma

David Pulis
Maritime College, State University of New York

David Thornton
Jacksonville State University

Dawn Medlin
Appalachian State University

Debby Keen
University of Kentucky

Debra Chapman
University of South Alabama

Derrick Huang
Florida Atlantic University

Diana Baran
Henry Ford Community College

Diane Cassidy
The University of North Carolina at Charlotte

Diane Smith
Henry Ford Community College

Don Danner
San Francisco State University

Don Hoggan
Solano College

Doncho Petkov
Eastern Connecticut State University

Donna Ehrhart
State University of New York at Brockport

Elaine Crable
Xavier University

Elizabeth Duett
Delgado Community College

Erhan Uskup
Houston Community College–Northwest

Eric Martin
University of Tennessee

Erika Nadas
Wilbur Wright College

Floyd Winters
Manatee Community College

Frank Lucente
Westmoreland County Community College

G. Jan Wilms
Union University

Gail Cope
Sinclair Community College

Gary DeLorenzo
California University of Pennsylvania

Gary Garrison
Belmont University

George Cassidy
Sussex County Community College

Gerald Braun
Xavier University

Gerald Burgess
Western New Mexico University

Gladys Swindler
Fort Hays State University

Heith Hennel
Valencia Community College

Henry Rudzinski
Central Connecticut State University

Irene Joos
La Roche College

Iwona Rusin
Baker College; Davenport University

J. Roberto Guzman
San Diego Mesa College

Jan Wilms
Union University

Jane Stam
Onondaga Community College

Janet Bringhurst
Utah State University

Jeanette Dix
Ivy Tech Community College

Jennifer Day
Sinclair Community College

Jill Canine
Ivy Tech Community College

Jim Chaffee
The University of Iowa Tippie College of Business

Joanne Lazirko
University of Wisconsin–Milwaukee

Jodi Milliner
Kansas State University

John Hollenbeck
Blue Ridge Community College

John Seydel
Arkansas State University

Judith A. Scheeren
Westmoreland County Community College

Judith Brown
The University of Memphis

Juliana Cypert
Tarrant County College

Kamaljeet Sanghera
George Mason University

Karen Priestly
Northern Virginia Community College

Karen Ravan
Spartanburg Community College

Kathleen Brenan
Ashland University

Ken Busbee
Houston Community College

Kent Foster
Winthrop University

Kevin Anderson
Solano Community College

Kim Wright
The University of Alabama

Kristen Hockman
University of Missouri–Columbia

Kristi Smith
Allegany College of Maryland

Laura McManamon
University of Dayton

Leanne Chun
Leeward Community College

Lee McClain
Western Washington University

Linda D. Collins
Mesa Community College

Linda Johnsonius
Murray State University

Linda Lau
Longwood University

Linda Theus
Jackson State Community College

Linda Williams
Marion Technical College

Lisa Miller
University of Central Oklahoma

Lister Horn
Pensacola Junior College

Lixin Tao
Pace University

Loraine Miller
Cayuga Community College

Lori Kielty
Central Florida Community College

Lorna Wells
Salt Lake Community College

Lorraine Sauchin
Duquesne University

Lucy Parakhovnik (Parker)
California State University, Northridge

Lynn Mancini
Delaware Technical Community College

Mackinzee Escamilla
South Plains College

Marcia Welch
Highline Community College

Margaret McManus
Northwest Florida State College

Margaret Warrick
Allan Hancock College

Marilyn Hibbert
Salt Lake Community College

Mark Choman
Luzerne County Community College

Mary Duncan
University of Missouri–St. Louis

Melissa Nemeth
Indiana University-Purdue University
Indianapolis

Melody Alexander
Ball State University

Michael Douglas
University of Arkansas at Little Rock

Michael Dunklebarger
Alamance Community College

Michael G. Skaff
College of the Sequoias

Michele Budnovitch
Pennsylvania College of Technology

Mike Jochen
East Stroudsburg University

Mike Scroggins
Missouri State University

Muhammed Badamas
Morgan State University

NaLisa Brown
University of the Ozarks

Nancy Grant
Community College of Allegheny
County–South Campus

Nanette Lareau
University of Arkansas Community
College–Morrilton

Pam Brune
Chattanooga State Community College

Pam Uhlenkamp
Iowa Central Community College

Patrick Smith
Marshall Community and Technical College

Paul Addison
Ivy Tech Community College

Paula Ruby
Arkansas State University

Peggy Burrus
Red Rocks Community College

Peter Ross
SUNY Albany

Philip H. Nielson
Salt Lake Community College

Ralph Hooper
University of Alabama

Ranette Halverson
Midwestern State University

Richard Blamer
John Carroll University

Richard Cacace
Pensacola Junior College

Richard Hewer
Ferris State University

Rob Murray
Ivy Tech Community College

Robert Dušek
Northern Virginia Community College

Robert Sindt
Johnson County Community College

Robert Warren
Delgado Community College

Rocky Belcher
Sinclair Community College

Roger Pick
University of Missouri at Kansas City

Ronnie Creel
Troy University

Rosalie Westerberg
Clover Park Technical College

Ruth Neal
Navarro College

Sandra Thomas
Troy University

Sheila Gionfriddo
Luzerne County Community College

Sherrie Geitgey
Northwest State Community College

Sophia Wilberscheid
Indian River State College

Sophie Lee
California State University,
Long Beach

Stacy Johnson
Iowa Central Community College

Stephanie Kramer
Northwest State Community College

Stephen Jourdan
Auburn University Montgomery

Steven Schwarz
Raritan Valley Community College

Sue McCrory
Missouri State University

Susan Fuschetto
Cerritos College

Susan Medlin
UNC Charlotte

Suzan Spitzberg
Oakton Community College

Sven Aelterman
Troy University

Sylvia Brown
Midland College

Tanya Patrick
Clackamas Community College

Terri Holly
Indian River State College

Thomas Rienzo
Western Michigan University

Tina Johnson
Midwestern State University

Tommy Lu
Delaware Technical and Community College

Troy S. Cash
Northwest Arkansas Community College

Vicki Robertson
Southwest Tennessee Community

Weifeng Chen
California University of Pennsylvania

Wes Anthony
Houston Community College

William Ayen
University of Colorado at Colorado Springs

Wilma Andrews
Virginia Commonwealth University

Yvonne Galusha
University of Iowa

VBA for Office 2010 Reviewer:
Brian Kovar
Kansas State University

Special thanks to our development and technical team:

Nancy Lamm

Julie Boyles

Lisa Bucki

Janet Pickard

Elizabeth Lockley

Heather Hetzler

Preface

The Exploring Series and You

Exploring is Pearson's Office Application series that requires students like you to think "beyond the point and click." In this edition, we have worked to restructure the Exploring experience around the way you, today's modern student, actually use your resources.

The goal of Exploring is, as it has always been, to go further than teaching just the steps to accomplish a task—the series provides the theoretical foundation for you to understand when and why to apply a skill.

As a result, you achieve a deeper understanding of each application and can apply this critical thinking beyond Office and the classroom.

You are practical students, focused on what you need to do to be successful in this course and beyond, and want to be as efficient as possible. Exploring has evolved to meet you where you are and help you achieve success efficiently. Pearson has paid attention to the habits of students today, how you get information, how you are motivated to do well in class, and what your future goals look like. We asked you and your peers for acceptance of new tools we designed to address these points, and you responded with a resounding "YES!"

Here Is What We Learned About You

You are goal-oriented. You want a good grade in this course—so we rethought how Exploring works so that you can learn the how and why behind the skills in this course to be successful now. You also want to be successful in your future career—so we used motivating case studies to show relevance of these skills to your future careers and incorporated Soft Skills, Collaboration, and Analysis Cases in this edition to set you up for success in the future.

You read, prepare, and study differently than students used to. You use textbooks like a tool—you want to easily identify what you need to know and learn it efficiently. We have added key features such as Step Icons, Hands-On Exercise Videos, and tracked everything via page numbers that allow you to navigate the content efficiently, making the concepts accessible and creating a map to success for you to follow.

You go to college now with a different set of skills than students did five years ago. The new edition of Exploring moves you beyond the basics of the software at a faster pace, without sacrificing coverage of the fundamental skills that you need to know. This ensures that you will be engaged from page 1 to the end of the book.

You and your peers have diverse learning styles. With this in mind, we broadened our definition of "student resources" to include Compass, an online skill database; movable Student Reference cards; Hands-On Exercise videos to provide a secondary lecture-like option of review; Soft Skills video exercises to illustrate important non-technical skills; and the most powerful online homework and assessment tool around with a direct 1:1 content match with the Exploring Series, MyITLab. Exploring will be accessible to all students, regardless of learning style.

Providing You with a Map to Success to Move Beyond the Point and Click

All of these changes and additions will provide you with an easy and efficient path to follow to be successful in this course, regardless of your learning style or any existing knowledge you have at the outset. Our goal is to keep you more engaged in both the hands-on and conceptual sides, helping you to achieve a higher level of understanding that will guarantee you success in this course and in your future career. In addition to the vision and experience of the series creator, Robert T. Grauer, we have assembled a tremendously talented team of Office Applications authors who have devoted themselves to teaching you the ins and outs of Microsoft Word, Excel, Access, and PowerPoint. Led in this edition by series editor Mary Anne Poatsy, the whole team is equally dedicated to providing you with a **map to success** to support the Exploring mission of **moving you beyond the point and click.**

Key Features

- **White Pages/Yellow Pages** clearly distinguish the theory (white pages) from the skills covered in the Hands-On Exercises (yellow pages) so students always know what they are supposed to be doing.

- **Enhanced Objective Mapping** enables students to follow a directed path through each chapter, from the objectives list at the chapter opener through the exercises in the end of chapter.
  - **Objectives List:** This provides a simple list of key objectives covered in the chapter. This includes page numbers so students can skip between objectives where they feel they need the most help.
  - **Step Icons:** These icons appear in the white pages and reference the step numbers in the Hands-On Exercises, providing a correlation between the two so students can easily find conceptual help when they are working hands-on and need a refresher.
  - **Quick Concepts Check:** A series of questions that appear briefly at the end of each white page section. These questions cover the most essential concepts in the white pages required for students to be successful in working the Hands-On Exercises. Page numbers are included for easy reference to help students locate the answers.
  - **Chapter Objectives Review:** Appears toward the end of the chapter and reviews all important concepts throughout the chapter. Newly designed in an easy-to-read bulleted format.

- **Key Terms Matching:** A new exercise that requires students to match key terms to their definitions. This requires students to work actively with this important vocabulary and prove conceptual understanding.

- **Case Study** presents a scenario for the chapter, creating a story that ties the Hands-On Exercises together.

- **End-of-Chapter Exercises** offer instructors several options for assessment. Each chapter has approximately 12–15 exercises ranging from multiple choice questions to open-ended projects. Newly included in this is a Key Terms Matching exercise of approximately 20 questions, as well as a Collaboration Case for every chapter.

- **Enhanced Mid-Level Exercises** include a **Creative Case** (for PowerPoint and Word), which allows students some flexibility and creativity, not being bound by a definitive solution, and an **Analysis Case** (for Excel and Access), which requires students to interpret the data they are using to answer an analytic question, as well as **Discover Steps**, which encourage students to use Help or to problem-solve to accomplish a task.

Instructor Resources

The Instructor's Resource Center, available at www.pearsonhighered.com, includes the following:

- **Instructor Manual** provides an overview of all available resources as well as student data and solution files for every exercise.

- **Solution Files with Scorecards** assist with grading the Hands-On Exercises and end-of-chapter exercises.

- **Prepared Exams** allow instructors to assess all skills covered in a chapter with a single project.

- **Rubrics** for Mid-Level Creative Cases and Beyond the Classroom Cases in Microsoft Word format enable instructors to customize the assignments for their classes.

- **PowerPoint Presentations** with notes for each chapter are included for out-of-class study or review.

- **Objectives Lists** map chapter objectives to Hands-On Exercises and end-of-chapter exercises.

- **Multiple Choice, Key Terms Matching, and Quick Concepts Check Answer Keys**

- **Test Bank** provides objective-based questions for every chapter.

- **Syllabus Templates**

- **Scripted Lectures** offer an in-class lecture guide for instructors to mirror the Hands-On-Exercises.

Student Resources

Companion Web Site

www.pearsonhighered.com/exploring offers expanded IT resources and self-student tools for students to use for each chapter, including:

- Online Chapter Review

- Glossary

- Chapter Objectives Review

Getting Started with VBA

OBJECTIVES | AFTER YOU READ THIS CHAPTER, YOU WILL BE ABLE TO:

1. Use VBA and get help p. 2
2. Identify code in the Code window p. 5
3. Create, run, and debug a procedure p. 8
4. Create a message box p. 9
5. Declare and use variables and constants p. 20
6. Create an input box p. 25
7. Perform calculations p. 27
8. Use decision structures p. 37
9. Perform data validation p. 42
10. Use logical operators p. 43
11. Use the For…Next structure p. 51
12. Use the Do…Loop structure p. 52

CASE STUDY | ACME Consulting

ACME has four regional offices that are located in different geographical regions of the United States: the East, Midwest, Rocky Mountains, and West. ACME consultants are located in cities throughout the regions, and each employee reports to the closest regional office. ACME stores a lot of important company data in Microsoft Excel workbooks and Microsoft Access databases. In particular, the head financial officer, Tina McAfee, stores customer loan information in Excel workbooks, and her assistant, Anthony Trujilo, stores employee payroll in an Access database.

During the past six months, you helped other ACME managers automate tasks with macros in Excel and Access. Because of this experience, Tina and Anthony have asked you to help them automate additional files using Visual Basic for Applications. Although you have limited programming experience, you have studied macro syntax (rules that you must follow for constructing code).

Introduction to VBA

Visual Basic for Applications (VBA) is a programming language that you can use to create and customize Office applications to enhance their functionality. VBA—which is included with Microsoft Office 2013—is a subset of Visual Basic, a stand-alone robust programming language that is part of Visual Studio. Programmers use Visual Basic to create Windows and Web-based applications. Unlike Visual Basic, VBA requires a host application, such as Excel or Access.

You can use VBA to customize Excel workbooks or to enhance Access database objects. For example, you might want to modify a command button for exiting an Access database so that the user has an opportunity to cancel the procedure if he or she clicks the button by mistake. You can use VBA to create data entry forms, add custom menus, and hide or display interface elements depending upon user access. Office developers also use VBA to create custom functions, perform calculations using variables and constants, and process database records.

In this section, you will use the VBA interface and identify types of code in the Code window. You will learn then how to create, run, and debug a procedure. Finally, you will learn how to display message boxes.

Using VBA and Getting Help

When you record a macro in Excel, Excel generates VBA code for the actions you take, such as changing margins and clearing cell contents. When you use a wizard to create an Access control, such as a command button, Access creates the VBA code to provide functionality for actions, such as clicking the button. If you have created macros in a Microsoft Office program, you might have had to edit the macro code to add functionality to the macro or correct an error. To modify macros, you use VBA.

STEP 1

Table 1.1 lists the different ways you can launch VBA in Excel and Access.

TABLE 1.1 Launch VBA	
Excel	**Access**
1. Click the DEVELOPER tab*. 2. Click Visual Basic in the Code group.	1. Click the DATABASE TOOLS tab. 2. Click Visual Basic in the Macro group.
1. Click the DEVELOPER tab*. 2. Click Macros in the Code group. 3. Click a macro name in the Macro dialog box. 4. Click Edit.	1. Open a form or report in Design view. 2. Display the Property Sheet. 3. Click a specific control (such as a button). 4. Click the Event tab in the Property Sheet. 5. Click an event such as On Click. 6. Click Build.
1. Click the VIEW tab. 2. Click the Macros arrow in the Macros group. 3. Select View Macros. 4. Click a macro name in the Macro dialog box. 5. Click Edit.	
1. Press Alt+F11.	1. Press Alt+F11.
*If the DEVELOPER tab is not displayed, click the FILE tab, click Options, click Customize Ribbon, click the Developer check box in the Main Tabs list, and then click OK.	

Use the VB Editor

The Microsoft Visual Basic for Applications window is called the VB Editor. Figure 1.1 shows the VB Editor for an Excel workbook, and Figure 1.2 shows the VB Editor for an Access database. Notice the similarities between the windows: a menu bar, a toolbar, Project Explorer, Properties window, and the Code window. If these items do not display on your screen, click View on the menu bar and select the item you want to display.

FIGURE 1.1 VB Editor for Excel ➤

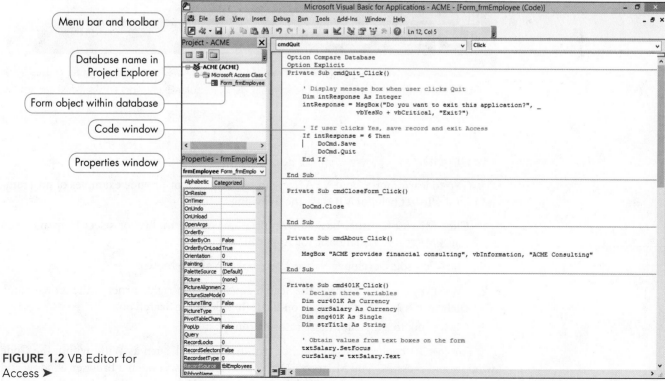

FIGURE 1.2 VB Editor for Access ➤

Menu Bar and Toolbar. The menu bar and toolbar provide access to commands similar to how the Ribbon organizes commands in Excel and Access. The toolbar also indicates the location of the insertion point by line number and column number, such as Ln 49, Col 5 (see Figure 1.1) or Ln 12, Col 5 (see Figure 1.2), within the Code window.

Project Explorer. The Project Explorer is on the left side of the VB Editor. A *project* is a collection of modules and objects needed to run an application. In VBA, a project is a particular Microsoft Office file, such as a particular Excel workbook or an Access database, and its associated modules and macros. The Project Explorer lists all open projects. If three Excel workbooks are open, Project Explorer lists three projects. The project or file includes objects within that file (such as Sheet1 in Excel or Form_frmEmployee in Access) and *modules*, which are containers to organize programming code. Click an object or module to display or write code for that selected object or module in the Code window.

Properties Window. The Properties window displays the *properties* or attributes for the selected object in the Project Explorer. In Figure 1.1, the Properties window shows the properties for Module1 that is selected in Project Explorer. In Figure 1.2, the Properties window shows the properties for the selected Form_frmEmployees object. The Properties window is similar to the Property Sheet you use to set properties for database objects in Access. For example, in Access, you can display the Property Sheet to set properties such as the number of decimal points for a calculated field in a query. If the Properties window is not displayed, select View from the menu and select Properties Window.

Code Window. The *Code window* is a workspace text editor for writing and editing VBA programming statements. When the Code window is maximized, it takes up most of the screen area. Programming statements include procedures, variable and constant declarations, mathematical expressions, and so on. A module consists of one or more *procedures*, which are named sequences of statements that perform a series of actions for a defined task. When you create several macros in a workbook, Excel stores each macro as a procedure in one module. The macro name becomes the name of an individual procedure in VBA.

When you create a VBA procedure using the VB Editor, you enter your code statements in *design time*, the mode for designing or creating programming code. When you execute a procedure, VBA executes the procedure's code in *runtime*, the mode during which a program is being executed.

 TIP **Macro-Enabled Excel Workbook**

When you create macros or write VBA procedures for an Excel workbook, you must save it in the Macro-Enabled Workbook file format (.xlsm). Regular Excel workbooks (.xlsx) cannot store VBA code.

Get Help

Use Help to learn more about VBA, explain terminology, or provide examples of programming code. To get help for VBA, do the following:

1. Click Microsoft Visual Basic for Applications on the toolbar or select Help and then select Microsoft Visual Basic for Applications Help.

   The Microsoft Developer Network will open in a Web browser.

2. Type a keyword or phrase in the Search box in the top-right corner of the browser and click Search MSDN, the button on the right side of the Search box.

3. Click a link to a topic for more information.

For specific context assistance, click within a keyword, such as With, within the Code window and press F1. The Microsoft Developer Network will open a browser window and display specific help for that keyword. Figure 1.3 shows Help information about the keyword With.

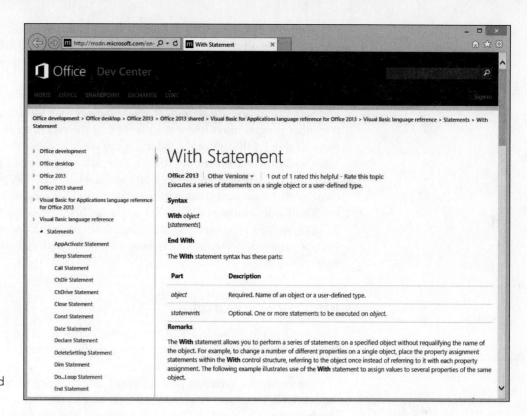

FIGURE 1.3 Help for Keyword *With* ➤

Identifying Code in the Code Window

Before you edit existing code or start to write code, you should learn how to identify different elements in the Code window. The more you study VBA statements generated by creating macros, the more you will be able to identify the code and start editing it or writing your own code. Programming code must follow proper syntax or rules. Programming syntax is similar to grammar and punctuation rules you follow when writing a paper for an English class. If you do not follow proper programming syntax, the program will fail to execute fully. Figure 1.4 identifies code elements.

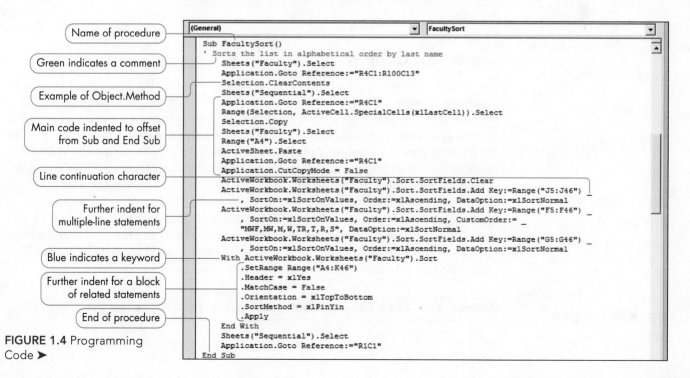

FIGURE 1.4 Programming Code ➤

A procedure begins with Sub and ends with End Sub. Sub includes the procedure name, such as Sub FacultySort(). Statements between Sub and End Sub define the tasks that will be executed when you run the procedure. You must define each procedure separately. You cannot nest one procedure within another procedure.

For readability, indent the statements within a procedure to offset them from Sub and End Sub. In addition, if a statement takes up more than one line, indent the carryover lines so that other programmers know at a glance that the carryover lines are part of the same statement. Figure 1.4 illustrates the indented carryover lines for the ActiveWorkbook statements. You should further indent additional, related blocks of code to indicate coding hierarchy. In Figure 1.4, several statements relate to the With ActiveWorkbook statement. Therefore, those related statements that start with the period are indented.

The Code window color-codes words in black, blue, green, and red. Black indicates properly written programming statements that are free from syntax errors. In addition, the Code window supports automatic completion of certain statements you enter or adjusts capitalization if needed.

Identify Keywords

Blue words, such as *Sub* and *End Sub*, are keywords. **Keywords** are words or symbols particular to a programming language and have specific purposes. Some general keywords include With, End With, True, False, Do, and Loop.

Keywords are grouped into different categories. For example, procedural keywords include Call, Function, Property Get, Sub, and so on. Decision-control structures use keywords such as Choose, If…Then…Else, Select Case, and Switch. Use Help to learn about the keywords specific to VBA. A **syntax error** occurs when you misuse or misspell a keyword, use incorrect punctuation, have not defined a procedure, or violate any other programming rules specific to the language.

> **TIP** **Errors in Keywords**
>
> If you enter code incorrectly, the VB Editor displays the syntax error in red.

Document Code with Comments

Documenting programs is important. As you write programming code, you know what it should do. However, after a few months you might not remember what the code does. Or, if you take over a project from another programmer or are working on a program with multiple programmers, you could spend a considerable amount of time deciphering the code. Therefore, a good programming practice is to include comments within the code. Often programmers in an organization follow a set of coding conventions, such as comments, indenting, and naming techniques so that all programmers on a development team will create consistent programming code.

A **comment** is a remark or text that documents or explains what a section of code does. Comments are not executable code. A comment appears in green and begins with an apostrophe or the keyword Rem (derived from the word *remark*) followed by a space. Keep comments brief yet descriptive, such as the comment in Code Window 1.1.

CODE WINDOW 1.1 ➤

```
'Sorts the list in alphabetical order by last name
```

Identify Objects and Methods

When you create objects, such as Excel macros and Access controls, the host application creates a procedure. Procedures are uniquely named and contain a sequence of programming statements to execute an algorithm. These procedures are contained within modules. VBA has two types of modules: standard modules and class modules. A **standard module** stores procedures that can be used by any object in the application. When you use the macro recorder in some Office applications such as Excel or Word or add a module to a workbook, the code for the macro is stored in a standard module.

A **class module** enables you to create an object template along with the properties and methods that decide how the object behaves. These custom objects can have properties and methods similar to the built-in objects, and you can create multiple copies of these objects. Microsoft Access uses class modules to store the procedures associated with objects on a form or report. You can also create class modules in Excel to store procedures for specific objects, such as forms that a VBA procedure displays in a workbook.

VBA is an **object-oriented programming language** in which methods revolve around objects and actions that manipulate those objects. For example, Excel objects include worksheets, charts, and ranges. In Access, objects include tables, queries, forms, and reports. **Methods** are actions pertaining to the objects. For example, you can Select (method name) an Excel range (object). When you record a macro to select cell A4 or range B4:B10 in an Excel worksheet, the VBA code identifies the object, such as Range("A4") or Range("B4:B10"), and then the action, such as Select. In Access, you can manage macros in dialog boxes or convert macros to VBA code. The first line of code in Code Window 1.2 shows how to select a cell or a range in Excel. The second line of code shows how to use the ClearContents method to clear the data in the specified range.

CODE WINDOW 1.2 ➤

```
Range("A4").Select
Range("B4:B10").ClearContents
```

In some cases, you need to qualify methods within the hierarchy of objects. For example, a workbook object contains a worksheet object, and a worksheet object contains range objects. When you specify the hierarchy of objects, separate the object names with periods. Code Window 1.3 shows an example of using Excel objects and methods. ActiveWorkbook is the main object. Worksheets is an object within the ActiveWorkbook. ("Sheet3") defines which worksheet object you are referring to. The sheet name is enclosed in quotation marks. *Sort* is a method acting on the Sheet3 data, *SortFields* is an object referring to the list of data to sort, and *Clear* is a method or an action acting on the SortFields object.

CODE WINDOW 1.3 ➤

```
ActiveWorkbook.Worksheets("Sheet3").Sort.SortFields.Clear
```

 TIP Auto List Members

When you type a period, the Auto List Members feature displays a list of potential objects, properties, or methods that can logically complete the statement. For example, after you type ActiveWorkbook, VBA displays a list of applicable items that relate to the active workbook. If you type W, VBA will scroll through the list to the first item starting with a W. You can continue typing the object, property, or method name, or you can double-click the word in the list to insert it into the code.

Creating, Running, and Debugging Procedures

Custom applications use VBA to process information or perform actions in response to events. An *event* is an action that occurs when the code is running, such as the user clicking a button at runtime that triggers a program instruction. For example, you can write VBA code to specify what an object does in response to the event. The system triggers some events, such as when Access opens a form. Users trigger other events by performing specific actions, such as selecting an item in a list or a menu option.

VBA supports three kinds of procedures. A *sub procedure* is a procedure that performs an action but does not return a specific value, such as Sub FacultySort in Figure 1.1. A *function procedure* is a procedure that performs an action and returns a value, similar to how functions return values in Excel. A *property procedure* is a procedure that creates or manipulates a custom property. Most procedures you create with VBA will be sub procedures or function procedures.

All procedures are either public or private. A *public procedure* is available to any object in an application; the code for an object anywhere in the application can use the code statements. A *private procedure* is available only to a specific object or module. Procedures are public by default, unless the procedure is associated with a specific event, such as clicking a button.

Create a Procedure

Sub procedures begin with the Sub statement and end with End Sub. The code for a procedure must be contained between these two statements. In Figure 1.1, the Sub FacultySort() statement begins the procedure, which is contained in a standard module. The procedure is public and is available to any object in the Class Schedule1 workbook. This is useful when more than one procedure must perform the same action, such as changing user preferences or validating an action before closing the application. Rather than writing the code in each procedure that performs the action, you can write the code once and access the procedure from multiple objects.

STEP 2 ⟫ To create a procedure within the Code window in the VB Editor, do the following:

1. Type Sub in Excel or type Private Sub in Access, press Spacebar, and type a name for the procedure. The procedure name cannot have spaces. However, you can use CamelCasing (where you capitalize the first letter of each word) to type a multi-word procedure name such as FacultySort.
2. Press Enter, and VBA will enter the End Sub statement automatically.
3. Press Tab to indent the procedure code and type the procedure statements between the Sub and End Sub statements.
4. Click Save on the toolbar.

STEP 4 ⟫ If you are adding a procedure for a control (such as a command button) on an Access form, start the procedure with Private Sub cmdCloseForm_Click() where cmdCloseForm is the name of the control, such as a command button, and Click is the event to trigger the procedure.

Run and Debug a Procedure

After you create a procedure, you can run it. Running a procedure is the process of executing the statements in the procedure. To run a procedure from within the VB Editor, do the following:

STEP 3 ⟫ 1. Click Run Sub/UserForm on the toolbar or click Run from the menu bar and select Run Sub/UserForm.

The Debug menu helps you identify errors in programming code by stepping through the code to isolate the specific problem. If a procedure contains an error, you can debug it to identify the error. To debug a procedure, do the following within the VB Editor:

1. Click within a procedure to position the insertion point within the Code window and then click Debug on the menu bar and select Step Into.

   VBA will highlight the first statement.

2. Click Continue (the same as Run) on the toolbar to step through the procedure statements.

   VBA displays an error message if a statement contains an error. Figure 1.5 shows an error message if the property or method is incorrect within a statement.

3. Click Help to display information about the error or click Debug to highlight the statement that contains an error so that you can correct it.

4. Look for an error, such as a word that does not start with a capital letter. The lowercase word may indicate an incorrect object, method, or property name.

5. Click Reset on the toolbar to exit debugging mode.

FIGURE 1.5 Debugging Error Message ➤

Creating a Message Box

A common task for programmers is to display a message to the user. For example, you might want to display a message that announces that changes were saved to a database table or that the user entered an incorrect value in an Excel cell. Programmers also create message boxes to display intermediate or final calculations in a process. *Message boxes* are small dialog boxes that contain a title bar, a message, an icon, and one or more buttons. During runtime, the program halts until the user clicks a button on the message box. When the user clicks the button, the message box closes, and a specific action programmed to that button executes.

Use the MsgBox Statement and Function

STEP 5 ➤

To create a message box in VBA, use either the MsgBox statement or the MsgBox function. The *MsgBox statement* displays a message onscreen. This statement is useful when you need to provide a message, such as a confirmed change or error alert, to the user. The default options for a message box include the title of the application in the title bar, the message, and an OK button. The code statement that defines a message box is identical in Access and Excel. Code Window 1.4 illustrates the code to display a message box. Figure 1.6 shows an example of a message box created using the MsgBox statement in Access.

CODE WINDOW 1.4 ➤

```
Sub Display_Message()
    'Display a message box with a prompt"
    MsgBox "Welcome to ACME Consulting!"
End Sub
```

FIGURE 1.6 Message Box in Access ➤

The **MsgBox function** displays a message on the screen and returns an integer value indicating which button the user clicked in the message box. The MsgBox function is useful when the program needs to have the user make a choice by clicking a particular button, such as OK or Cancel, and you need to store a specific value depending upon that choice. In addition, the MsgBox function enables you to customize the title bar, include an icon, and specify which buttons to display. Like Excel functions, VBA functions include a function name and the arguments. An **argument** is a value in the form of a constant, variable, or expression that provides necessary information to a procedure or function, similar to how arguments provide necessary data for Excel functions. The MsgBox function contains four arguments in a specific sequence. If you omit an argument, VBA assigns a default value. The syntax for the MsgBox function is as follows:

`MsgBox("prompt"[, buttons] [, "title"] [, helpfile, context])`

The *prompt* argument is the message or information that appears within the main area of the message box. It is called the prompt argument because it prompts the user to click a button within the message box. The *title* argument is the text that will appear in the title bar of the message box when you run the procedure. You must type the text for the prompt and title arguments within quotation marks.

Prompt is the only required argument; the other arguments—indicated by brackets above—are optional but typically included. If you omit an optional argument that occurs before another argument you define, you must enter a comma as a placeholder for the omitted argument.

Display Buttons and Icons in a Message Box

The second argument in the MsgBox function enables you to specify buttons and icons you want to display in the message box. If you want to use the default OK button only but want to specify the message box title, type the prompt, two commas, and then the title. Table 1.2 lists some of the button syntax and the buttons displayed by the syntax.

TABLE 1.2	Message Box Buttons and Icons
Button Syntax	**Displays**
vbOKOnly	OK
vbOKCancel	OK Cancel
vbAbortRetryIgnore	Abort Retry Ignore
vbYesNoCancel	Yes No Cancel
vbYesNo	Yes No
vbRetryCancel	Retry Cancel
vbCritical	⊗
vbQuestion	❓
vbExclamation	⚠
vbInformation	ⓘ

You can specify buttons, icons, or both. For example, you might want to display the OK button and the Exclamation icon. Because the default displays the OK button, you can specify only vbExclamation for the second argument. You cannot combine two or more button sets (such as both vbYesNo and vbRetryCancel) or two or more icon sets (such as both vbCritical and vbInformation) in the same statement. However, you can combine a button set with an icon set by typing a + between the button and icon codes, such as vbYesNo + vbExclamation.

Code Window 1.5 shows three sample buttons or icons and sample combinations. The prompt argument is *Welcome!* in all three lines of code. In the first line of code, the title bar displays *VBA in Access*, and the vbExclamation symbol displays in the message box. Without explicitly stating buttons, OK is the default button that displays. See if you can recognize what will display in the message boxes for the second and third lines of code.

```
Dim intValue As Integer

intValue = MsgBox("Welcome!", vbExclamation, "VBA in Access")
intValue = MsgBox("Welcome!", vbYesNo, "VBA in Access")
intValue = MsgBox("Welcome!", vbYesNo + vbExclamation, "VBA in Access")
```

CODE WINDOW 1.5 ▲

Because the MsgBox function returns an integer value based on which button the user clicks, you must assign the returned value to a variable or to do something else with the returned integer. You will learn about the Dim statement and how to assign values to variables in the next section. Table 1.3 lists the buttons and their return values.

TABLE 1.3 Integers Returned by Button	
Button	**Integer Returned**
OK	1
Cancel	2
Abort	3
Retry	4
Ignore	5
Yes	6
No	7

Code Window 1.6 illustrates the use of the MsgBox function. The first argument *"Welcome to ACME Consulting!"* contains the text for the message box shown in Figure 1.7. Because the statement is long, divide it into two physical lines by typing the *line-continuation character*, which is a space followed by an underscore (_). The second argument *vbYesNo + vbInformation* creates the Yes and No buttons and the Information icon. The third argument "VBA in Access" displays the text for the message box title bar. When the message box displays, the user clicks Yes or No. If the user clicks Yes, the MsgBox function returns the integer 6. If the user clicks No, the MsgBox function returns the integer 7. The integer is stored in the intMsgBoxReturn variable, and you can execute different statements depending on the value of 6 or 7 that is stored in that variable.

CODE WINDOW 1.6 ➤

```
Dim intMsgBoxReturn As Integer
intMsgBoxReturn = MsgBox("Welcome to ACME Consulting!", _
                  vbYesNo + vbInformation, "VBA in Access")
```

FIGURE 1.7 Message Box
Created by MsgBox
Function ➤

TIP | MsgBox Function Integer

Remember that the MsgBox function returns an integer value based on which button the user clicks. The statement must do something with that returned value. Often, you will assign that value to a variable. Variables are discussed after Hands-On Exercise 1.

Quick
Concepts ✓

1. What three colors are used in the Code window, and what do these colors mean? *p. 6*

2. Explain when and why you should indent code in the Code window. Also explain what the line-continuation character is. *pp. 5–6*

3. Write the code to create a message box that displays "Record Changed in the title bar, Do you want to save the changes?" as the prompt, the question mark icon, and the Yes and No buttons. *p. 11*

Hands-On Exercises

1 Introduction to VBA

Tina and Anthony provided you with an Excel workbook and an Access database so that you can experiment with implementing VBA code. They want to make sure you can succeed on some basic VBA commands before having you work on larger files.

Skills covered: Use VBA and Get Help • Create a Procedure • Run and Debug a Procedure • Create a Procedure in Access • Create a Message Box

STEP 1 ≫ USE VBA AND GET HELP

You will open an Excel workbook and use the Help menu to find a glossary of VBE terms. Refer to Figure 1.8 as you complete Step 1.

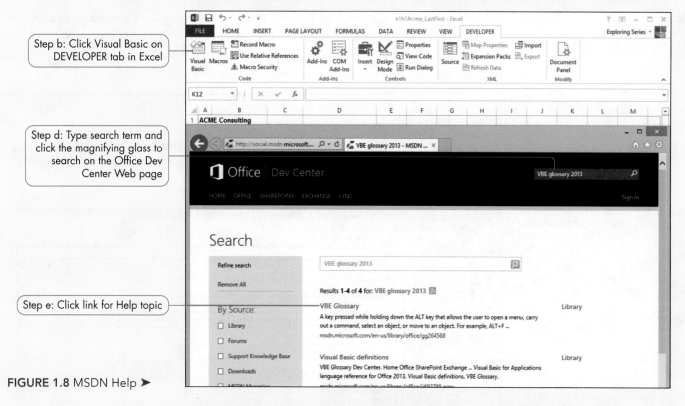

Step b: Click Visual Basic on DEVELOPER tab in Excel

Step d: Type search term and click the magnifying glass to search on the Office Dev Center Web page

Step e: Click link for Help topic

FIGURE 1.8 MSDN Help ➤

a. Start Excel, open *v1h1Acme.xlsm* (an Excel macro-enabled workbook) and save it as **v1h1Acme_LastFirst.xlsm**.

> **TROUBLESHOOTING:** If the Security Warning toolbar displays, click Enable Content. If you make any major mistakes in this exercise, you can close the file, open *v1h1Acme* again, and then start this exercise over.

b. Click the **DEVELOPER tab** and click **Visual Basic** in the Code group.

> **TROUBLESHOOTING:** If the DEVELOPER tab is not displayed, click the FILE tab, click Options, click Customize Ribbon, click the Developer tab check box in the Main Tabs list on the right side, and click OK. Maximize the VB Editor and Code window if necessary.

The VB Editor opens and shows existing VBA code for a macro.

c. Click **Microsoft Visual Basic for Applications Help** (the question mark) on the toolbar.

The Microsoft Developer Network (MSDN) for Excel 2013 Web page opens in a browser.

d. Type **VBE glossary 2013** in the Search help box and click **Search MSDN** (the magnifying glass).

The Web page changes to the Office Dev Center, and the results window displays a list of hyperlinked topics.

e. Click the **VBE Glossary** link to open a window containing the glossary of terms. Scroll through the list and read some of the definitions.

f. Adapt steps d and e to search for **Create a Procedure** and **MsgBox Function**. Read a few articles from each of the search results. Close the browser window after reading about each topic.

g. Leave the VB Editor open to continue with the next step.

STEP 2 ⟫ CREATE A PROCEDURE

The Excel workbook contains a macro to sort the list in alphabetical order by last name and then to further sort in alphabetical order by first name. You will study this macro code to create a new procedure that sorts the list by salary in descending order. Refer to Figure 1.9 as you complete Step 2.

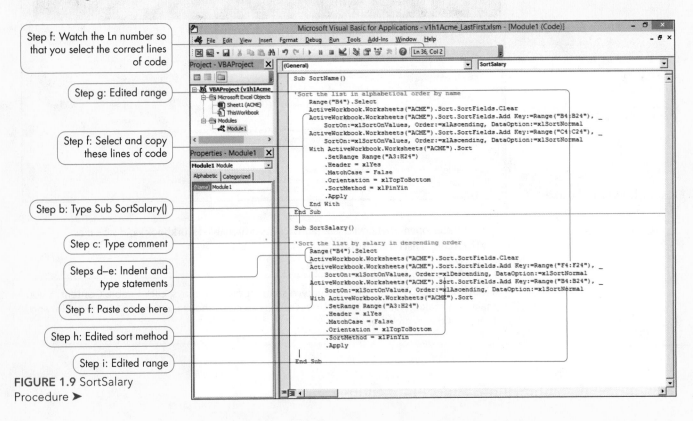

FIGURE 1.9 SortSalary Procedure ➤

a. Position the insertion point in the Code window, press **Ctrl+End** to position the insertion point on the line below the SortName procedure's End Sub statement, and press **Enter**.

The existing SortName procedure sorts the list in alphabetical order by last name and further sorts the list in alphabetical order by first name.

b. Type **Sub SortSalary()** and press **Enter** twice.

The VB Editor creates a corresponding End Sub statement and displays a horizontal line between the SortName procedure's End Sub statement and the Sub SortSalary() statement to separate the procedures visually.

c. Type **'Sort the list by salary in descending order** and press **Enter**.

The comment displays in green in the Code window.

d. Press **Tab**. Type **Range("B4").Select** and press **Enter**.

You indented the main code to offset it from the *Sub* and *End Sub* statements for readability. After you type *Range("B4").*, VBA's Auto List Members feature displays a list of potential items to complete the statement. The Range("B4").Select statement selects a cell in the range to be sorted.

e. Type **ActiveWorkbook.Worksheets("ACME").Sort.SortFields.Clear** and press **Enter**.

After you type *ActiveWorkbook* and the period, VBA displays a list of potential objects that relate to the ActiveWorkbook object. You can select from the list or continue typing the programming statement. This statement clears any prior sort settings in the current ACME worksheet in the active workbook.

f. Select **Ln 6 through the end of Ln 17** of code in the SortName procedure (look at Figure 1.9 and the toolbar to identify the line numbers) stopping after the *End With* statement, click **Copy** on the toolbar, click below the line of code you typed in the SortSalary procedure (Ln 25), and click **Paste** on the toolbar.

> **TROUBLESHOOTING:** Depending on what you selected and where you pasted exactly, you may need to press Tab to indent the first line of the pasted code in the SortSalary procedure. Check your code with Figure 1.9 to ensure correct placement and indenting of pasted code.

You copied most of the code from the SortName procedure to the SortSalary procedure to minimize time typing code and to avoid creating syntax errors. Now you need to edit the code so that the procedure will sort by salary instead of by name.

 TIP **Location Status**

Look at the toolbar to identify the lines (Ln) within the Visual Basic Editor to make sure you are copying and editing code as instructed in these steps.

g. Select **B4:B24** on Ln 25 in the SortSalary procedure and type **F4:F24**.

Range F4:F24 in the worksheet contains the salary data.

h. Select **xlAscending** on Ln 26 in the SortSalary procedure and type **xlDescending**.

> **TROUBLESHOOTING:** Make sure you type the letters xl, not the letter x and the number 1. The *xl* prefix refers to an object in the Excel object library that you can use in your code.

Steps g and h will sort the list of salaries in descending order so that the largest value is listed first.

i. Select **C4:C24** on Ln 27 in the SortSalary procedure and type **B4:B24**.

The range B4:B24 contains the last names in worksheet. Step i will further sort the list by last names in alphabetical order when employees have identical salaries.

j. Delete the **End With** statement at the end of the procedure and leave a blank line between *.Apply* and *End Sub* to introduce an error that you will debug when you run the procedure in Step 3.

k. Click **Save** on the toolbar.

STEP 3 ≫ RUN AND DEBUG A PROCEDURE

You want to run the SortSalary procedure to ensure it sorts the list correctly. As you run the procedure, an error message displays. You will correct the error and run the procedure again. Refer to Figure 1.10 as you complete Step 3.

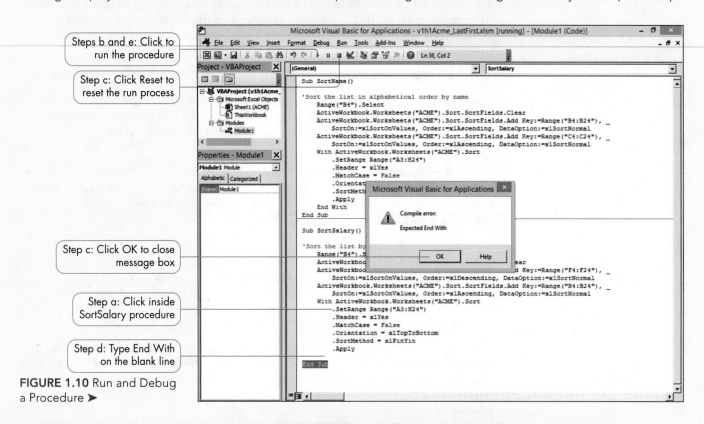

FIGURE 1.10 Run and Debug a Procedure ➤

a. Make sure the insertion point is within the SortSalary procedure you just created.

b. Click **Run Sub/UserForm** (the green triangle) on the toolbar.

A message box displays, informing you that a compile error occurred. The message includes *Expected End With* because you deleted a required ending statement in the last step. VBA highlights the procedure name, indicating a problem exists.

c. Click **OK** to close the message box and click **Reset** on the toolbar to remove the highlighting in the Code window so that you can correct the error and run the procedure again.

d. Type **End With** on Ln 36 Col 5, the blank line between *.Apply* and *End Sub*. Make sure *End With* is indented to align with the With statement on Ln 29. Click **Save** on the toolbar.

e. Click **Run Sub/UserForm** on the toolbar.

Nothing changes in the VB Editor; however, the procedure runs in the Excel workbook.

f. Minimize the VB Editor and look at the Excel workbook.

The list is sorted in descending order (largest to smallest) by salary. Patricia Hansen's row is listed first because her salary is the highest at $90,500, and Mark Knoff's row is listed last because his salary is the lowest at $54,000. For the two employees who earn $55,000, the list is further sorted by last name so that Collins appears before Smith.

g. Click **Macros** in the Code group on the DEVELOPER tab, select **SortName** in the dialog box, and click **Run**.

The list is sorted in alphabetical order by last name and then by first name. You can run procedures from either the Macros dialog box or from within the VB Editor.

h. Click **Macros** in the Code group on the DEVELOPER tab, select **SortSalary** in the dialog box, and click **Run**.

The list is sorted in descending order (largest to smallest) by salary again.

i. Save the workbook. Exit Excel, which will also close the VB Editor.

STEP 4 ≫ CREATE A PROCEDURE IN ACCESS

Anthony's Access database contains one table and one form. He has created five buttons on the form; however, only the Quit button works. He has asked you to write the VBA code for the Close Form button. Refer to Figure 1.11 as you complete Step 4.

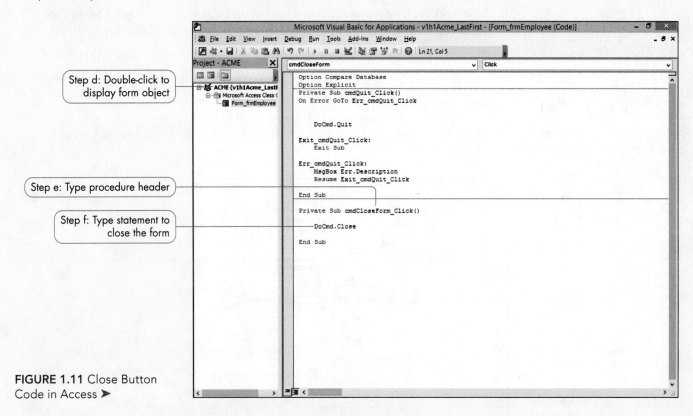

FIGURE 1.11 Close Button Code in Access ➤

a. Start Access, open *v1h1Acme.accdb* (an Access database) and save it as **v1h1Acme_LastFirst.accdb**.

> **TROUBLESHOOTING:** If the Security Warning bar displays, click Enable Content. If you make any major mistakes in this step, you can close the file, open *v1h1Acme* again, and then start this step over.

b. Open the frmEmployee form, and then click each button at the bottom of the form: **About**, **401K**, **Bonus**, **Close Form**, and **Quit**.

The Quit button is the only button that has been programmed. The Quit button quits or closes the entire database. You will write the code for the Close Form and About buttons.

c. Open *v1h1Acme_LastFirst.accdb*, click the **DATABASE TOOLS tab**, and click **Visual Basic** in the Macro group to open the VB Editor.

d. Double-click **ACME** in the Project Explorer, double-click **Microsoft Access Class Objects**, and double-click **Form_frmEmployee**.

The programming code for the form displays in the Code window.

e. Click in the Code window and press **Ctrl+End** to go to the end of the code. Type **Private Sub cmdCloseForm_Click()** and press **Enter** twice.

VBA adds the End Sub statement. You created a procedure named cmdClose that corresponds to the Close Form button's name (cmdCloseForm). After typing the command button name, you type an underscore and specify the event (Click). You are about to specify the action to take when the user clicks that button.

f. Press **Tab**. Type **DoCmd.Close** and press **Enter**. Compare your code to the code shown in Figure 1.11.

g. Click **Save** on the toolbar and close the VB Editor.

The frmEmployee form is open in Design view in Access.

h. Right-click the **frmEmployee tab** at the top of the form window and select **Form View** to display the form in Form view. Click **Close Form** at the bottom of the form.

The form closes, but the database remains open (unlike when you click the Quit button).

STEP 5 ≫ CREATE A MESSAGE BOX

Anthony wants a message box to appear when users click the About button. You need to add a MsgBox statement to do this. Refer to Figure 1.12 as you complete Step 5.

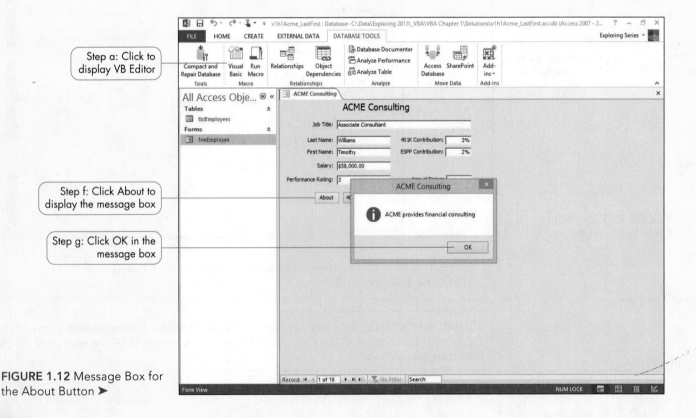

FIGURE 1.12 Message Box for the About Button ➤

a. Click the **DATABASE TOOLS tab** if necessary and click **Visual Basic** in the Macro group.

b. Press **Ctrl+End** to go to the end of the code and press **Enter**.

c. Type **Private Sub cmdAbout_Click()** and press **Enter** twice.

d. Press **Tab**. Type **MsgBox "ACME provides financial consulting", vbInformation, "ACME Consulting"** and press **Enter**.

You used the MsgBox statement instead of the MsgBox function because you do not need a return value.

e. Click **Save** on the toolbar and close the VB Editor.

f. Display the form in Form view. Click **About** at the bottom of the form.

The MsgBox statement displays the message, an Information icon, and the title. By default, the message box will also display the OK button.

g. Click **OK** in the message box, click **Close Form** at the bottom of the form, and exit Access.

Variables, Constants, Inputs, and Outputs

When a program is running, it needs to be able to accept input, perform calculations, and then display output. For example, in a payroll program, the inputs need to include an employee's name or ID, the hours worked, and the hourly pay rate. The processing takes the inputs to calculate the regular pay, overtime pay, total gross pay, income taxes and other deductions withheld, and net pay. The output displays the results of the calculations. In addition to specifying the inputs, processing, and outputs, the program needs mechanisms for storing data. Programmers create variables and constants to store values that are then used in other statements to perform calculations or manipulate data during execution.

In this section, you will learn how to declare variables and constants, assign descriptive names, and select appropriate data types. In addition, you will learn how to obtain user input, store the input in variables, and display output.

Declaring and Using Variables and Constants

Variables are programmer-defined names that store values that can change while the application is running. Variables store values in computer memory, and your code statement can change the value at any time. Because variables are stored in computer memory, a value for a variable exists only while a program is running. When the program ends, the ability to access the value in memory is lost. The advantage to using variables is that the value can change. For example, you might originally record an order of one dessert at a restaurant and then change the order to two desserts.

Constants store values that are specified at design time and that remain the same (or constant) while the application is running. Only a programmer can change a constant's value at design time; users cannot change a constant's value during runtime. Declaring and using constants is important in a program because it prevents the use of raw, unidentified values within mathematical expressions. VBA supports three types of constants:

- *Intrinsic constant* is a constant specific to an application, such as Microsoft Excel or Microsoft Access. You can use the Object Browser to view constants in the object library. You cannot create a user-defined constant that uses the same name as an intrinsic constant.

- *Symbolic or user-defined constant* is a constant created by a programmer.

- *Conditional compiler constant* is defined in the host application. The compiler uses it to determine when or if specific Visual Basic code blocks are compiled. (Because this type of constant is more specialized, it will not be discussed or illustrated in this chapter.)

 TIP **Variable or Constant?**

When deciding whether to create a variable or a constant, ask yourself if a user should be able to change a value. For example, if you want the user to specify hours worked, create a variable to accept and store that input. If the user should not be changing a value, such as a sales tax rate, create a constant to store the tax rate.

Select a Data Type

All variables and constants have a ***data type***, which refers to the kind of data the variable or constant can hold and how the data is stored in the computer's memory. Data types assigned to variables in programming code are similar to assigning data types to fields in Access tables. You must specify the type of data that can be stored in an Access table field. Because variables and constants are stored in memory, good programmers select the appropriate data type that uses the least amount of memory necessary to store various kinds of information, such as text and numbers. Because each data type has different memory requirements, you can conserve computer memory, increase the speed of your application, and minimize programming errors by carefully selecting the most appropriate data type for the kind of data your application needs to store. Table 1.4 lists the data types in VBA.

TABLE 1.4 Data Types

Data Type	Data Stored in the Variable	Memory Used
Boolean	Only two possible values: True or False.	2 bytes
Byte	A whole number ranging from 0 to 255.	1 byte
Currency	Value ranging from −922,337,203,685,477.5808 to 922,337,203,685,477.5807. Use Currency data type to store values that you will use to calculate monetary amounts.	8 bytes
Date	Dates or times.	8 bytes
Decimal	Value that contains decimal numbers scaled by a power of 10.	12 bytes
Double	Double-precision floating-point numbers with 14 digits of accuracy. See VBA Help for exact value ranges.	8 bytes
Integer	Whole numbers ranging from −32,768 to 32,767.	2 bytes
Long	Whole numbers ranging from −2,147,483,648 to 2,147,483,647.	4 bytes
Object	A reference to an application object.	4 bytes
Single	Single-precision floating-point numbers with six digits of accuracy. See VBA Help for exact value ranges.	4 bytes
String (fixed length)	Alphanumeric data including letters, numbers, spaces, punctuation, and other characters with a fixed length.	1 to approximately 63K characters
String (variable length)	Alphanumeric data including letters, numbers, punctuation, and other characters with variable length.	0 to 2 billion characters
Variant	Default type if no specific data type is assigned.	Up to 22 bytes plus the length of a text string
Type (user defined)	Structured data that contains data appropriate to the required elements in a range.	Size depends on the data definition

How do you determine the appropriate data type? If you need to store a text string such as a person's name, use the String data type. If you need to perform calculations between dates, use the Date data type.

For numeric data, such as 100 items in stock, a tax rate of 5%, gross pay of $1,500, or a number expressed as an exponent, such as 3.2×10^{23}, the data type requires more consideration.

Table 1.4 shows that the Integer and Long data types store whole number (nondecimal) values. Because these data types store only whole numbers, they are called *integral data types*. Therefore, if you need to store a whole value for calculations, such as the number of items in stock or the term of a loan, use an integral data type.

Nonintegral data types, such as Single and Double, represent numbers with integer and fractional parts. The Single and Double data types store floating-point numbers. You can use these types to store numbers that are extremely small or extremely large.

Floating-point (Single and Double) numbers have larger ranges but can be subject to rounding errors. Thus, if you use two decimal point numbers in calculations, very small rounding errors might occur. The errors are too small to be of any significance unless you are working with complex monetary calculations. If your application makes complex calculations using money, use the Currency or Decimal data type.

TIP Variables for Currency Values

For monetary calculations, such as calculating the value of inventory or a monthly loan payment, some programs perform best if you use the Single data type, whereas others perform best with the Currency data type. This book uses the Currency data type for monetary calculations.

Choosing the appropriate data type for variables is important. Table 1.5 provides examples of the recommended data types for various kinds of data.

TABLE 1.5 Recommended Data Types

Data to Store	Data Type	Example
Employee address	String	100 Elm Street
Number of graduating students	Integer	1234
Marital status	Boolean	0 (married) or 1 (not married)
Speed of light	Double	2.99 10^8
Age of a person in years	Integer	24
Population of a major metropolitan city	Integer	250763
Gross pay for a pay period	Currency	2526.41
Net 30 payment due date	Date	12/01/2016
Term of a loan in months	Integer	360
Total sale amount	Currency	360.27
Constant *pi*	Double	3.1415926535897
Local sales tax rate	Single	0.065
Estimated world population in 2020	Long	7000000000

Name Variables and Constants

In addition to choosing a data type, you must choose a name for your variables and constants. You will then use those names to store and retrieve values to manipulate when the program is running. The standards for naming variables and constants in VBA follow requirements and recommendations.

Requirements

- Use a letter as the first character for a variable or constant name.
- Avoid disallowed characters: space, period (.), exclamation mark (!), @, &, $, and #.
- Create names that are 255 or fewer characters in length.

Recommendations

- Use descriptive names that tell the purpose of a variable or constant and the kind of data it contains.
- Begin the name with the first three characters indicating the data type (in lowercase) and the remainder specifying the variable's purpose (beginning with an uppercase letter). For example, a variable for storing the number of units might be named intQuantity, where *int* indicates the data type (Integer) and *Quantity* is a descriptive name for the values the variable holds (number of units). The first three characters appear in lowercase, with the remaining part of the variable name appearing as descriptive words that begin with uppercase letters. Use CamelCase for descriptive names with more than one word. Table 1.6 lists the Hungarian notation—the three-character designation for each data type—and gives an example of how to apply the CamelCase convention. Some programmers use the Hungarian notation, whereas other programmers omit the three-letter prefix to simplify code. You should use the naming style preferred by your organization.

TABLE 1.6 Variable Prefixes and Sample Names

Data Type	Prefix	Example Variable Name
Boolean	bln	blnMaritalStatus
Currency	cur	curNetPay
Date	dtm	dtmNet30
Double	dbl	dblSpeedOfLight
Integer	int	intQuantity
Long	lng	lngPopulation
Object	obj	objCurrent
Single	sng	sngSalesTax
String	str	strAddress

In previous versions of Visual Basic, programmers capitalized constant names and used an underscore between words, such as TAX_RATE. However, the current naming convention for user-defined constants is CamelCase, such as TaxRate.

Intrinsic constants defined by an application for specific objects use a two-character prefix and mixed-case format. For example, the prefix vb represents a constant in the VBA object library, and xl represents a constant from the Microsoft Excel object library.

Declare Variables and Constants

When you want to define a variable, you must include a declaration statement. The ***declaration*** statement assigns a name and data type and allocates memory to store a value for the variable or constant. When you declare a variable or a constant, you can specify its accessibility or ***scope***. The scope specifies which program statements can access the value stored in the variable or constant. If you declare a variable or constant within a procedure that you want to be available to only that procedure, it is a local variable or constant and has procedure scope. This means that other procedures cannot directly access the variable or constant. If you want to make a variable or constant accessible to any procedure within an Access form, for example, you create a module-level (or form-level) variable or constant, which has module scope.

STEP 1

Declare a local variable at the top of a procedure or declare a module-level variable at the top of the module code in the Code window using the *Dim* statement. After you type the *Dim* keyword, type the variable name, type As, and then type the data type. Code Window 1.7 provides examples of variable declarations.

```
Dim blnMaritalStatus As Boolean
Dim curNetPay As Currency
Dim intQuantity As Integer
Dim strAddress As String
```

CODE WINDOW 1.7 ➤

To declare a user-defined constant, start with the keyword *Const* and include the constant name. In addition, you must assign a value that will not change during the runtime of the application. The value must match the data type you specify. For example, if you declare an integer constant, you cannot assign a value of 0.065 to it because integers store whole numbers only. Code Window 1.8 shows sample constant declarations.

```
Const SalesTaxRate As Double = 0.065
Public Const Taxrate As Double = 0.065
Private Const CityTaxRate As Double = 0.065
```

CODE WINDOW 1.8 ➤

To be able to use a value stored in a variable or constant in all procedures in a project, use the *Public* statement instead of the *Dim* statement. To ensure that variables are properly declared before being used, you should type the statement *Option Explicit* at the top of the Code window. If *Option Explicit* is on, you must explicitly declare a variable before assigning a value to it. If you do not enter that statement, VBA allows you to create variables on the spot, which can lead to problems in an application. It is good programming practice to always declare variables before using them.

By default, constants are private, as shown in Code Window 1.8. You cannot change a constant's availability within a procedure. However, in a standard module, you can add the keyword *Public* at the beginning of the declaration statement to make a constant available to "all procedures in all modules." You can limit a constant's availability to a specific module only by including the keyword *Private* at the beginning of the declaration. Help further explains *Public* and *Private* and the usage in class modules.

TIP Auto Syntax Corrections

VBA checks for and corrects some errors for you when the Auto Syntax Check check box is selected in the Options dialog box. For example, if you forget to add a space before and after the assignment operator (=), VBA will insert the spaces for you when you press Enter. Other automatic corrections include changing case, such as changing *as integer* to *As Integer* or making a variable's case match its case in the declaration statement. Select Tools on the menu, and then select Options to verify the Auto Syntax Check setting.

Assign Values to Variables

An assignment statement is one that assigns a value to a variable or constant. With constants, the declaration and assignment must occur within one statement because once the constant is declared and assigned a value that value cannot change during runtime. For variables, you create separate declaration and assignment statements. Code Window 1.9 shows examples of variable declaration and assignment statements for an integer and a string. The variable name goes on the left side of the = operator, and the value being assigned goes on the right side of the = operator. When you assign text to a string, you must enclose the text within quotation marks.

```
Dim intQuantity As Integer
intQuantity = 100

Dim strLastName As String
strLastName = "Johnson"
```

TIP | Date Literals

When you assign dates to a Date variable or constant, you must enclose the date in a mm/dd/yyyy (two digits for the month and day, and four digits for the year) format within two pound sign (#) characters, such as #07/01/2016#. This value, known as a date literal, assigns the proper date to the variable or constant.

Creating an Input Box

Variables and constants simplify the calculations your applications perform. However, you need to plan how the data assigned to variables gets into an application. An application can include specific controls, such as a text box, to obtain data from the user. You create an *input box*, a dialog box that displays on the screen to prompt the user to enter a value. Like a message box, the program halts after displaying an input box until the user enters data and then clicks OK. Unlike message boxes, input boxes do not have icons.

Programmers use functions to simplify program code statements. VBA includes numerous functions to return values. Predefined VBA functions often require one or more arguments, similar to Excel functions such as the IF function. A code statement with a function contains the function name and one or more arguments. The arguments are the values supplied to the function. Arguments can be required or optional. If an argument is required, it must be included in the code statement. As you type a function in the Code window, the VB Editor displays a pop-up window listing the required functions.

Obtain User Input with the InputBox Function

The *InputBox function* (InputBox) prompts the user to enter a value that the application needs to perform an action. This function returns the value supplied by the user as a string. The syntax for the InputBox function is as follows:

`InputBox(prompt[, title] [, default] [, xpos] [, ypos] [, helpfile, context])`

The *prompt* is the message inside the input box; the *title* is an optional argument. When specified, it displays the text that appears on the input box title bar. The optional *xpos* and *ypos* arguments specify the horizontal distance from the left edge of the screen and the vertical distance from the top of the screen, respectively, to display the input box.

STEP 2 ≫

Code Window 1.10 shows the InputBox function used to get a person's name, store it in a string variable, and then display a message box that contains a text string and the contents of the strLastName variable. Because the InputBox statement is long, it is divided into two lines by using the line-continuation character. If you do not use a line-continuation character at the end of the first line or if you use a line-continuation within string quotes enclosed within quotation marks, VBA will display an error. To combine two text strings together into one string, type & between them. Figure 1.13 shows the input box, and Figure 1.14 shows the resulting message box.

```
'Declare string variable
Dim strLastName As String
    'Display input box, get user input,& store in variable
    strLastName = InputBox("Please enter your last name.", _
                  "Data Entry: Last Name")


    'Display results in a message box
    MsgBox "Last Name is: " & strLastName

End Sub
```

CODE WINDOW 1.10 ➤

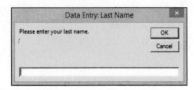

FIGURE 1.13 Input Box ➤

FIGURE 1.14 Message Box ➤

TIP | Concatenation Character

Use the ampersand character (&) or plus sign (+) to *concatenate*, or join, two values, such as MsgBox "Last Name is: " & strLastName shown in Code Window 1.10. Figure 1.14 displays the result of the code, Last Name is: Johnson. The message box displays the text string Last Name is: and the value of the strLastName variable, which in this case is Johnson. Concatenation is useful for joining text strings.

Convert Strings to Numeric Values Using the Val Function

When you obtain user input using the InputBox function, the value that the user supplies is returned to the procedure as a text string by default. This is fine for text data, but if you need to perform calculations on numbers entered into an input box, you need to use the *Val function*, which converts the value into numeric data for calculations.

The Val function stops reading the string when it encounters the first character it does not recognize as part of a number. Symbols and characters frequently added to numeric values (like currency symbols and commas) are not recognized. When the Val function encounters a nonnumeric character, it ignores the remaining characters in the string.

You can use the Val function in conjunction with the InputBox function to convert the string value into a numeric value for calculations. For example, Code Window 1.11 shows a procedure that uses the Val function to convert numbers entered as text into numeric values that can be used in calculations. This code declares and assigns text to string variables so that you can use the string variable names in the InputBox() function to simplify that line of code.

CODE WINDOW 1.11 ➤

```
Dim strMessage As String
Dim strTitle As String
Dim curSalary As Currency

strMessage = "Please enter your annual salary."
strTitle = "Salary Data Entry"


    curSalary = Val(InputBox(strMessage, strTitle, "45000"))
    MsgBox "You entered: " & curSalary
```

This procedure prompts the user for his or her salary. The title of the input box uses the strTitle variable contents, *Salary Data Entry*, and the message uses the strMessage variable contents, *Please enter your annual salary*. Including 45000 as the third argument in the InputBox function displays that value as a default value in the input box when the program runs. However, the user can type over that value. The Val function converts the user's entry from a text string to a numeric value, assigns it to the variable curSalary, and a message box displays the entry.

 TIP | **Val Function and Text Entries**

What happens if you enter a text string into the input box that requires a value? The Val function converts any values it cannot interpret as a number to the value of zero. If you enter nonnumeric characters into the input box, the Val function returns a value of zero. If you enter leading numbers followed by characters, the Val function converts the numeric values to numbers. When a custom application has an input box for data input, programmers often include a sentence or two explaining how to enter data. You can include these instructions as a part of the prompt for the input box.

Performing Calculations

To perform calculations within a procedure using variables, you need to create an arithmetic expression. Expressions use operators to perform calculations and join text strings. You can also format the results of calculations.

Use Operators and Order of Precedence

Many of the expressions you create to perform calculations contain functions and operators. An *operator* is a character or combination of characters that accomplishes a specific computation. VBA supports six kinds of operators: arithmetic, assignment, comparison, concatenation, logical, and miscellaneous. Table 1.7 lists the arithmetic operators supported in VBA.

TABLE 1.7　VBA Arithmetic Operators

Operator Symbol	Operator Name	Purpose
^	Exponentiation	Raises a number to the power of another number.
*	Multiplication	Multiplies two numbers.
/	Division	Divides two numbers and returns a floating-point result.
\	Integer Division	Divides two numbers and returns an integer result.
Mod	Modulus arithmetic	Modulus arithmetic, which divides two integer numbers and returns only the remainder.
+	Addition, concatenation	Adds two numbers. Also used to concatenate two strings.
–	Subtraction, negation	Yields the difference between two numbers or indicates the negative value of a numeric expression.
+ or &	String concatenation	Combines two strings.

When several operations occur in an expression, each part is evaluated and used in a predetermined order called operator precedence. **Order of precedence** is the order in which arithmetic expressions are performed. Understanding operator precedence is important for creating expressions that produce the results you want. VBA performs arithmetic calculations left to right in the order: parentheses, exponentiation, multiplication or division, and finally addition or subtraction.

You can use parentheses to override the order of precedence and force some parts of an expression to evaluate before others. When you use parentheses, operations within parentheses occur before those outside. Expressions with parentheses occur according to operator precedence (multiplication, division, addition, subtraction). Code Window 1.12 shows example expressions that perform calculations using constants that have already been declared and variable values obtained from worksheet cells.

```vba
'Declare constants
Const conStTax As Single = 0.065
Const conCityTax As Single = 0.035

'Declare variables
Dim curSaleAmount As Currency
Dim curTotalTax As Currency
Dim curTotalSale As Currency

'Obtain the sale amount
curSaleAmount = Val(InputBox("Enter the sale amount: "))

'Calculate taxes and total sale amount
curTotalTax = curSaleAmount * (conStTax + conCityTax)
curTotalSale = curSaleAmount + curTotalTax

'Display result
MsgBox "The total sale is " & curTotalSale
```

CODE WINDOW 1.12 ➤

Given the two constants in Code Window 1.12, if a user enters 123.45 as the sales amount, the result is 135.795. The addition operation within parentheses occurs first: conStTax (0.065) is added to the conCityTax (0.035). The result of 0.1 is then multiplied by the curSaleAmount (123.45) to calculate the curTotalTax (12.345). Then, the curSaleAmount (123.45) is added to the curTotalTax (12.345); the result (135.795) is then stored in the curTotalSale variable and displayed in the message box.

Format Output Results

You should format values that you display onscreen as results. Unformatted results might display more decimal places than required or not include a currency symbol when you are displaying monetary units. For example, the result of the calculation appears as a decimal value with three digits to the right of the decimal: 135.795.

You can use the **Format function** to format the results of calculations. This function uses predefined formats to change the appearance of text. In its simplest form, the Format function has the following syntax:

Format (expression, style)

Expression refers to the string you want to format, and *style* refers to a named format. Table 1.8 lists the named number styles that you can use with the Format function. VBA also includes named formats for dates. Use Help to learn about other named formats.

TABLE 1.8 Named Styles for Number Formats

Format Name	Description
General Number	Displays a value without a comma for the thousand separator.
Currency	Displays a value with the comma as a thousand separator and displays two digits to the right of the decimal point.
Fixed	Displays a value with at least one digit to the left and two digits to the right of the decimal point.
Standard	Displays a value with a comma as a thousand separator with at least one digit to the left and two digits to the right of the decimal point.
Percent	Displays values multiplied by 100 with two digits to the right of the decimal point with a percent sign (%) on the right side of the value.
Scientific	Uses standard scientific notation.
Yes/No	Displays the word *No* if the value is 0. Displays the word *Yes* for any other value.
True/False	Displays the word *False* if the value is 0. Displays the word *True* for any other value.
On/Off	Displays the word *Off* if the number is 0. Displays the word *On* for any other value.

Code Window 1.13 illustrates the use of Format functions.

```
Dim curSalary As Currency
Dim sngBonus As Single
Dim blnExempt As Boolean

curSalary = 47000
sngBonus = 0.065
blnExempt = 21

MsgBox "Salary: " & Format(curSalary, "Currency") _
       & Chr$(10) & Chr$(13) _
       & "Bonus: " & Format(sngBonus, "Percent") _
       & Chr$(10) & Chr$(13) _
       & "Exempt: " & Format(blnExempt, "Yes/No")
```

CODE WINDOW 1.13 ➤

The procedure in Code Window 1.13 declares three variables and then assigns each a value. The MsgBox statement returns each variable formatted using a named style. To make the code easier to read, the statement uses the line-continuation character. Figure 1.15 displays the formatted results.

FIGURE 1.15 Message Box ➤

TIP | Chr Function

The Chr function requires an integer as its argument and then returns a character associated with that integer. For example, Chr$(10) returns a line feed, and Chr$(13) returns a carriage return. You can create a hard return in a text string by combining the line feed and carriage return characters, as in the previous code example.

Quick Concepts ✓

1. What is the difference between a variable and a constant? Provide an example of each. **p. 20**

2. What is the purpose of an input box? What should the statement do with the return value? **p. 25**

3. What is the purpose of the Format function? **p. 29**

Hands-On Exercises

2 Variables, Constants, Inputs, and Outputs

Tina and Anthony need you to create procedures that perform calculations in the Excel workbook and Access database. You will utilize your knowledge of message boxes, input boxes, variables, and constants to add the desired functionality. Tina asks you to create a procedure to automate the Excel workbook so that she can search for an employee by unique ID, locate that person's salary, and then calculate a 5% bonus for that person.

Skills covered: Declare Variables and Constants • Create an Input Box • Perform Calculations • Use Variables, Constants, Inputs, and Outputs in Access

---

STEP 1 ≫ DECLARE VARIABLES AND CONSTANTS

You need to create a procedure and declare a constant to store the 5% bonus rate and three variables: ID selection, salary, and bonus amount. Refer to Figure 1.16 as you complete Step 1.

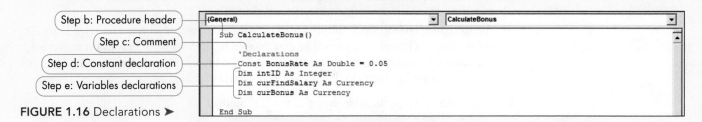

Step b: Procedure header
Step c: Comment
Step d: Constant declaration
Step e: Variables declarations

```
(General)                                    CalculateBonus

Sub CalculateBonus()

    'Declarations
    Const BonusRate As Double = 0.05
    Dim intID As Integer
    Dim curFindSalary As Currency
    Dim curBonus As Currency

End Sub
```

FIGURE 1.16 Declarations ➤

a. Open the macro-enabled *v1h1Acme_LastFirst* workbook in Excel, save it as **v1h2Acme_LastFirst**, and display the VB Editor.

> **TROUBLESHOOTING:** If the Security Warning toolbar displays, click Enable Content.

b. Click at the top of the Code window, type **Sub CalculateBonus()** and press **Enter** twice.

c. Press **Tab**. Type **'Declarations** and press **Enter**.

It is good programming practice to enter comments for blocks of code.

d. Type **Const BonusRate As Double = 0.05** and press **Enter**.

You declared a constant to store the bonus rate. You must enter 5% as a decimal point equivalent in programming code: 0.05.

e. Type **Dim intID As Integer** and press **Enter**.

Type **Dim curFindSalary As Currency** and press **Enter**.

Type **Dim curBonus As Currency** and press **Enter**.

Compare your declarations to those in Figure 1.16. You declared an Integer to store the employee ID, a Currency variable to store the employee's salary, and a Currency variable to store the calculated bonus amount.

f. Click **Save** on the toolbar.

The procedure needs to prompt the user to enter an employee's ID, store it in a variable, and use that variable to find the ID in the list. After the procedure finds the ID, it must make the respective salary the active cell. With the salary as the active cell, the procedure saves the salary value in a variable.

a. Press **Enter**, type the code shown in Code Window 1.14, and press **Enter** twice.

The Application.Goto statement makes the third row (R3) in the first column (C1) the active cell. In VBA, use the abbreviations R and C for row and column respectively.

CODE WINDOW 1.14 ➤

```
'Set the active cell to A3
Application.Goto Reference:="R3C1"

'Display input box to get employee ID
intID = Val(InputBox("Enter ID", "Find Employee's Data"))
```

TROUBLESHOOTING: Look at Code Window 1.14 carefully as you type each statement. Pay close attention to spaces, periods, and spelling to avoid syntax errors.

The last line of code in Code Window 1.14 displays an input box with the message *Enter ID* and the title *Find Employee's Data*. The data entered by the user is a string and is converted to a value with the Val function, which surrounds the InputBox function. Once the input is converted to a value, the value is assigned to the intID variable.

b. Press **Enter** and type the code shown in Code Window 1.15.

CODE WINDOW 1.15 ➤

```
'Use Find dialog box to find ID and select respective salary
Cells.Find(What:=intID, After:=ActiveCell, _
    LookIn:=xlFormulas, LookAt:=xlWhole, _
    SearchOrder:=xlByColumns, SearchDirection:=xlNext, _
    MatchCase:=False, SearchFormat:=False).Activate
ActiveCell.Offset(0, 5).Select
curFindSalary = ActiveCell.Value
```

What:=intID is the equivalent of typing a value in the Find dialog box. You want to use the value in the intID variable. LookAt:=xlWhole requires that the entire cell must be identical to the data entered. If you search for 8, it finds 8 and not 86. SearchOrder:=xlByColumns searches down the current (ID) column rather than across by rows.

TROUBLESHOOTING: A syntax error will occur if you forget to use a line-continuation character to continue a line of code. If you get a syntax error, check to see if the line-continuation character is missing. If so, insert it at the end of each line (except the last) of a complete programming statement. In addition, make sure you type the letters xl, not x and the number 1.

The ActiveCell statement keeps the active cell on the same row (0) and moves over to the right by five cells (5) and makes that cell the active cell. That cell contains the salary for the ID you found. The last statement uses the active cell's value and assigns it to the curFindSalary variable.

c. Click **Save** on the toolbar.

STEP 3 ▶▶ PERFORM CALCULATIONS

To complete the procedure, you need to add an expression to calculate the bonus amount based on the identified salary and the constant bonus rate. After calculating the bonus, you need to format it and display it in a message box. Refer to Figure 1.17 as you complete Step 3.

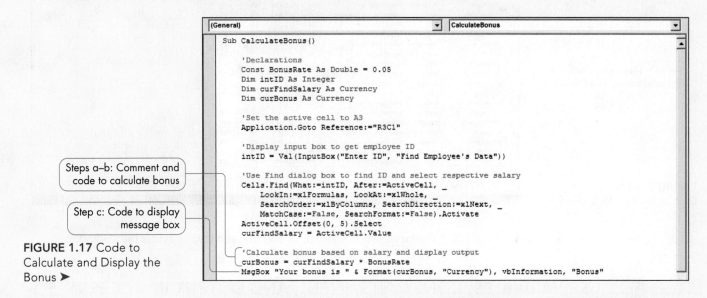

(General)	CalculateBonus

```
Sub CalculateBonus()

    'Declarations
    Const BonusRate As Double = 0.05
    Dim intID As Integer
    Dim curFindSalary As Currency
    Dim curBonus As Currency

    'Set the active cell to A3
    Application.Goto Reference:="R3C1"

    'Display input box to get employee ID
    intID = Val(InputBox("Enter ID", "Find Employee's Data"))

    'Use Find dialog box to find ID and select respective salary
    Cells.Find(What:=intID, After:=ActiveCell, _
        LookIn:=xlFormulas, LookAt:=xlWhole, _
        SearchOrder:=xlByColumns, SearchDirection:=xlNext, _
        MatchCase:=False, SearchFormat:=False).Activate
    ActiveCell.Offset(0, 5).Select
    curFindSalary = ActiveCell.Value

    'Calculate bonus based on salary and display output
    curBonus = curFindSalary * BonusRate
    MsgBox "Your bonus is " & Format(curBonus, "Currency"), vbInformation, "Bonus"
```

Steps a–b: Comment and code to calculate bonus

Step c: Code to display message box

FIGURE 1.17 Code to Calculate and Display the Bonus ➤

a. Press **Enter** twice after the *curFindSalary - Active.Cell.Value* statement. Type **'Calculate bonus based on salary and display output** and press **Enter**.

b. Type **curBonus = curFindSalary * BonusRate** and press **Enter**.

The expression takes the value in curFindSalary and multiplies it by 0.05 in the constant BonusRate. The result is then assigned to the curBonus variable.

c. Type **MsgBox "Your bonus is " & Format(curBonus, "Currency"), vbInformation, "Bonus"** and press **Enter**. Click **Save**.

This statement uses the Format() function to format the curBonus value in Currency format. That result is displayed with the text *Your bonus is* and then displayed in a message box. The message box also contains the Information icon.

> **TROUBLESHOOTING:** Check your code with Figure 1.17 to ensure you entered the statements correctly. The code should contain a space between *is* and the quotation mark to ensure a space displays between the word *is* and the actual salary value.

d. Click **Run Sub/UserForm** on the toolbar.

The Find Employee's Data message box opens.

e. Type **75** and click **OK**.

The procedure finds 75 in the ID column, goes to the right by five cells to find the $81,000 salary, multiplies it by 5%, and displays $4,050.00 in the message box (see Figure 1.18).

Step e: Active cell 5 cells to the right of the ID

Step e: ID value found from input box

Step e: Message box with icon, calculated bonus, and OK button

Step f: Click OK

	A	B	C	D	E	F	G	H
1	ACME Consulting							
2								
3	ID	Last Name	First Name	Job Title	Bill Rate	Salary	401K	ESPP
4	54	Hansen	Patricia	Senior Project Manager	$215	$90,500	2%	2%
5	86	Hunt	Rita	Project Manager	$215	$90,250	4%	5%
6	76	Keating	Brian	Project Manager	$210	$89,500	5%	2%
7	15	Hunt	Robert	Senior Project Manager	$225	$89,000	9%	5%
8	8	Epstein	Abraham	Project Manager	$215	$88,000	4%	3%
9	58	VanGelder	Ben	Senior Project Manager	$210	$87,600	0%	2%
10	12	Tucker	Bill	Project Manager	$200	$87,000	6%	2%
11	75	Willman	Tricia	Senior Consultant	$190	$81,000	2%	2%
12	2	Jackson	Samantha	Senior Consultant				1%
13	99	Bolton	Marianne	Senior Consultant				1%
14	29	Sandoval	Ari	Senior Consultant				4%
15	25	Anderson	Denise	Associate Consul				1%
16	81	Andersen	Dennis	Associate Consul				2%
17	33	Keller	Sally	Associate Consul				0%
18	38	Sandoval	Melissa	Associate Consul				3%
19	63	Watson	Matthew	Senior Consultant				1%
20	9	Williams	Timothy	Associate Consult				1%
21	66	Collins	Jeff	Associate Consultant	$165	$55,000	2%	1%
22	97	Smith	Amanda	Associate Consultant	$175	$55,000	4%	0%
23	39	Martinez	Paul	Associate Consultant	$170	$54,250	3%	3%
24	13	Knoff	Mark	Associate Consultant	$170	$54,000	4%	2%
25								

Bonus dialog box: Your bonus is $4,050.00 — OK

FIGURE 1.18 Bonus Calculated and Displayed ➤

ACME

f. Click **OK** in the message box. Close the VB Editor, and save and close the workbook.

STEP 4 ➤ USE VARIABLES, CONSTANTS, INPUT, AND OUTPUT IN ACCESS

Anthony wants to expand the frmEmployee form so that it calculates and displays the monthly 401K contribution for an employee.

a. Open the *v1h1Acme_LastFirst* database in Access, and save the database as **v1h2Acme_LastFirst**.

> **TROUBLESHOOTING:** If the Security Warning toolbar displays, click Enable Content.

b. Click the **DATABASE TOOLS tab** and click **Visual Basic** in the Macro group.

> **TROUBLESHOOTING:** If you do not see the Visual Basic Editor containing code, double-click Microsoft Access Class Objects in the Project Explorer, and double-click Form_frmEmployee to display its code.

c. Click in the Code window, press **Ctrl+End** to position the insertion point after all existing code and press **Enter**.

d. Type the code shown in Code Window 1.16.

```
Private Sub cmd401K_Click()
    'Declare three variables
    Dim cur401K As Currency
    Dim curSalary As Currency
    Dim sng401K As Single

    'Obtain values from text boxes on the form
    txtSalary.SetFocus
    curSalary = txtSalary.Text

    txt401K.SetFocus
    sng401K = Val(txt401K.Text) / 100

    'Calculate and display the monthly 401K contribution
    cur401K = curSalary / 12 * sng401K
    MsgBox "Your monthly 401K contribution is: " _
            & Format(cur401K, "Currency"), vbInformation, "401K"

End Sub
```

CODE WINDOW 1.16 ➤

You declared two Currency variables and one Single variable.

The txtSalary.SetFocus code makes the txtSalary box have the focus during runtime. That is, when a user clicks the 401K button, the procedure makes the txtSalary box active to select its current value. The curSalary = txtSalary.Text code uses the Text property, which contains the current value of the txtSalary box and then assigns that value to the curSalary variable.

The txt401K.SetFocus code then sets the focus to the txt401K box. The sng401K = Val(txt401K.Text) / 100 statement uses the Text property that contains the current value in the txt401K box, converts it to a value, divides that value by 100 to convert it to a decimal amount, and then assigns the result to the sng401K variable.

The next statement calculates the 401K value and stores the result in the cur401K variable. The last statement in the procedure displays a message box with the value in the cur401K variable formatted as Currency.

e. Click **Save** on the toolbar and close the VB Editor.

f. Open the form in Form view and click **401K** in the form.

Timothy Williams's 401K contribution is $145.00 (see Figure 1.19).

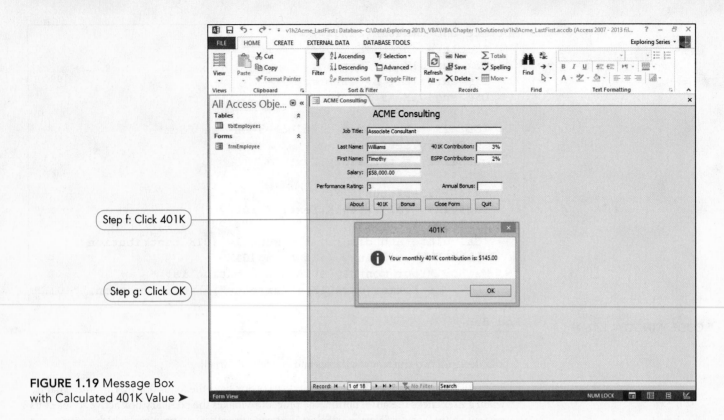

FIGURE 1.19 Message Box
with Calculated 401K Value ➤

g. Click **OK** and exit Access.

Decision Structures

When you customize applications with VBA, you write code using program statements that tell the computer exactly what to do based on a programming structure. A *programming structure* is the sequence in which the program statements execute at runtime. Programmers use programming structures to organize code statements in one of three ways: with a sequence structure, a decision structure, or a repetition structure.

If the program executes statements in the order that they appear, it uses the *sequence structure*. All of the sub procedures you have written up to this point use the sequence structure because the program statements execute in a direct sequence when the procedure runs. That is, the first statement runs, followed by each successive statement until all statements have run, with no statements skipped. Sequence structures are the simplest programming structures.

In this section, you will learn how to use decision structures in VBA procedures. Specifically, you will create procedures that use the If…Then, If…Then…Else and Select Case decision structures. You will then learn how to use decision structures to perform data validation and how to include logical operators in decision structures.

Using Decision Structures

A *decision structure* is a programming structure that makes a comparison between values, variables, and/or constants. Based on the result of that comparison, the program executes statements in a certain order. If the result of the comparison is true (or yes), one statement executes, but if the result of the comparison is false (or no), an alternative statement executes. Thus the result of the comparison determines which path the program takes.

By phrasing the conditions in terms of a question, you can determine the appropriate course of action. For example, *Is the curGrossPay value greater than or equal to 500?* A *condition* is an expression that uses a *relational operator* (such as = and <=) to compare two values (through variables, constants, or expressions) and determine whether the result of the comparison is true or false. An expression is a combination of variables and operators that performs a calculation or returns a value. A comparison that uses relational operators is a *logical test*, which is always contained within a decision structure. In programming, you can use a logical test within your program statements to respond to conditions that vary. VBA uses the relational operators listed in Table 1.9.

TABLE 1.9 Relational Operators		
Format Name	**Tests Whether the Value of …**	**Example**
=	two operands are equal.	txtLastName.Text = Smith
<>	two operands are not equal.	Val(txtLoanAmont.Text)<>0
<	the first operand is less than the value of the second operand.	Val(txtLoanAmount.Text)<25000
>	the first operand is greater than the value of the second operand.	Val(txt401K.Text)>100000
<=	the first operand is less than or equal to the second operand.	sngConversionResult<=300
>=	the first operand is greater than or equal to the second operand.	curGrossPay>=500

Decision structures use relational operators to make comparisons that perform a logical test. You can use a decision statement to test whether a condition is true or false, to test a series of conditions, or to make a selection when a condition is true. Table 1.10 lists the decision structures supported in VBA.

TABLE 1.10 Decision Structures Supported in VBA	
Decision Statement	**Usage**
If...Then	Performs a logical test. If the test evaluates to True, the program executes a specific statement or block of statements.
If...Then...Else	Performs a logical test. If the test evaluates to True, the program executes a specific statement or block of statements. If the test evaluates to False, the program executes a different statement or block of statements.
Select Case	Compares the same expression to several different values. The Select statement evaluates a single expression only once and uses it for every comparison. When the test evaluates to True, the case is applied.

Create an If...Then Structure

The *If...Then structure* represents the simplest kind of decision structure. An If...Then structure performs a logical test; if the test evaluates to True, the program code specifies what action to take. No alternative statements are executed if the logical test is false, however.

Suppose an employer wants to encourage its employees to make a year-end contribution to the company's 401K retirement plan. The standard match is 25%. If an employee contributes more than $500, the company will match the contribution at 50%. You can phrase this decision as a question:

- Is the contribution greater than $500?
- Yes: Match is 50%
- No: Match is 25% (keep the original 25% match)

STEP 1 Code Window 1.17 shows how to implement this decision in a VBA procedure.

```
Dim curContribution As Currency
Dim sngMatch As Single
sngMatch = 0.25

curContribution = Val(InputBox("Enter the contribution amount", _
                  "401K Contribution"))

'Test if contribution is greater than 500
'If true, assign 0.5 to sngMatch
'If false, maintain existing value (0.25)
If curContribution > 500 Then
    sngMatch = 0.5
End If

MsgBox "We will match your contribution by " & _
        Format(sngMatch, "Percent")
```

CODE WINDOW 1.17 ➤

This procedure declares two variables: a Currency data type for contribution amount and a Single data type for the match percentage, which is assigned a default value of 0.25. An input box prompts the user to enter a contribution amount. The If...Then structure performs the logical test; if the contribution exceeds 500, it assigns a new value to the sngMatch variable. A message box displays the match percentage. For example, if a user types 600 in the input box, the message box will display 50.00%. If the user types 500 in the input box, the message box will display 25.00%.

Create an If...Then...Else Structure

You can use an *If...Then...Else structure* to test for a condition and specify one option if the test evaluates to True and another if it evaluates to False. Use the If...Then...Else structure to determine the appropriate matching percentage for an employee's 401K contribution. Because the structure tests a condition and specifies a path for a True and a False result, you do not need to set a default value for the sngMatch variable. Figure 1.20 illustrates the process using a flowchart, and Code Window 1.18 shows the code. The code in Code Window 1.18 does the same thing as the code in Code Window 1.17. However, some programmers prefer to explicitly assign a value to a variable instead of relying on the program to maintain a previous value for a variable.

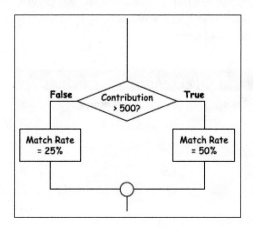

FIGURE 1.20 If...Then...Else Flowchart ➤

```
Dim curContribution As Currency
Dim sngMatch As Single

curContribution = Val(InputBox("Enter the contribution amount", _
                "401K Contribution"))

'Test if contribution is greater than 500
'If true, assign 0.5 to sngMatch
'If false, assign 0.25 to sngMatch
If curContribution > 500 Then
    sngMatch = 0.5
Else
    sngMatch = 0.25
End If

MsgBox "We will match your contribution by " & _
        Format(sngMatch, "Percent")
```

CODE WINDOW 1.18 ➤

STEP 2》 The structure begins with *If* and ends with *End If*. The word *Then* must appear after the logical test. In this example, the procedure performs the logical test before assigning a value to the sngMatch variable. Note that the logical test sngContribution > 500 is executed only once. The test evaluates to either True or False. If the result is True, the statement after Then is executed. If the result is False, the statement after the Else is executed.

Create a Select Case Structure

The conditions you need to test sometimes become complex and require one or more If statements nested within another If statement. Suppose ACME Consulting pays employees an annual bonus that is a percentage of the employee's salary. The percentage used is determined by the employee's performance rating. Managers rate employee performance on a 10-point scale (see Table 1.11). For example, if an employee gets a rating between 1 and 3, that person earns a 5% bonus.

TABLE 1.11 Ratings and Bonus Percentages	
Performance Rating	**Bonus Percentage**
0	No Bonus
1–3	5%
4–8	7.5%
9 and above	10%

You can determine each employee's rating using nested If structures. Figure 1.21 models this decision in a flowchart. The circle at the bottom of the flowchart indicates the end of the algorithm.

FIGURE 1.21 Flowchart Modeling Nested If Structure ➤

You can nest as many levels of If structures as your application requires; however, nesting too deeply makes code hard to model, write, and manage. The Select Case structure is a good alternative to nested If structures when you need to test a single variable or expression for multiple values, such as testing for an employee's performance rating and returning one of four possible values depending upon the rating. The Select Case structure is simpler than a nested If structure; the code is more concise for testing one value against multiple conditions.

The **Select Case structure** compares an expression or a value to a case block, which is the set of cases that might apply. A case is an individual condition to test. You can easily code this complex decision structure using the Select Case structure. Figure 1.22 models this decision with a flowchart, and Code Window 1.19 illustrates the use of a Select Case statement.

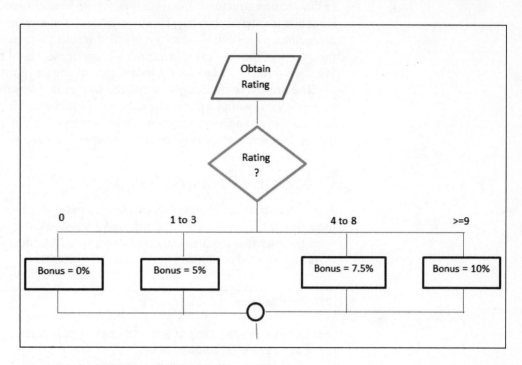

FIGURE 1.22 Flowchart Modeling Select Case Structure ➤

```
Dim curSalary As Currency
Dim curBonusPay As Currency
Dim sngBonus As Single
Dim intRating As Integer

curSalary = InputBox("Enter your salary", "Salary")
intRating = InputBox("Enter your performance rating", "Rating")

Select Case intRating
    Case Is < 1
        sngBonus = 0
    Case 1 To 3
        sngBonus = 0.05
    Case 4 To 8
        sngBonus = 0.075
    Case Is > 8
        sngBonus = 0.1
End Select

curBonusPay = curSalary * sngBonus
MsgBox "Your bonus is " & Format(curBonusPay, "Currency")
```

CODE WINDOW 1.19 ➤

The case block begins with *Select Case* and ends with *End Select*. The Select Case structure uses the case block to determine the appropriate bonus rate based on the performance rating value. When the structure tests a single value, the *Case Is* statement is used. When the structure tests a range of values, the words *Case Is* are followed by the range of values. If a user enters 45500 for the salary and 5 for the performance rating, the calculated bonus is $3,412.50. Not shown in the example is an optional *Case Else* statement. You can use this statement after all *Case Is* statements to catch all other conditions and perform an action.

Performing Data Validation

In the decision structures discussed thus far, we have assumed that the data entered into an input box is entered correctly. However, users can inadvertently enter text where a number is required, which can produce unintended results. Because computer output depends on the quality of the data the user supplies, programmers need to check the values entered in Windows forms to make sure the data is appropriate for its intended use.

The process of checking data entered by a user to ensure it meets certain conditions, such as a value within a particular range or values instead of text, is called **data validation**. You can use decision structures to display a message if the user fails to enter the required data or to ensure that users enter numbers where they are needed to perform calculations.

Check for a Required Value

A common data validation task is checking to make sure users input required data. You can use a simple If…Then…Else structure and a message box to confirm the data entered or to warn the user that required data is missing. Code Window 1.20 checks to make sure that users have entered an annual salary greater than 25000.

```
Dim curSalary As Currency

curSalary = Val(InputBox("Enter your salary", "Salary"))
If curSalary > 25000 Then
    MsgBox "You entered " & curSalary
Else
    MsgBox "Not a valid entry", vbCritical, "Invalid Data"
End If
```

CODE WINDOW 1.20 ➤

The Val function converts the user's entry into a numeric value. If text is entered instead of a valid number, the function returns a value of zero. The decision structure displays one of two messages, depending upon the value supplied.

Check for a Numeric Value

You have used the Val function to convert data entered into a text box to a numeric value for performing calculations. However, if the Val function encounters an empty text string, it converts the empty string to a value of zero. Therefore, it is important to validate numeric data before performing calculations.

VBA includes a function designed to determine whether data entered is a numeric value. The **IsNumeric function** checks a text string and determines whether it evaluates as a number. If the string does evaluate as a number, the function returns a Boolean value of True. Otherwise, the function returns False. The function requires one argument: the expression to evaluate. The required argument can be a variable, a property of a control, or a text string. Code Window 1.21 illustrates the use of the IsNumeric function.

```
Dim varSalary
varSalary = InputBox("Enter your salary", "Salary")

If IsNumeric(varSalary) = False Then
    MsgBox "Enter your salary as a number"
Else
    MsgBox "You entered " & varSalary
End If
```

This procedure declares a variable for the salary without specifying a data type, so the default data type is variant. The If…Then…Else structure checks the value. If the user has not made an entry or if the user enters invalid characters, the function returns False. A numeric or decimal value returns a Boolean result of True. For example, if the user enters 25000, the return value is True. If the user enters nothing, the return value is False.

Using Logical Operators

You can test for more than one condition in a decision structure by using logical operators. A *logical operator* is an operator that uses Boolean logic to test conditions. The *And operator* requires that all conditions included in the statement evaluate to True. The *Or operator* requires that any one of the conditions evaluate to True.

Use the Or Logical Operator

Code Window 1.22 shows a procedure that declares a string variable and then prompts the user for a text string to assign to the variable. The procedure then uses the Or operator to validate the text string as being either Smith or Jones.

```
Dim strText As String
strText = InputBox("Enter either 'Smith' or 'Jones'")
If strText = "Smith" Or strText = "Jones" Then
    MsgBox "Your data entry passes the test: " & strText
Else
    MsgBox "Invalid Data", vbCritical, "Error"
End If
```

If the user enters Smith or Jones, a message informs the user that the data is valid. If the user enters anything else or does not make an entry, a message informs the user that the data is invalid. The text comparisons are case sensitive. If the user enters smith or sMiTh, the data entry does not match the text string specified in the logical test; therefore, the Invalid Data message box would appear.

Use the And Logical Operator

STEP 4 ➤ You might need to perform a logical test to ensure that two or more conditions are true. For example, you might need the user to enter a value within a particular range. Use the And logical operator to ensure the user input meets the minimum value and another test to ensure the user input does not exceed the maximum value. Code Window 1.23 declares an integer variable and then prompts the user for a value between 10 and 90. The procedure then uses the And operator to validate the entry as being greater than or equal to 10 and less than or equal to 90.

```
Dim intValue As Integer
intValue = InputBox("Enter an integer between 10 and 90")

If Val(intValue) >= 10 And Val(intValue) <= 90 Then
    MsgBox "Your data passes the test: " & intValue
Else
    MsgBox "Invalid Data", vbCritical, "Error"
End If
```

CODE WINDOW 1.23 ➤

If the user enters a number that is greater than or equal to 10 and less than or equal to 90, a message appears indicating that the data is valid. If the user enters anything else or does not make an entry, a message appears indicating that the data is invalid.

Quick
Concepts

1. Explain when to use an If…Then…Else structure and a Select Case structure. ***pp. 39–40***

2. Why should programmers write data validation code? ***p. 42***

3. What is the difference in using the Or and And logical operators in decision structures? ***p. 43***

Hands-On Exercises

3 Decision Structures

Anthony wants you to complete the programming code for the buttons on the frmEmployee form in the Access database. Specifically, you need to write procedures for the Quit, 401K, and Bonus buttons.

Skills covered: Create an If...Then Structure • Create an If...Then...Else Decision Structure • Create a Select Case Structure • Use the And Logical Operator to Perform Data Validation

---

STEP 1 ≫ CREATE AN IF...THEN STRUCTURE

Anthony wants a confirmation message box to display when the user clicks Quit. Currently, when a user clicks Quit, the database closes without any confirmation. Refer to Figure 1.23 as you complete Step 1.

FIGURE 1.23 Message Box ➤

a. Open the *v1h2Acme_LastFirst* database and save it as **v1h3Acme_ LastFirst**.

> **TROUBLESHOOTING:** If the Security Warning toolbar displays, click Enable Content.

b. Open the VB Editor and display the code in the Code window.

c. Select the code in the Private Sub cmdQuit_Click() procedure. Do not select the header or the End Sub statements. Press **Delete** to delete the statements within this procedure.

d. Type the code shown in Code Window 1.24. The procedure header and End Sub statements should already exist.

```
Private Sub cmdQuit_Click()

    'Display message box when user clicks Quit
    Dim intResponse As Integer
    intResponse = MsgBox("Do you want to exit this application?", _
                 vbYesNo + vbCritical, "Exit?")

    'If user clicks Yes, save record and exit Access
    If intResponse = 6 Then
        DoCmd.Save
        DoCmd.Quit
    End If

End Sub
```

CODE WINDOW 1.24▲

The MsgBox function returns an integer that is assigned to the intResponse variable. You use the If…Then decision structure to determine if the user clicked Yes, which is assigned an integer of 6. If so, the procedure saves the current record and quits the application. If the user clicks No, nothing happens. The database remains open with the form onscreen.

e. Click **Save** on the toolbar and close the VB Editor.

f. Display the form in Form view and click **Quit** in the form (see Figure 1.23).

g. Click **No**.

The form and Access remain open.

h. Click **Quit** again and click **Yes** in the message box to close the database.

STEP 2 ≫ CREATE AN IF…THEN…ELSE DECISION STRUCTURE

Your next task is to revise the procedure for the 401K button. You need to create an If…Then…Else decision structure to determine whether to add a 5% contribution to the existing percent for senior project managers or add a 3% contribution to the existing percent for other employees. Refer to Figure 1.24 as you complete Step 2.

FIGURE 1.24 Message Box ➤

a. Open the *v1h3Acme_LastFirst* database.

b. Open the VB Editor and display the code in the Code window.

c. Place the insertion point on the blank line below the *Dim sng401K As Single* variable declaration in the Sub cmd401K_Click() procedure.

d. Type **Dim strTitle As String** and press **Enter** to declare a string variable.

You declared a string variable that you will use to store the text the user enters in a field in the form.

e. Place the insertion point on the blank line below *sng401K = Val(txt401K.Text) / 100* statement and type the code shown in Code Window 1.25. Press **Enter** to leave a blank line between this block of code and the comment below it.

CODE WINDOW 1.25 ➤

```
If strTitle = "Senior Project Manager" Then
    sng401K = sng401K + 0.05
Else
    sng401K = sng401K + 0.03
End If
```

f. Click **Save** and close the VB Editor.

g. Display the form in Form view and click **401K** in the form.

The current employee is an associate consultant. Therefore, the conditional expression is false. The procedure adds 3% to the current 401K contribution of 3% and then multiplies it by the salary and divides by 12. The result is $290.00.

h. Click **OK**, navigate to the fifth record in the form, and click **401K**.

Patricia is a senior project manager. Therefore, the conditional expression is true. The procedure adds 5% to the current 401K contribution of 2%. The result of 7% is multiplied by the salary and divided by 12. The result is $377.08.

i. Click **OK** to close the message box and click **Close Form**.

STEP 3 ›› CREATE A SELECT CASE STRUCTURE

Anthony wants to create a set of rules to calculate employees' bonuses based on their respective performance ratings. A rating of 0 means no bonus. A rating of 1–3 earns a 5% bonus, a rating of 4–7 earns a 7.5% bonus, and a rating of 8–10 earns a 10% bonus. You will create a Select Case decision structure to identify the correct bonus rate and use that rate to calculate the bonus amount. Refer to Figure 1.25 as you complete Step 3.

Step e: Bonus calculated and displayed on the form

Step e: Click Bonus

FIGURE 1.25 Results of Select Case Structure ➤

a. Open the VB Editor again.

b. Position the insertion point after the last procedure's End Sub statement and press **Enter**.

c. Type the code shown in Code Window 1.26.

```
Private Sub cmdBonus_Click()

    'Declare variables
    Dim curSalary As Currency
    Dim intRating As Integer
    Dim sngBonus As Single
    Dim curBonus As Currency

    'Obtain salary and performance rating
    txtSalary.SetFocus
    curSalary = txtSalary.Text

    txtRating.SetFocus
    intRating = txtRating.Text

        'Calculate the bonus
        Select Case intRating
            Case Is = 0
                sngBonus = 0
            Case 1 To 3
                sngBonus = 0.05
            Case 4 To 7
                sngBonus = 0.075
            Case 8 To 10
                sngBonus = 0.1
        End Select

        'Calculate the bonus and assign to the txtBonus text box
        curBonus = curSalary * sngBonus
        txtBonus.SetFocus
        txtBonus.Text = curBonus

End Sub
```

CODE WINDOW 1.26 ➤

You declared four variables. The second block of code sets the focus to text boxes to obtain values and assign those values to two variables. The Select Case statement uses the performance rating to determine which bonus rate to select. The last block of code multiplies the bonus rate by the current salary, calculates the bonus, and displays the bonus on the form.

d. Click **Save** on the toolbar and close the VB Editor.

e. Display the form in Form view and click **Bonus** in the form.

The Bonus text box displays $2,900 for the first employee. The performance rating of 3 qualifies Timothy for the 5% bonus rate. Five percent of his $58,000 salary equals his $2,900 bonus. This value is added to Timothy's record in the tblEmployees table.

f. Click the **Next record button** at the bottom of the form window to accept the entry.

 TIP **Assigning a Value to a Text Box**

The procedures you have written to obtain a value from a text box use the SetFocus method to set the focus to the text box and then assign the text value to a variable. In this procedure, you assigned the value of a variable to the Text property of a text box by setting the focus to the text box and then assigning the value of the variable to the Text property of the text box.

STEP 4 ≫ USE THE AND LOGICAL OPERATOR TO PERFORM DATA VALIDATION

Before implementing the database for other users to use, you want to add one data validation structure. You want to make sure the user enters a whole number between 0 and 10 in the Performance Rating text box on the form. If a user enters a negative value or a number over 10, you want to display an error message and select the text box contents so the user can try again. Refer to Figure 1.26 as you complete Step 4.

FIGURE 1.26 Message When User Enters Invalid Rating ➤

a. Display the VB Editor.

b. Use Code Window 1.27 to insert the If statement between the *txtRating.SetFocus* and *intRating = txtRating.Text* statements. Press **Enter** to leave a blank line after the If statement and press **Tab** to indent the intRating = txt.Text statement.

```
txtRating.SetFocus

If Val(txtRating.Text) >= 0 And Val(txtRating.Text) <= 10 Then

    intRating = txtRating.Text

    'Calculate the bonus
    Select Case intRating
        Case Is = 0
            sngBonus = 0
        Case 1 To 3
            sngBonus = 0.05
        Case 4 To 7
            sngBonus = 0.075
        Case 8 To 10
            sngBonus = 0.1
    End Select

    'Calculate the bonus and assign to the txtBonus text box
    curBonus = curSalary * sngBonus
    txtBonus.SetFocus
    txtBonus.Text = curBonus
Else
    MsgBox "Rating must be a whole number between 0 and 10. Try again.", _
        vbCritical, "Error"
    txtRating.SetFocus
End If
```

CODE WINDOW 1.27 ▲

c. Position the insertion point on the blank line below txtBonus.Text = curBonus. Use Code Window 1.27 to insert the Else, Message Box, and End If lines of code.

The If structure tests to see if the data contained in the Performance Rating text box is a value between 0 and 10. If so, the data is valid, and the rest of the code to calculate the bonus executes. If the data is not valid (that is, the value is negative or above 10), a message box displays the error and selects the text box value so that the user can enter a correct value and try again.

d. Click **Save** on the toolbar and close the VB Editor.

e. Select the value in the **Performance Rating text box** on the form, type **14**, and click **Bonus**.

A message box displays (see Figure 1.26) because the data you entered is not valid.

f. Click **OK** in the message box, type **3**, and click **Bonus** on the form.

Because the performance rating 3 is valid, the message box does not display. The remaining code in the procedure executes, and the calculated bonus $2,900 displays in the Annual Bonus text box.

g. Exit Access.

Repetition Structures

Programmers use decision structures when an application requires a program to analyze conditions. Sometimes, however, you need to complete an operation a specific number of times while a certain condition is true or until a condition is true. For example, a payroll application may need to calculate employee bonuses for all eligible employees. To accomplish this, you can use a *repetition structure*, which repeats the execution of a series of program statements. You can use two types of statements to define repetition structures: For…Next and Do…Loop.

In this section, you will learn how to use For…Next and Do…Loop repetition structures.

Using the For…Next Structure

The *For…Next structure* repeats a *loop*—a set of statements or a procedure—a specific number of times. As the computer processes the statements, one execution of the loop is an *iteration*. When you use looping, which is the process of repeating a procedure until a condition is met, the statements repeat until the condition is true, until the condition is false, or until they have repeated for a specified number of times.

The For…Next statement requires a *counter variable*, which is used to count the number of times the loop repeats. The counter increases or decreases in value during each repetition of the loop. An increment is an increase in the value of the counter; a decrement is a decrease in the value of the counter. The start value is the value at which it begins incrementing. The end value is the final value of the counter. When the counter reaches this value, the loop ends. The *step value* is the amount by which the counter is incremented during each cycle of the loop. The step value, which is optional, can be positive or negative. If it is omitted, VBA supplies a default value of 1.

STEP 1 >>

Code Window 1.28 shows an incrementing For…Next loop and a decrementing For…Next loop. In the first loop, the intCounter counter variable starts at 1 and ends at 5, incrementing by 1 each time. During each iteration, the loop produces a message box that displays the counter variable's value. After five iterations, the loop ends. In the second loop, the intCount counter variable starts at 5 and ends at 1, decreasing by 1 each time. During each iteration, the loop produces a message box that displays the counter variable's value. After five iterations, the loop ends. When one procedure uses two loops, you should declare two separate counter variables, each with its own name such as intCount and intCounter.

```
'Counter increments by 1 each time
Dim intCounter As Integer
For intCounter = 1 To 5 Step 1
    MsgBox intCounter
Next

'Counter decrements by 1 each time
Dim intCount As Integer
For intCount = 5 To 1 Step -1
    MsgBox intCount
Next
```

CODE WINDOW 1.28 ➤

As you create For...Next loops, it is important to consider under which conditions a loop will never reach the end value. For example, you could inadvertently add a statement that resets the counter, as shown in the following code statements:

```
For intCounter = 1 To 4
        strName = strName & InputBox("Please enter a name.")
        intCounter = 1
Next
```

This loop is infinite, meaning that it will never reach the end value because the counter value is reset to 1 during each iteration of the loop. Avoid introducing an infinite loop into your programs; this is considered a poor programming practice. Test your loops to make sure they will not run endlessly.

Using the Do...Loop Structure

For...Next loops are an appropriate choice when you know how many iterations the loop will require. However, sometimes, you do not know in advance when a loop will end because the loop will continue until a certain condition is met. Do...Loops are appropriate when you do not know in advance how many times you need to execute the statements in the loop. A ***Do...Loop structure*** differs from the For...Next structure in that it executes a block of statements while a condition remains true or until a condition is true. In either case, you do not define an end value for the loop. Do...Loop statements execute a series of statements an indefinite number of times, depending on the Boolean value of the condition. The Do...Loop structure uses the keywords *While* or *Until*.

Loop While the Condition Is True

Use the While keyword in a Do...Loop to repeat the iterations of the loop *while* the condition is true. VBA provides two ways to use the While keyword to check the condition: by specifying the condition *before* entering the loop or by checking for the condition *after* the loop runs. Because the loop performs a test to check for the condition, specifying the condition before entering the loop uses a ***pretest*** to test for the condition, and testing the condition after entering the loop uses a ***posttest*** to check the condition. In either case, looping continues for as long as the condition remains true.

STEP 2 ▶▶   Code Window 1.29 illustrates pretest and posttest Do While loop structures. In both examples, the loops iterate five times.

```
'Pretest Loop
Dim intCounter As Integer
intCounter = 1
Do While intCounter <= 5
    MsgBox "intCounter is " & intCounter, _
            vbInformation, "Do While Pretest"
        intCounter = intCounter + 1
Loop

'Posttest Loop
Dim intCount As Integer
intCount = 1
Do
    MsgBox "intCount is " & intCount, _
            vbInformation, "Do While Posttest"
        intCount = intCount + 1
Loop While intCount <= 5
```

CODE WINDOW 1.29 ➤

Loop Until a Condition Becomes True

Use the Until keyword in a Do…Loop to repeat the iterations of the loop until the specified condition evaluates to True. The structure is similar to the While keyword. As with the While keyword, you can check the condition before you enter the loop by using a pretest or after the loop has run at least once by using a posttest. In either case, looping continues until the condition evaluates to True.

Code Window 1.30 illustrates pretest and posttest Do Until loop structures. In the pretest loop, the logical test intCounter > 5 is False to start because intCounter starts at 1. The loop iterates until the logical test is true. After the fifth iteration, intCounter is 6. When the logical test is performed again, the condition is met and the loop does not iterate a sixth time. In the posttest loop, the loop iterates at least one time before performing the logical test. After the first iteration, intCount is 2, the logical test intCount > 5 is False, so the loop iterates again. After the fifth iteration, intCount is 6. When the logical test is performed again, the condition is met, and the loop does not iterate a sixth time.

```
'Pretest Loop
Dim intCounter As Integer
intCounter = 1
Do Until intCounter > 5
    MsgBox "intCounter is " & intCounter, _
            vbInformation, "Do Until Pretest"
        intCounter = intCounter + 1
Loop

'Posttest Loop
Dim intCount As Integer
intCount = 1
Do
    MsgBox "intCount is " & intCount, _
            vbInformation, "Do Until Posttest"
        intCount = intCount + 1
Loop Until intCount > 5
```

CODE WINDOW 1.30 ➤

Quick Concepts

1. Explain how a For…Next loop structure works. *p. 51*

2. What is the difference between a pretest and posttest in repetition structures? *p. 52*

3. What is an infinite loop? *p. 52*

Hands-On Exercises

4 Repetition Structures

Tina wants you to create two procedures in the Excel workbook to display cumulative monthly salary data. You will use the For…Next loop structure to create a procedure to show cumulative gross salary for a 12-month period. You will then use a Do…Loop structure to display cumulative gross salary, cumulative taxes, and cumulative net pay for a 12-month period.

Skills covered: Use the For…Next Structure • Loop While a Condition Is True

---

STEP 1 ➤ USE THE FOR…NEXT STRUCTURE

Tina wants a user to enter an employee's ID, look up the salary, and then display a message box that shows the cumulative salary for a 12-month period. You can copy some code you created in Hands-On Exercise 2 to find a salary for a particular ID. Then you need to create a For…Next repetition structure to store the data in a string and then display the string in a message box. Refer to Figure 1.27 as you complete Step 1.

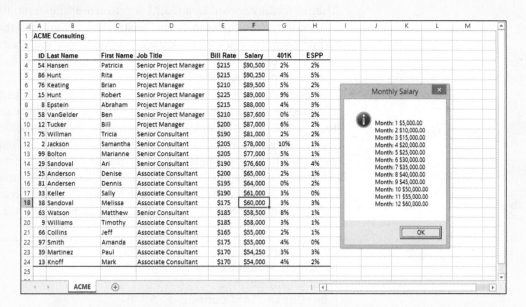

FIGURE 1.27 Results of For… Next Structure ➤

a. Open *v1h2Acme_LastFirst.xlsm* in Excel, save it as **v1h4Acme_LastFirst.xlsm**, and open the VB Editor.

b. Position the insertion point before the Sub CalculateBonus() statement. Type the procedure header, comment, and four declarations shown in Code Window 1.31.

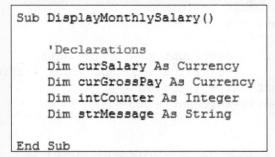

```
Sub DisplayMonthlySalary()

    'Declarations
    Dim curSalary As Currency
    Dim curGrossPay As Currency
    Dim intCounter As Integer
    Dim strMessage As String

End Sub
```

CODE WINDOW 1.31 ➤

c. Scroll to the CalculateBonus() procedure and start selecting with the comment *Set the active cell to A3* through *curFindSalary = ActiveCell.Value*. Click **Copy** on the toolbar, position the insertion point on the blank line below the declarations in the Sub DisplayMonthlySalary() procedure, press **Enter**, and click **Paste** on the toolbar.

You copied the statements that set cell A3 as the active cell, display a dialog box to enable the user to find an ID, locate the respective salary for that ID, and then save it in a variable.

d. Change *curFindSalary* to **curSalary** in the Sub DisplayMonthlySalary procedure.

The CalculateBonus() procedure declared and used a variable named curFindSalary. However, you need to edit the variable name in the current procedure, which uses curSalary as a variable name instead.

e. Click at the end of the curSalary statement, press **Enter** twice, and type the rest of the code shown in Code Window 1.32. Leave one blank line between the MsgBox statement and the End Sub statement.

```
'Calculate monthly pay and display cumulative pay
intCounter = 1
curGrossPay = curSalary / 12

For intCounter = 1 To 12
    strMessage = strMessage & vbCrLf & "Month: " & intCounter & " " _
            & Format(curGrossPay * intCounter, "Currency")
Next

MsgBox strMessage, vbInformation, "Monthly Salary"
```

CODE WINDOW 1.32 ⟁

The code initializes the counter variable, intCounter, to 1 and divides the annual salary by 12 to get a monthly salary. The For...Next loop adds to the existing string, which accumulates during each iteration. The vbCrLf inserts a carriage return within the string, adds the text *Month:*, and enters the current counter variable's value. The monthly salary is multiplied by the current loop's iteration for the month number, formats the value as currency, and adds that to the string.

After the 12th iteration, the loop ends, and a message box displays the cumulative salary by month. You indented the carryover line for the strMessage assignment statement so that the variable name stands out.

f. Click **Save** on the toolbar, click **Run** on the toolbar, and select **Run Sub/UserForm**.

g. Type **38** in the input box and click **OK**.

The procedure finds the ID containing 38, identifies and stores the respective salary ($60,000), and uses that salary to calculate the monthly pay and the cumulative pay. The message box displays a string containing the entire 12-month data.

h. Click **OK** in the message box.

Anthony and Tina like the last procedure you wrote and want one that displays cumulative taxes and cumulative net pay. You will use the Do While repetition structure this time. Refer to Figure 1.28 as you complete Step 2.

FIGURE 1.28 Result of Do While Repetition Structure ➤

a. Display the VB Editor in Excel again, if necessary. Position the insertion point before the Sub DisplayMonthlySalary() statement, and press **Enter** twice.

b. Press **Ctrl+Home** and then type the procedure name, comment, declarations, and assignment as shown in Code Window 1.33.

```
Sub DisplayMonthlyDetails()

    'Declarations
    Dim curSalary As Currency
    Dim curGrossPay As Currency
    Dim curTaxes As Currency
    Dim intCounter As Integer
    Const TaxRate As Single = 0.125
    strMessage = "Month" & vbTab & "Gross" & vbTab & "Taxes" & vbTab & "Net"

End Sub
```

CODE WINDOW 1.33 ▲

The strMessage assignment statement adds the words *Month*, *Gross*, *Taxes*, and *Net*. You use the vbTab character constant to insert tabs between the words within the string variable.

c. Select and copy the *'Set the active cell* comment through *curGrossPay = curSalary / 12* in the DisplayMonthlySalary procedure, and paste it below the strMessage assignment statement in the DisplayMonthlyDetails procedure. Check spacing to make sure the pasted code does not continue with existing code. If needed, press **Enter** to separate pasted code from existing code.

d. Edit the first pasted comment to be **Set the active cell to A3 and display input box to get ID**. Delete the blank line below the *Application.Goto* statement and delete the *Display input to get employee ID* comment.

e. Position the insertion point after the *curGrossPay = curSalary / 12* statement and press **Enter**. Type **curTaxes = curGrossPay * TaxRate** and press **Enter**.

This expression multiplies the employee's gross pay by the constant tax rate. The product is then stored in the curTaxes variable.

f. Type **curNetPay = curGrossPay – curTaxes** and press **Enter** twice.

This expression subtracts the value in the curTaxes variable from the value in the curGrossPay variable. The result is then stored in the curNetPay variable.

g. Type the comment and the Do While statement block and the MsgBox statement shown in Code Window 1.34. Leave one blank line between the last statement and the End Sub statement.

```
'Calculate, store, and display cumulative salary data
Do While intCounter <= 12
    strMessage = strMessage & vbCrLf & intCounter & " " _
                & vbTab & Format(curGrossPay * intCounter, "$#,###") _
                & vbTab & Format(curTaxes * intCounter, "$#,###") _
                & vbTab & Format(curNetPay * intCounter, "$#,###")
    intCounter = intCounter + 1
Loop

MsgBox strMessage, vbInformation, "Monthly Salary Details"
```

CODE WINDOW 1.34 ⬆

The loop iterates 12 times, once for each month. The loop continues to add to the existing strMessage variable using the & concatenation character. The vbCrLf character constant inserts a carriage return to store each month's data on a separate line in the string variable.

For each iteration, the current intCounter's value is added to the string to indicate month 1, month 2, and so on. The vbTab character constant inserts tabs between data. The Format function formats values with a custom Currency type: $#,### to avoid zeros for cents. The last line of the loop increments the counter.

After the loop terminates, the MsgBox statement displays the contents of the strMessage.

h. Click **Save** and run the DisplayMonthlyDetails procedure.

i. Type **38** in the input box and click **OK**.

j. Click **OK** in the message box, close the VB Editor, and exit Excel.

Chapter Objectives Review

After reading this chapter, you have accomplished the following objectives:

1. **Use VBA and get Help.**
   - The VB Editor contains the tools needed to write code or edit macros for Microsoft Office applications. The window contains a toolbar, a menu bar, a Project window, a Property window, and a Code window.
   - If you click Help within the VB Editor, the Microsoft Developer Network opens in a web browser so that you can search for information. For specific help on a keyword, click within the keyword and press F1.

2. **Identify code in the Code window.**
   - Keywords are words or symbols particular to a programming language. They appear in blue within the Code window.
   - Comments are text that explain programming code, but these statements do not execute. Comments start with an apostrophe or Rem and display in green in the Code window.
   - Methods revolve around objects. For example, an Excel workbook contains objects, such as worksheets and charts. You must use the object name followed by a period and a method to perform an action for the object.

3. **Create, run, and debug a procedure.**
   - Start a procedure with the word Sub and end the procedure with End Sub in the Code window.
   - You can run a procedure directly within the Code window, although the results will display the application window.
   - Use the Debug option to step through a procedure to determine where it contains a problem so that you can fix it.

4. **Create a message box.**
   - A message box is a dialog box that contains a title bar, message, an icon, and one or more buttons.
   - The prompt argument specifies the text that appears within the message box. The title argument specifies the text that appears on the title bar.

5. **Declare and use variables and constants.**
   - A variable stores values that can change during runtime. A constant stores a value declared by the programmer and cannot be changed during runtime.
   - When declaring variables and constants, you must specify a data type, such as integer or double.
   - Use a letter to start a variable or constant name, do not use disallowed characters, use descriptive names, and start the name with the designated prefix, such as int for integer.
   - Use the assignment statement to assign values to variables.

6. **Create an input box.**
   - An input box prompts the user to enter data. The data is then often stored in a variable.
   - Use the Val function to convert data entry from an input box to a value before assigning it to a variable.

7. **Perform calculations.**
   - The variable name goes on the left side of the assignment (=) operator, and the arithmetic calculation goes on the right side of the operator.
   - Calculations follow the order of precedence: exponentiation, multiplication, division, integer division, modulus, addition and concatenation, subtraction and negation, and string concatenation.
   - Use the Format function to format values on displayed output.

8. **Use decision structures.**
   - The If…Else structure performs a logical test. If the test is True, the program code executes specific code. If not, that specific code is not executed.
   - The If…Then…Else structure tests for a condition. Different code is executed based on the results of the logical test.
   - The Select Case structure compares an expression or value to a case block. Once the program identifies the correct case, it executes the respective statement.

9. **Perform data validation.**
   - The process of checking data entered by a user to ensure it meets certain conditions is called data validation.
   - Programmers use If…Then…Else structures to perform data validation to determine if user input contains a value that meets a condition.
   - Programmers also test to determine if users entered a value instead of text for numeric data.

10. **Use logical operators.**
    - The OR logical operator requires that any of the conditions evaluate to true to execute code.
    - The AND logical operator requires that all conditions evaluate to true to execute code. Programmers use the AND logical operator to ensure a value is both less than a value and greater than another value.

11. **Use the For…Next Structure.**
    - The For…Next structure repeats a loop a specific number of times using a counter variable and a step process to increment or decrement the counter during each iteration.

12. **Use the Do…Loop Structure.**
    - Use the Do While…Loop to perform a pretest loop. Use the Do…Loop While to perform a posttest loop.
    - Use Do Until…Loop to perform a pretest loop until a condition becomes true. Use a Do…Loop Until to perform a posttest loop that loops until a condition becomes true.

Key Terms Matching

Match the key terms with their definitions. Write the key term letter by the appropriate numbered definition.

a. Comment
b. Constant
c. Design Time
d. Do...Loop Structure
e. Event
f. For...Next Structure
g. If...Then Structure
h. Input Box
i. Keyword
j. Loop

k. Message Box
l. Method
m. Module
n. Project
o. Runtime
p. Select Case Structure
q. Sub Procedure
r. Syntax Error
s. Variable
t. Visual Basic for Application

1. _____ The mode for designing, writing, and editing programming statements. **p. 4**

2. _____ A dialog box that displays a message of information and contains buttons for the user to click to perform actions. **p. 9**

3. _____ Performs a logical test and executes one or more statements if the test is true. **p. 38**

4. _____ Text or a symbol used for a specific purpose in a programming language. **p. 6**

5. _____ A textual description that explains a section of programming code. **p. 6**

6. _____ A dialog box that prompts the user to enter data. **p. 25**

7. _____ An action at runtime that triggers the execution of code. **p. 8**

8. _____ Stores values that remain the same during runtime. **p. 20**

9. _____ The mode for executing a program. **p. 4**

10. _____ The set of statements that repeat for a repetition structure. **p. 51**

11. _____ A repetition structure that repeats designated statements as long as a condition is true or until a condition is satisfied. **p. 52**

12. _____ Performs an action but does not return a specific value. **p. 8**

13. _____ A repetition structure that repeats statements a specific number of times. **p. 51**

14. _____ A programmer-defined name that stores values that can change or vary during runtime. **p. 20**

15. _____ An action that can be taken for an object. **p. 7**

16. _____ Occurs when code contains a misspelled or misused keyword, incorrect punctuation, or undefined elements. **p. 6**

17. _____ A programming language to enhance the functionality of Office applications. **p. 2**

18. _____ Compares an expression and then executes the code for the matching case. **p. 41**

19. _____ A collection of modules and objects in an Office file. **p. 4**

20. _____ A container to organize programming procedures within a project. **p. 4**

Multiple Choice

1. Which of the following Workbook file extensions support macros?

   (a) .xlsm

   (b) .xlsx

   (c) .xls

   (d) All of the above

2. What is the default color for comments in the VB Editor?

   (a) Blue

   (b) Green

   (c) Black

   (d) Yellow

3. What keystroke opens the VB Editor?

   (a) Alt+F12

   (b) F4

   (c) Alt+F11

   (d) Control+Shift+Enter

4. VBA cannot be used:

   (a) To create code in Access.

   (b) To create code in Excel.

   (c) To create stand-alone applications.

   (d) To create code in PowerPoint.

5. Which of the following should be used to create a procedure that can be accessed by any object in the application?

   (a) Public procedure

   (b) Function procedure

   (c) Property procedure

   (d) Private procedure

6. A For...Next loop:

   (a) Allows the code to execute from top to bottom.

   (b) Is required in all subroutines.

   (c) Can only be used when incrementing by 1.

   (d) Allows a section of the code to repeat x number of times.

7. Which statement can be used to compare the same expression to several different values?

   (a) InputBox()

   (b) If...Then

   (c) Select Case

   (d) Else...Then

8. The purpose of declaring variables in VBA is:

   (a) To make it easier to debug the code at a later date.

   (b) For enhanced memory management.

   (c) To follow standard programming techniques.

   (d) To use the variables later in calculations.

9. The difference between a MsgBox statement and an InputBox statement is:

   (a) InputBox allows the user to enter data.

   (b) MsgBox is easier to use.

   (c) Only InputBox can be customized.

   (d) No difference.

10. All of the following are examples of data types except which one?

    (a) Decimal

    (b) Boolean

    (c) String

    (d) Simplex

Practice Exercises

1 Library Budget

You have been appointed to the executive board of your local library. As part of your duties, you need to create the budget for the next fiscal year. Using the previous year's budget worksheet, you decide to create a procedure that will ask for the percent increase (or decrease) from the previous year, and then create the next fiscal year's budget amounts. This exercise follows the same set of skills as used in Hands-On Exercises 1 and 2 in the chapter. Refer to Figures 1.29 and 1.30 as you complete this exercise.

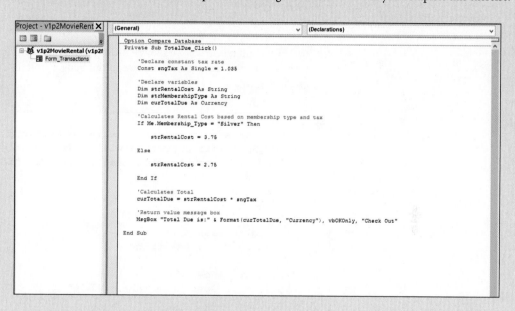

FIGURE 1.29 ➤

FIGURE 1.30 ➤

a. Open the *v1p1Library.xlsm* Excel workbook, click **Enable Content**, and then save it as **v1p1Library_ LastFirst.xlsm**.

b. Type =C5*1.05 in **cell D5** and press **Enter**.

This represents a 5% increase in the Federal Funding account compared to the previous year.

c. Click the **DEVELOPER tab** and click **Visual Basic** in the Code group to open the VB Editor. You will create a VBA procedure to automate what you did in step b.

d. Type **Sub CopyNextYearsBudget()** in the Code window and press **Enter**. The End Sub statement appears, as shown in Code Window 1.35.

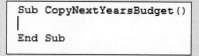

CODE WINDOW 1.35 ➤

```
Sub CopyNextYearsBudget()

End Sub
```

e. Type the code shown in Code Window 1.36 to verify that the user wants to continue.

```
Sub CopyNextYearsBudget()
    'Check to see if the user wants to continue
    If MsgBox("This procedure will create next year's budget." & vbCrLf & _
        "Do you want to continue?", vbYesNo, "Confirmation") = vbNo Then
        Exit Sub
    End If
```

CODE WINDOW 1.36 ➤

f. Press **Enter** and type the code shown in Code Window 1.37. This code declares a variable, sets the active cell, obtains the percent increase in the budget from the user, and inserts the new amount into the first row.

```
Sub CopyNextYearsBudget()
    'Check to see if the user wants to continue
    If MsgBox("This procedure will create next year's budget." & vbCrLf & _
        "Do you want to continue?", vbYesNo, "Confirmation") = vbNo Then
        Exit Sub
    End If

    ' Declare variables
    Dim sngIncrease As Single
    Dim strLastCell As String

    ' Set active cell
    Application.Goto Reference:="R5C4"

    ' Display input box to get percent increase in budget
    sngIncrease = Val(InputBox("Enter percent increase (ex. .05 for 5%)", _
                "Enter Percent Increase"))

    ' Insert new budget amount into first cell
    ActiveCell.FormulaR1C1 = "=RC[-1]"
    ActiveCell = ActiveCell * (1 + sngIncrease)

End Sub
```

CODE WINDOW 1.37 ➤

g. Click **Save** on the toolbar and minimize the VB Editor. Type **0** in **cell D5** and press **Enter** to reset the Federal Funding amount, and click **Visual Basic** on the Ribbon to restore the VB Editor. Make sure the insertion point is within the CopyNextYearsBudget procedure you just created. Click **Run Sub/UserForm** on the toolbar. Click **Yes** to confirm you want to continue, type **.05** in the input box, and click **OK**. Press **Alt + F11** to preview your results in the worksheet. Next, you will modify the procedure to calculate the new budget for all accounts.

h. Press **Alt + F11** to open the VB Editor. Place the insertion point after the Dim sngIncrease As Single statement in the *Declare variables* section and press **Enter**. As highlighted in Code Window 1.38, type **Dim strLastCell As String**.

i. Place the insertion point below the *sngIncrease = Val(InputBox("Enter percent increase (ex. .05 for 5%)", "Enter Percent Increase"))* statement, and then press **Enter** twice. Type the remaining code as shown in Code Window 1.38 to create a Do…Loop that will calculate the new budget amounts for all accounts. Save the code.

```
Sub CopyNextYearsBudget()
    'Check to see if the user wants to continue
    If MsgBox("This procedure will create next year's budget." & vbCrLf & _
        "Do you want to continue?", vbYesNo, "Confirmation") = vbNo Then
        Exit Sub
    End If

    ' Declare variables
    Dim sngIncrease As Single
    Dim strLastCell As String

    ' Set active cell
    Application.Goto Reference:="R5C4"

    ' Display input box to get percent increase in budget
    sngIncrease = Val(InputBox("Enter percent increase (ex. .05 for 5%)", _
            "Enter Percent Increase"))

    ' Use a Do loop to calculate the new amounts for all accounts
    Do Until strLastCell = "Net Budget:"
        ' Set the value of strLastCell
        strLastCell = ActiveCell.Offset(0, -2).Value

        ' Insert new budget amount into first cell
        ActiveCell.FormulaR1C1 = "=RC[-1]"
        ActiveCell = ActiveCell * (1 + sngIncrease)

        ' Move down one row
        ActiveCell.Offset(1, 0).Select
    Loop

End Sub
```

CODE WINDOW 1.38 ➤

j. Press **Alt+F11** to return to the worksheet and type **0** in **cell D5** in the worksheet to reset the Federal Funding amount. In the VB Editor, make sure the insertion point is within the CopyNextYearsBudget procedure you just created. Click **Run Sub/UserForm** on the toolbar, click **Yes**, enter **.05** in the input box, and click **OK**. Close the VB Editor.

k. Delete the zeros in **cells D10**, **D17**, and **D26**.

Sometimes, manual manipulation of a worksheet is still needed after a VBA procedure runs. Additional code could be added to remove the contents of these cells.

l. Compare your results to Figure 1.30.

m. Save the workbook and close Excel.

n. Submit the workbook based on your instructor's directions.

2 Larry's Movie Rentals

Larry McGown, the owner of a local movie rental store, currently uses Access to manage his clients, transactions, and movie inventory. His database is comprised of four tables and a data entry transaction form. He offers two types of memberships for his customers, Gold and Silver. Silver members pay $3.75 per rental while Gold members pay $2.75. He would like you to use VBA to create a message box to automatically calculate rental price including 5% sales tax based on client membership type. Refer to Figure 1.31 as you complete this exercise.

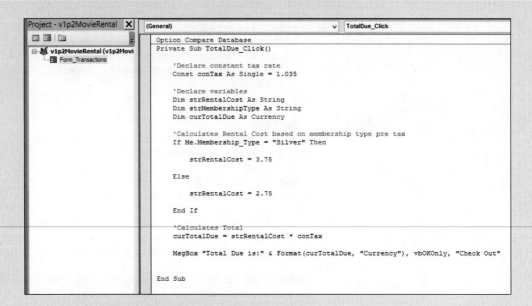

FIGURE 1.31 ➤

a. Open the *v1p2MovieRental* database and save it as **v1p2MovieRental_LastFirst**.

b. If necessary, click **Enable Content** in the yellow warning bar underneath the Ribbon. Double-click the **Transactions form** in the object viewer to display the form. From the **HOME tab** on the Ribbon, click the **Design View** button to begin editing the form.

c. Click **Property Sheet** on the Ribbon. Select the **Total Due button** and click the **EVENT tab** within the **Property Sheet** menu. Add an event **On Click** and click the **Build button** to enter the VBA editor.

d. If necessary, place the insertion point underneath the first line and press **Enter** and press **Tab**. Type **'Declare constant Tax Rate as *sngTax*** and press **Enter**. Enter the constant **conTax** with a Single data type format as shown in Code Window 1.39 and **Enter** twice.

```
Private Sub TotalDue_Click()

    'Declare constant tax rate
    Const sngTax As Single = 1.035

    'Declare variables
    Dim strRentalCost As String
    Dim strMembershipType As String
    Dim curTotalDue As Currency

    'Calculates Rental Cost based on membership type and tax
    If Me.Membership_Type = "Silver" Then

        strRentalCost = 3.75

    Else

        strRentalCost = 2.75

    End If

End Sub
```

CODE WINDOW 1.39 ➤

e. Type **'Declare variables** and press **Enter**. Enter variables for **strRentalCost** with a string data format, **strMembershipType** with a string data format, and **curTotalDue** with a currency data format as shown in Figure 1.31 and press **Enter.**

f. On the current line type the comment **'Calculates Rental Cost based on membership type and tax**, then enter the If...Then...Else statement as shown in Code Window 1.40. Next you will create code to calculate the Total Due.

CODE WINDOW 1.40 ➤

```
'Calculates Total
curTotalDue = strRentalCost * sngTax
```

g. Press **Enter** twice and type the comment **'Calculates Total**. Press **Enter** and type **curTotalDue = strRentalCost * conTax**. This calculates the total by multiplying the rental cost and the constant tax rate.

h. Press **Enter** and type the comment **'Return value message box**. Next use VBA to create a message box that when active will display the words "Total due is:" with the calculate dollar amount as created above. Use the Format function to return the results as currency. Use the code in Code Window 1.41 as a guide.

```
Option Compare Database
Private Sub TotalDue_Click()

    'Declare constant tax rate
    Const sngTax As Single = 1.035

    'Declare variables
    Dim strRentalCost As String
    Dim strMembershipType As String
    Dim curTotalDue As Currency

    'Calculates Rental Cost based on membership type and tax
    If Me.Membership_Type = "Silver" Then

        strRentalCost = 3.75

    Else

        strRentalCost = 2.75

    End If

    'Calculates Total
    curTotalDue = strRentalCost * sngTax

    'Return value message box
    MsgBox "Total Due is: " & Format(curTotalDue, "Currency"), vbOKOnly, "Check Out"

End Sub
```

CODE WINDOW 1.41▲

i. Save your changes and press **Alt+F22** to close the VB Editor.

j. In Form view press the **Total Due button** to test your work.

k. Save and close the database.

l. Submit the database based on your instructor's directions.

Mid-Level Exercises

1 | Food Service Company

A food service company needs to increase the price of its products based on category. Categories include Beverages, Condiments, Confections, and so on. The company's database contains a list of products and the corresponding category for each product. You need to create a new VBA procedure to display the new price based on the category. Refer to Figure 1.32 as you complete this exercise.

FIGURE 1.32 ➤

a. Open *v1m1FoodService*. Save the database as **v1m1FoodService_LastFirst**. Enable the content.

b. Open the Categories table and review the categories. Close the table.

c. Open the Products table and review the products. Take note that each product has a CategoryID designation. Close the table.

d. Run the Average Price query to review the average price of products in each category. Close the query.

e. Open the VB Editor.

f. Place the insertion point under *Option Compare Database*, type **Option Explicit**, and press **Enter**.

g. Type **Sub cmdDisplayNewPrice_Click()** and press **Enter**.

h. Press **Tab**, type **'Declare variables** and press **Enter**. Type **Dim intCategory As Integer** and press **Enter** twice. Continue typing the remainder of the code shown in Code Window 1.42. This section establishes the VBA category variable.

```
Sub cmdDisplayNewPrice_Click()
    ' Declare variables
    Dim intCategory As Integer

    'Verify that CategoryID is not blank
    If IsNull(Me.CategoryID) Then
        Exit Sub
    End If

    intCategory = Me.CategoryID

End Sub
```

CODE WINDOW 1.42 ➤

i. On the current line type the comment **'Set the price increase based on category.** Next type **Select Case intCategory** and press **Enter**. Continue typing the code as shown in Code Window 1.43.

```
Sub cmdDisplayNewPrice_Click()
    ' Declare variables
    Dim intCategory As Integer

    'Verify that CategoryID is not blank
    If IsNull(Me.CategoryID) Then
        Exit Sub
    End If

    intCategory = Me.CategoryID

    ' Set the price increase based on category
    Select Case intCategory

    Case 1 To 4
    MsgBox "New Price: " & Format(Me.UnitPrice * 1.05, "currency"), vbOKOnly, "New Price"

    Case 5, 7, 8
    MsgBox "New Price: " & Format(Me.UnitPrice * 1.03, "currency"), vbOKOnly, "New Price"

    Case 6
    MsgBox "New Price: " & Format(Me.UnitPrice * 1.1, "currency"), vbOKOnly, "New Price"

    Case Else
    MsgBox "New Price not on file."

    End Select

End Sub
```

CODE WINDOW 1.43▲

j. Save the code and close the VB Editor. Open the Products form in Form view and click the **New Price command button** to test the procedure. The new price should appear in a message box. Use a calculator to verify the new price is correct.

k. Advance to the next record and test the New Price button again. Repeat for several more records.

DISCOVER

l. Create a new category in the Categories table and assign any product in the Products table to the new category. Test the New Price procedure to verify it displays the *New Price not on file* message.

m. Exit Access.

n. Submit the database based on your instructor's directions.

2 Retirement Calculation

You have been hired as a financial analyst for RLB investments. As part of your daily tasks you help clients plan for retirement. You have decided to use VBA to create a simple retirement calculator that utilizes the future value function along with several client inputs to perform its calculations. Refer to Figure 1.33 while you complete this exercise.

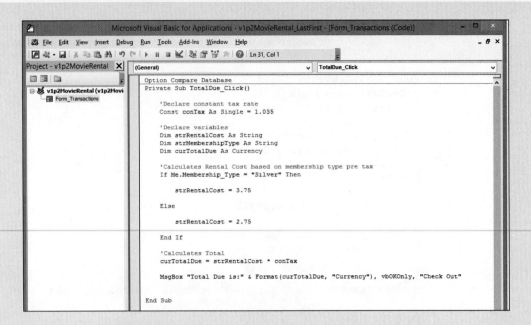

FIGURE 1.33 ➤

a. Open the *v1m2Retirement* document and save it as **v1m2Retirement_LastFirst**.

b. Open the VB Editor and in the already created module, declare the constant Interest Rate as **.0275** with the data type Single.

c. Declare variables for the following inputs with the corresponding data types.
   - *Monthly contribution as Currency*
   - *Retirement age as Single*
   - *Current age as Single*
   - *Total value at retirement as Currency*

d. Define the current age variable value by creating an Input box that requests the user's current age. Use the prompt **Enter Current Age** and the title **Age Input**.

e. Define the retirement age variable value by creating an Input box that requests the users to enter the desired retirement age. Use the prompt **Enter Ideal Retirement Age** and the title **Retirement Input**.

f. Define the monthly contribution variable value by creating an Input box that requests the users to enter the estimated monthly contribution as a dollar amount. Use the prompt **Enter Monthly Contribution** and the title **Monthly Contribution**.

g. Define the Total Value at Retirement variable by using the built in FV function as follows **=FV(InterestRate / 12, (sngRetirementAge – sngCurrentAge) * 12, -curMonthlyContribution)**

h. Create a message box to return the results. Use concatenated text with the words **"Your Total Value at retirement is:"** & and the value of the curTotalValueAtRetirement variable formatted as currency.

i. Exit the VB Editor and assign the Macro to the **Calculate Retirement button**.

j. Test the button by entering your own information and answer the question that is listed on the analysis tab.

k. Submit the file based on your instructor's directions.

Beyond the Classroom

Calculate Financial Aid

GENERAL CASE

You have been hired as a financial aid advisor for incoming freshmen at a local university. To help reduce frequently asked questions regarding financial aid eligibility, you have decided to use VBA in Excel to create a calculator that will determine students' financial aid awards based on household income. To complete this task you will create a decision structure using Select Case, perform validation with logic, and display the financial award in both a message box and within the student worksheet.

Open *v1b1FinAid* and save the file as **v1b1FinAid_LastFirst**. Open the VB Editor. Declare variables for household income as Currency and the aid multiplier as Single. Create a Select Case for the curHouseHoldIncome variable based on the following information.

Any household with an income of less than 10,000 receives a multiplier of 3, any household with an income between 10000 and 60000 receives a multiplier of 2, and any household with a total Income greater than 60000 receives a multiplier of 0. Next create an **If...Then...Else** statement that returns the message "**You must enter total household income**" if the cell H14 has a zero value. If the value entered is greater than zero, then the message box should return a statement displaying the amount available as of the current graduation date. Your last step is to use VBA to enter the amount available for aid in **cell H14**. Exit the VB Editor and assign the newly created macro to the **Calculate Financial Aid** button. Save the worksheet as a macro enabled workbook. Submit based on your instructor's directions.

Case Sensitive Input

RESEARCH CASE

Date validation is an important aspect of data entry. Validation can be used to minimize human error as well as insure all required data is entered. In the file *v1b2Logical*, VBA has been used to insure that data entered into your company's accounting system is being entered for either Refunds or Expenses. Open the file *v1b2Logical*, and then save it as **v1b2Logical_LastFirst.xlsm.** Open the VB Editor and run the procedure. The code will loop three times for demo purposes. Enter a response. Is your input case sensitive? Run a search on the Internet and find out how to change the code so that it is NOT case sensitive. Modify the code so it is not case sensitive, save the workbook and submit based on your instructor's directions.

Revise the Scholarship Database

DISASTER RECOVERY

You decide to review the scholarship database to see if you can improve the code. You decide that the message box text could be more efficient if the repeating phrases were assigned to constants. Open the *v1b3Scholarship* file, and then save the database as **v1b3Scholarship_LastFirst**. Open the VBA code and review the message box components. Declare a new variable and assign the repeating text phrases to the new variable. Replace the text phrases in the message boxes with the new variable; join the phrase using the "&" character. Test your results and make corrections if necessary. Test the procedure further by introducing an error into the code. Insert a space between the first ElseIf statement so it becomes *Else If*. Click **Debug** in the toolbar and select **CompileVBA4** from the list. The compile process should stop at the Else If error. Correct the error and run the compile process again. Close the database. Submit based on your instructor's directions.

Capstone Exercise

You have been hired as an office manager for Drexel and Associates dentistry. As part of your tasks you calculate the patients' visit fee as well as determine their follow-up visit date. The office currently uses an Access database; therefore you have decided to use VBA to automate your tasks.

Create a Procedure

Your first task is to create a procedure that is activated when the Check out button on the VisitHistory form is pressed.

a. Open the file *v1c1Dentist* and save the database as **v1c1Dentist_LastFirst**.

b. If necessary, enable content, open the **VisitHistory form**, and click **Design View** on the HOME tab.

c. Select the **Check Out button** and if necessary click **Property Sheet** on the Ribbon.

d. Add a new event that is triggered on click and open the VB Editor.

Declare Constants and Variables

Your next step is to declare tax, standard payment, and nonstandard payment as constants. You will then declare follow-up date as a variable.

a. Press return after line 1 and declare **Tax** as a constant with the value of *1.0475* and the data type Single. Declare **Standard Pmt** with the value *125* and the data type Currency as well as **NonStandard Pmt** with a value of *275* and the data type Currency.

b. Declare **Date of FollowUp** as a variable. Then add the following code: **dtmDateOfFollowUp = Me.Date + 30**.

Use Logical Operators

After declaring the constants and variables you need to use an IF function to determine if the patient has Ampson insurance. If the patient has Ampson insurance then he or she is charged a nonstandard rate of $275. All other patients will be charged $125.

a. Press return and enter an If...Then...Else statement that multiplies the constant **sngTax** by the constant **CurNonStandardPmt** if the customer received a crown or has Ampson insurance. All other customers receive the same tax rate with the **curStandardPmt**.

Create a Message Box

In the next step you will craft a message box that will return the date of next visit as well as the current balance based on the logic created in the prior step. You will place this code in the value if true and false arguments of the prior step.

a. In the true argument of the If statement created in the prior step, add a message box with the following code: **MsgBox ("Follow Up Visit is:" & dtmDateOfFollowUp & " Amount Owed is: " &CurNonStandardPmt * sngTax**

b. In the false argument of the If statement created in the prior step, add a message box using the following code: **MsgBox ("Follow Up Visit is: " & dtmDateOfFollowUp & " Amount Owed is: " &CurStandardPmt * sngTax**

c. Close the VB Editor and preview the results by pressing the Check out button.

Format Results

After previewing your results you determine that the calculations are correct, but the values are not formatted as currency. You will use the format function to correctly display the data.

a. Open the VB Editor and locate the value **IF true argument** within the IF statement created in the prior step. Add the **Format function** around the payment calculation and set the format to Currency.

b. Locate the value **If false argument** within the IF statement created in the prior step. Add the **Format function** around the payment calculation and set the format to Currency.

Perform Data Validation

Now that you have created logic and properly formatted the results, your last step is to use the ISNULL function to verify the patient has insurance information on file.

a. If not open, open the VB Editor and enter the following code as it appears in Code Window 1.44.

```
Option Compare Database

Private Sub CheckOut_Click()

    'declare constant
    Const sngTax As Single = 1.0475
    Const CurStandardPmt As Currency = 125
    Const CurNonStandardPmt As Currency = 275

    'declare variable
    Dim dtmDateOfFollowUp As Date

    dtmDateOfFollowUp = Me.Date + 30


    'Calculates payment based on insurance and type of service
    If Me.Service = "Crown" Or Me.InsuranceProvider = "Ampson" Then

    MsgBox ("Follow Up Visit is:" & dtmDateOfFollowUp & " Amount Owed is: " & Format((CurNonStandardPmt * sngTax), "currency"))

    Else

    MsgBox ("Follow Up Visit is: " & dtmDateOfFollowUp & " Amount Owed is: " & Format((CurStandardPmt * sngTax), "Currency"))
    End If

  'Verifies an insurance provider has been entered

    If IsNull(Me.InsuranceProvider) Then
    MsgBox ("Insurance Provider is missing")
    End If

End Sub
```

CODE WINDOW 1.44 ▲

b. Close the VB Editor and remove the current insurance information from the active patient.

c. Click the **CheckOut button** to verify the data validation feature is operational.

d. Save the database and exit Access.

e. Submit the database based on your instructor's directions.

Excel and VBA

Yuri Arcurs/Shutterstock

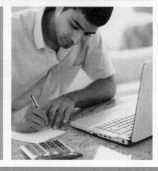

OBJECTIVES AFTER YOU READ THIS CHAPTER, YOU WILL BE ABLE TO:

1. Create forms p. 74

2. Add controls to forms p. 76

3. Adjust specialized properties p. 81

4. Insert controls on a worksheet p. 84

5. Add a procedure to a control p. 94

6. Create and call a function procedure p. 97

7. Create a list in a worksheet p. 106

8. Prepare an application for distribution p. 108

CASE STUDY | Expert Financial Services

Expert Financial Services (EFS) offers home mortgages. Several factors affect the interest rate. The interest rate depends upon the amount borrowed and the length of time of the loan repayment. EFS offers fixed interest rates from 4.25% to 5.25% based on the term (10 to 30 years) and the loan amount ($100,000 to $500,000).

All loans have closing costs, which are fees paid to obtain and process the loan. The original fees paid vary based on the mortgage scenario. All EFS loans have a 2% origination fee and additional points that vary depending upon the loan term and the initial loan amount. Customers who open a personal investment account with EFS qualify for a discount on the origination fees.

Cassandra Wilson, vice president of EFS, asked you to create an Excel application for representing mortgage loan options to customers. Your will create an interface to manage customer information, loan details, loan repayment schedule, and so on. You will create a customer information form and write the VBA code behind it. Next, you will insert buttons and write VBA code on an instructions worksheet to enable users to efficiently use the application. In addition, you will create a loan repayment schedule that lists the monthly principal payment, interest payment, cumulative principal, and cumulative interest payments for each monthly payment until the loan is paid in full. Finally, you will create a Truth-in-Lending disclosure form that summarizes the amount to be financed (the principal), the total finance charge (cumulative interest payments), the total payments (principal and finance charge), the interest rate, the term, and the dates the first and last payments are due.

Forms and Controls

You use forms regularly to enter data into various systems. For example, when you order products from an online store, you enter billing information, such as your name, billing address, credit card number, and expiration date. You can create forms within an Excel worksheet to provide an effective user interface to obtain data from a user. Forms in Excel are similar to forms in Access. However, when you create a form in Excel, you must also write the VBA code behind the controls so that the application can process the data entered.

In this section, you will create a form in a macro-enabled Excel workbook, insert controls, and change the control properties so that you can write VBA code later.

 TIP | **Macro-Enabled Workbook**

A regular Excel workbook (.xlsx) cannot store macros and VBA code. However, a macro-enabled workbook (.xlsm) is designed to store macros and VBA code. To save a workbook that contains VBA code for the first time, display the Save As dialog box, click the *Save as type* arrow, and choose Excel Macro-Enabled Workbook.

Creating Forms

An *object* represents an element, such as a worksheet, cell, chart, form, and so on. All code statements and the Excel objects that you reference in them fit into a logical framework called an *object model*. The object model organizes all objects into an object hierarchy, which defines how objects are related to one another. Objects in the hierarchy are organized in collections. A *collection* is a group of objects with similar characteristics.

The UserForm object contains the Control collection, which manages the individual controls, such as buttons, text boxes, and list boxes that provide a form with its functionality.

To add a UserForm object to an Excel workbook, do the following:

1. If the DEVELOPER tab is not displayed on the Ribbon, click the FILE tab, click Options, click Customize Ribbon, click the Developer check box in the Main Tabs list, and click OK.
2. Click the DEVELOPER tab and click Visual Basic in the Code group.
3. Click Insert on the VBA menu bar and select UserForm.

An empty form and the Toolbox display. The default UserForm name is *UserForm1*. Figure 2.1 shows the form after changing the name from UserForm1 to frmLoan and after changing the caption from UserForm1 to Loan Information.

Choose UserForm from the View menu

Caption property text displays on the title bar

Toolbox containing controls

Properties window for the selected form

Name of the selected form

Caption property

FIGURE 2.1 UserForm Object ➤

Set the Form Properties

After you insert a new UserForm object, you should set the form's properties. Most of the form properties control the appearance of the form. The Properties window lists the properties and their current values for the selected object, in this case the UserForm object. If the Properties window is not displayed, select View from the menu and select Properties Window. The Properties window contains two tabs: Alphabetic and Categorized. Click the Alphabetic tab to list property names in alphabetical order, although the Name property remains at the top of the property list, or click the Categorized tab to group the property names into related categories. The first column in the Properties window lists the name of the property; the second column lists the value or setting for the respective property.

STEP 1»
The ***Name property*** is a text string to identify an object, such as a form. The Name property can be used to identify and manipulate an object in VBA code. The naming scheme you choose for objects helps other VBA programmers understand the code better. Names should be meaningful but short enough to be easily read. Unique names differentiate the objects in your application. The first letter must be an alphabetic character or an underscore. Use the three-letter abbreviation *frm* followed by the descriptive name, such as frmData, to name a form.

The ***Caption property*** controls the text that appears on the form's title bar. The default name matches the default Name property, such as UserForm1. Unlike the Name property that must not contain spaces, the Caption property allows multiple words. Typically, you capitalize the first letter of each word for the caption.

Table 2.1 lists selected properties, their settings, and their purposes for the form shown in Figure 2.1.

TABLE 2.1 Properties of the frmData UserForm

Property	Setting	Purpose
Name	frmLoan	The name by which the form is referenced in code.
Caption	Loan Information	The caption appearing in the form's title bar.
Height	180	The height of the form in points where one vertical inch is measured in 72 points.
ShowModal	True	The modality setting of the form. A modal form must be closed before control is returned to any other object in the application; a non-modal form allows other objects in the application to be activated while the form is open.
Width	240	The width of the form in points where one horizontal inch is measured in 72 points.

TIP · UserForm Object

Technically, a custom form is an instance of the UserForm object. However, many developers refer to a UserForm as a form. This chapter uses *form* when referencing a UserForm object.

Adding Controls to Forms

Forms usually contain *controls* for entering data, displaying information, or evoking events. You can add controls to a form using the *Toolbox*, which is a palette that contains the standard controls. Common form controls include labels, text boxes, buttons, list boxes, check boxes, options buttons, command buttons, image controls, and so on. Each control provides specific functionality to a form. Table 2.2 lists the control name, shows the icon on the Toolbox, and provides a description of each standard control available in the Toolbox.

TABLE 2.2 Form Controls

Control	Icon	Purpose
Select Objects	▶	Selects a control on a form. After you add a control to a form, use the Selection Tool to select the control to modify it.
Label	A	Appears as text on a form, usually for the purpose of identifying controls. Use this for text that the user will not change.
TextBox	abl	Appears as a box in which text can be entered and changed by the user. A text box is often bound to an object in the application (such as an Excel range).
ComboBox	▦	Combines the functionality of a list box and a text box. The user can either choose an item from the list or enter a value in the text box.
ListBox	▦	Displays a list of items from which the user can make a choice. If there are more items in the list than will fit in the control space, a scrollbar appears.
CheckBox	☑	Creates a square box that can be checked or unchecked, to indicate a yes/no condition or a selection.

TABLE 2.2 Form Controls (continued)

Control	Icon	Purpose
OptionButton		Displays a small circular button for toggling options on or off. When multiple option buttons (also called radio buttons) are used together, only one selection can be made (see frame).
ToggleButton		Displays a button for toggling (turning on or off) a selection.
Frame		Displays a rectangular panel for grouping other controls. When option buttons are added to a frame, only one selection can be made.
CommandButton		Displays a button that evokes an event when clicked.
TabStrip		Displays tabs along the top of the window so that you can insert different controls on different tabs, similar to how the Page Setup dialog box in Excel has four tabs with each tab having a different set of controls.
MultiPage		Allows a form to store controls that appear on multiple pages in the form, much like a TabStrip control.
ScrollBar		Enables you to change a set of continuous values using a horizontal or vertical bar. The values are changed by dragging the button appearing in the scrollbar.
SpinButton		Increases and decreases values using up and down arrows. The values in the control are normally bound to a range in an Excel worksheet.
Image		Displays a bitmap, GIF, JPEG, metafile, or icon graphic.
RefEdit		Allows the user to select a range in a worksheet when the button is clicked.

TIP | Toolbox

Use the View menu to display and hide the Toolbox. To show or hide the Toolbox, select Toolbox on the View menu to toggle it on or off. Or, click Toolbox on the VB Editor toolbar to show or hide the Toolbox.

Name the Controls

The most common standard for naming controls in Visual Basic is Modified Hungarian Notation. This convention precedes the name of each instance of a control with a three-character prefix to the control and a descriptive title for the control. The prefix appears in lowercase, and the descriptive title starts with an uppercase character. If the descriptive title has more than one word, CamelCase is used to differentiate the words, such as txtFirstName. Table 2.3 lists the naming conventions for common form controls.

TABLE 2.3 Control Naming Conventions

Control	Prefix	Example
Frame	fme	fmeLoan
Label	lbl	lblTitle
TextBox	txt	txtFirstName
ListBox	lst	lstInterestRate
CheckBox	chk	chkSalariedEmployee
CommandButton	cmd	cmdExit
ComboBox	cbo	cboDays
OptionButton	opt	optTerm
Image	img	imgLogo

Insert a Frame Control

When you plan to insert multiple controls on a form, you might want to insert a Frame control first. The **Frame control** displays a frame or border around related controls on the form to increase readability for the user (see Figure 2.2).

TextBox control
Label control
Text box
Frame's caption
Label
Frame control

FIGURE 2.2 Frame, Label, and TextBox Controls ➤

STEP 2 ❯❯

To insert a Frame control, do one of the following from within the VB Editor:

- Drag Frame from the Toolbox and drop it at the location on the form where you want it and release the mouse. This approach creates a default-sized frame that fills most of the form.

- Click Frame in the Toolbox to make it the active control. Click and drag within the form to create and size the frame in a specific location.

After inserting the Frame control on the form, display the Properties window if it does not display automatically, type a name (such as fmeBankInfo) in the Name property and press Enter, type a descriptive title (such as Bank Information) in the Caption property, and press Enter to display text at the top of the frame. In Figure 2.2, the title bar displays Bank Information. Adjust the size by using the Height and Width properties in the Properties window. Remember that the Properties window reflects the currently selected object or control.

TIP Frame Controls for OptionButtons

Frame controls are mandatory when you need to include two or more sets of OptionButton controls on a form. If you do not insert OptionButton controls within a Frame control, the user can select only one option button on the form at a time. However, if the OptionButton controls are located in multiple Frame controls, the user can select one option button within each frame.

Insert Label and TextBox Controls

Forms usually contain several **Label controls** to display text. The text often indicates the purpose of other controls because those controls do not have Caption properties. For example, you might want to insert a **TextBox control** for the user to enter data. However, without a label displaying text, the user will not know what type of data to enter in the text box. The caption for first label in Figure 2.2 is Bank Name. A text box is located to the right side of the label so that the user can type the borrower's name.

To insert a Label control and change its properties, do one of the following:

- Drag Label from the Toolbox and drop it at the location on the form where you want it and release the mouse. This approach creates a default label that has a Width setting of 72.

- Click Label in the Toolbox to make it the active control. Click and drag within the form to create and size the label in a specific location.

After inserting the Label control on the form, type a name (such as lblName) in the Name property and press Enter, type a description in Caption property and press Enter, set the values for the Width and Height properties to control the size of the label, and set the TextAlign property to align text within the label. The **TextAlign property** is a property that specifies the horizontal alignment of a caption appearing in a label.

TIP Creating Multiple Labels Quickly

After you insert and format a Label control, you can copy the control and paste it several times to preserve the formatting property settings. Then you can change the Name and Caption properties of the copied controls as needed.

To insert a TextBox control and change its properties, do one of the following:

- Drag TextBox from the Toolbox and drop it at the location on the form where you want it and release the mouse. This approach creates a default text box that has a Width setting of 72.

- Click TextBox in the Toolbox to make it the active control. Click and drag within the form to create and size the text box in a specific location.

After inserting the TextBox control on the form, type a name (such as txtName) in the Name property and press Enter. Set the values for the Width and Height properties to control the size of the text box. Drag the TextBox control to align it to the right of its respective Label control.

Insert ListBox, CheckBox, and CommandButton Controls

Three other common controls include the ListBox, CheckBox, and CommandButton (see Figure 2.3). Insert a ***ListBox control*** to display a list of items from which the user may select. For example, you might want the user to select the number of years for a loan from a list of predefined years.

CheckBox control

ListBox control

Label and check boxes

Label and list box

CommandButton control

Command button

FIGURE 2.3 *ListBox, CheckBox, and CommandButton Controls* ➤

STEP 4 ❯❯

To insert a ListBox control and change its properties, do one of the following:

- Drag ListBox from the Toolbox and drop it at the location on the form where you want it and release the mouse. This approach creates a default list box that has a Width setting of 72.

- Click ListBox in the Toolbox to make it the active control. Click and drag within the form to create and size the list box in a specific location.

After inserting the ListBox control on the form, type a name (such as lstTerm) in the Name property and press Enter. Adjust other properties, such as BorderStyle, Width, and Height. (The ListBox control does not have a Caption property.)

Insert ***CheckBox controls*** when you want to user to select one or more options at the same time. For example, a user might want to select one or more accounts he or she has at a bank, such as Checking, Savings, and Certificate of Deposit.

To insert a CheckBox control and change its properties, do one of the following:

- Drag CheckBox from the Toolbox and drop it at the location on the form where you want it and release the mouse. This approach creates a default check box that has a Width setting of 108.

- Click CheckBox in the Toolbox to make it the active control. Click and drag within the form to create and size the check box in a specific location.

After inserting the CheckBox control on the form, type a name (such as chkAccount) in the Name property and press Enter. Adjust other properties, such as Caption and Width.

Insert a ***CommandButton control*** when you want to display a button to execute some action when the user clicks it. For example, you can insert a Close button to accept and apply settings when clicked and a Cancel button to reject changes made in a form.

To insert a CommandButton control, do one of the following:

- Drag CommandButton from the Toolbox and drop it at the location on the form where you want it and release the mouse. This approach creates a default command button that has a Width setting of 72.

- Click CommandButton in the Toolbox to make it the active control. Click and drag within the form to create and size the command button in a specific location.

After inserting the CommandButton control on the form, type a name (such as cmd-Close) in the Name property and press Enter. Adjust other properties, such as Caption and Width.

Adjusting Specialized Properties

After you insert each control, you might want to set many of that control's properties. However, some control properties may rely on other control properties. For these specialized properties, it may save you time to set these properties after you have inserted all the controls.

Set Enabled, TabStop, and TabIndex Properties

The **Enabled property** determines if a control can receive focus or attention and if that control can respond to the user. Set the Enabled property to True if you want the control to be able to receive focus or respond to the user. Set the Enabled property to False if you do not want the user to interact with the control when the application starts.

Commands on the Excel Ribbon exhibit Enabled status behavior. For example, the Enabled property of the Cut and Copy commands are set to False until you select something. After you select text, an image, or another object, the Enabled property of Cut and Copy changes to True. You can set a control's default Enabled property value in the Properties window; however, you might want to enable or disable a property based on an action when an application is running. The following code shows how to disable the Enabled property of a control:

```
cmdCut.Enabled=False
```

Some users press Tab to go to another form control to activate it so that they can enter data or select that control. When a control is active, it has *focus*. You should make sure the control property values are set correctly to ensure that controls can receive focus and that the form provides a logical flow when a user presses Tab to change focus when entering data on a form. Controls have two properties that determine the order in which the controls are activated as a user tabs through the form: TabStop and TabIndex.

STEP 5 ≫

The **TabStop property**, which accepts a value of True or False, determines whether the control receives the focus when the user presses Tab (True to receive the focus; False to skip the control when tabbing through the controls on the form). The **TabIndex property**, which accepts an integer value, determines the order in which a control receives the focus. A control with a TabIndex value of 0 receives the focus initially. The control with the next-highest value receives the focus when the user presses Tab.

Use Bound and Unbound Controls

A **bound control** is a control that is connected to a data source in the host application. In Excel, a bound control typically displays or changes the data in a worksheet cell or range. For example, a form might contain a text box for entering data and assign the data to a worksheet range object. An **unbound control** is a control that is not connected to data in the host application. Labels are common examples of unbound controls because they do not store text that is changed by the user. Another example of an unbound control is the command button because it most often triggers events.

To bind controls to a worksheet range, set the appropriate form properties. ListBox, ComboBox, and TextBox controls all have a ***ControlSource property*** that defines the cell to which the control is bound. VBA provides two ways to set control properties: the Properties window at design time or a code statement that executes at run time. To set the ControlSource property of a control using the Properties window, type the cell reference, such as A1 or D7, in the row for the ControlSource property. The column reference can be lower- or uppercase.

ListBox and ComboBox controls have a ***RowSource property*** that specifies the range that contains a list of the items that will appear in the list box or combo box control at run time. You can set this property using either the Properties window at design time or in a code statement that executes at run time. The value of the RowSource property is a worksheet range (such as B2:B7) that contains the items that will populate the list. Valid settings include any worksheet range. Just like the ControlSource property, the column references in the RowSource property are not case-specific.

Set Properties for the Loan Application Form

A good practice is to list the controls, their properties, and their desired settings when you plan to create a form. Doing so helps you remember control names and what properties you need to set. Figure 2.4 shows the EFS Residential Loan Application form that you will work on in Hands-On Exercise 1. Part of the form is created for you, and you will create the rest of it.

FIGURE 2.4 EFS Residential Loan Application Form ➤

The Borrower Information frame groups the controls for entering information about the borrower. The TabStop property for the frame is set to True, and the TabIndex property is set to 0. Table 2.4 lists the property settings for the controls in the Borrower Information frame.

The Property Information frame groups the controls for entering and editing information about the property being financed. This frame has a Name property of fmePropertyInfo and a Caption property of Property Information. Table 2.5 lists the controls and properties used in the Property Information frame.

TABLE 2.4 Properties for Controls in the Borrower Information Frame		
Control	Property	Setting
lblName	Caption	Borrower's Name:
txtName	ControlSource	B4
	TabIndex	0
	TabStop	True
lblSSN	Caption	Borrower's SSN:
txtSSN	ControlSource	B5
	TabIndex	1
	TabStop	True
lblAddress	Caption	Address:
txtAddress	ControlSource	B7
	TabIndex	2
	TabStop	True
lblCity	Caption	City:
txtCity	ControlSource	B8
	TabIndex	3
	TabStop	True
lblState	Caption	State:
txtState	ControlSource	B9
	TabIndex	4
	TabStop	True
lblZip	Caption	Zip:
txtZip	ControlSource	B10
	TabIndex	5
	TabStop	True

TABLE 2.5 Properties for Controls in the Property Information Frame		
Control	Property	Setting
lblAddress2	Caption	Address:
txtAddress2	ControlSource	B13
	TabIndex	0
	TabStop	True
lblCity2	Caption	City:
txtCity2	ControlSource	B14
	TabIndex	1
	TabStop	True
lblState2	Caption	State:
txtState2	ControlSource	B15
	TabIndex	2
	TabStop	True
lblZip2	Caption	Zip:
txtZip2	ControlSource	B16
	TabIndex	3
	TabStop	True
lblType	Caption	Type:
optSingle	Caption	Single Family
	ControlSource	B17
	TabIndex	4
	TabStop	True
optDuplex	Caption	Duplex
	ControlSource	B17
	TabIndex	5
	TabStop	True
optCondo	Caption	Condo/Townhome
	ControlSource	B17
	TabIndex	6
	TabStop	True

TIP   Option Buttons

Clicking an option button changes that control's Value to True. The Value property of the remaining option buttons within the same frame is set to False.

The Loan Information frame groups the controls for entering and editing information about the loan. This frame has a Name property of fmeLoanInfo and a Caption property of Loan Information. The TabStop property for the frame is set to True, and the TabIndex property is set to 2. Table 2.6 lists the controls and properties. This frame contains two Label controls for the interest rate. The first displays a descriptive label, and the second will eventually display the calculated interest rate, which is determined by the loan amount (principal), loan term, and whether the applicant has opened or will open an investment account.

Control	Property	Setting
lblPrincipal	Caption	Loan Amount:
	Left	12
	TextAlign	3-fmTextAlignRight
	Top	10
txtPrincipal	ControlSource	F6
	Left	90
	TabIndex	0
	TabStop	True
	Top	6
lblRate	Caption	Interest Rate:
	Left	12
	Top	33
lblRateValue	Caption	None: Delete the default caption
	BackColor	&H00FFFFC0&
	BorderStyle	1-fmBorderStyleSingle
	Left	90
	TextAlign	2-fmTextAlignCenter
	Top	30
lblTerm	Caption	Term (Years):
	Left	186
	Top	6
	Width	51
lstTerm	BorderStyle	0-fmBorderStyleNone
	ColumnWidths	0.15 pt
	Height	61.5
	Left	234
	TabIndex	1
	TabStop	True
	TextAlign	2-fmTextAlignCenter
	Top	6
chkAccount	Caption	I have/will open an Investment Account with EFS.
	Left	6
	TabIndex	2
	TabStop	True
	Top	48
	Width	200

TABLE 2.6 Properties for Controls in the Loan Information Frame

Inserting Controls on a Worksheet

STEP 6 >> In this project, the data entry form is launched from the Instructions worksheet. Therefore, this worksheet needs controls, such as command buttons, so the user can open the form and initialize the application. The first task is to insert a button on the Instructions worksheet that displays and initializes the frmData user form. To insert a control on a worksheet, do the following:

1. Click the DEVELOPER tab and click Insert in the Controls group (see Figure 2.5).

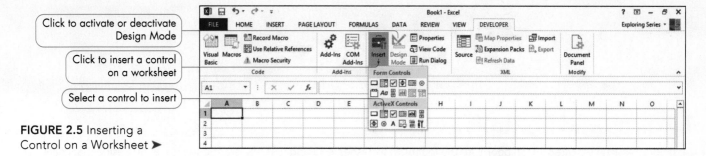

Click to insert a control on a worksheet

Select a control to insert

FIGURE 2.5 Inserting a Control on a Worksheet ➤

2. Click the icon for the type of control you want to insert on the worksheet.
3. Use the mouse pointer to drag to insert the control on the worksheet.

   When you add a control to an Excel worksheet, the worksheet is in Design mode, which enables you to edit the control and write VBA code.
4. Click Properties in the Controls group to display the Properties window for the selected control (see Figure 2.6).

Click to display or hide the Properties window

Properties window for selected control

Control placed on the worksheet

FIGURE 2.6 Properties Window for Control ➤

5. Click Design Mode to disable Design mode.

   When the Design mode is disabled and you click a control, the associated VBA code will run.

Quick Concepts

1. Why is it important to assign a name in the Name property for an object? *p. 75*
2. What is the difference between check boxes and option buttons on forms? *p. 80*
3. What does it mean when an object has focus? *p. 81*

Hands-On Exercises

1 Forms and Controls

Cassandra's assistant created a workbook with the four main worksheets. In addition, she started to create the Residential Loan Application form. However, Cassandra asked you to finish creating the interface of the form.

Skills covered: Set the Form Properties • Insert a Frame Control • Insert Label and TextBox Controls • Insert ListBox, CheckBox, and Button Controls • Adjust Specialized Properties • Insert Controls on a Worksheet

---

STEP 1 ≫ SET THE FORM PROPERTIES

Most of the properties have been set to match the settings listed in Tables 2.4 and 2.5. However, you need to set the Name, Caption, and Height properties for the form. Refer to Figure 2.7 as you complete Step 1.

> Step e: Caption displays on the form's title bar
>
> Step c: Double-click Forms; double-click UserForm1
>
> Step d: Type a name in the Name property
>
> Step e: Type a caption in the Caption property
>
> Step f: Set Height property

FIGURE 2.7 Form Properties ➤

a. Start Excel, open *v2h1Loan.xlsm* (an Excel macro-enabled workbook), and save it as **v2h1Loan_LastFirst.xlsm**.

> **TROUBLESHOOTING:** If the Security Warning toolbar displays, click Enable Content. If you make any major mistakes in this exercise, you can close the file, open *v2h1Loan* again, and then start this exercise over.

b. Click the **DEVELOPER tab** and click **Visual Basic** in the Code group.

> **TROUBLESHOOTING:** If the DEVELOPER tab is not displayed, click the FILE tab, click Options, click Customize Ribbon, click the Developer tab check box in the Main Tabs list on the right side, and click OK. Maximize the VB Editor if necessary.

The VB Editor opens. The Project Explorer window shows the worksheet names in the Microsoft Excel Objects section and a Forms folder.

c. Double-click **Forms** in the Project Explorer window and double-click **UserForm1** to display the form, if the form is not already displayed.

The default Name is UserForm1, and the default Caption is UserForm1.

> **TROUBLESHOOTING:** If the Properties window is not displayed, click View on the menu and select Properties Window.

d. Select *UserForm1* in the **Name property box** in the Properties window, type **frmData**, and press **Enter**.

e. Select *UserForm1* in the **Caption property box** in the Properties window, type **Expert Financial Services Loan Application**, and press **Enter**.

f. Select the existing value in the **Height property box** in the Properties window, type **400.5**, and press **Enter**.

g. Click **Save** on the toolbar.

STEP 2 ≫ INSERT A FRAME CONTROL

The Residential Loan Application form contains the top two frames: Borrower Information and Property Information. You will add the Loan Information frame and set its properties. Refer to Figure 2.8 as you complete Step 2.

Step a: Click Frame in the Toolbox

Step c: Caption text displays at the top of the frame

Step b: Set the Name property

Step c: Set the Caption property

Step d: Set the Height property

Step e: Set the Left property

Step f: Scroll down to set the Width property

FIGURE 2.8 Loan Information Frame ➤

a. Click **Frame** in the Toolbox and then click about two dots below the second frame in the form to create a default-sized frame.

You can drag the Toolbox to the right side of the form so that it is easier to see.

b. Select *Frame1* in the **Name property box** in the Properties window, type **fmeLoanInfo**, and press **Enter**.

c. Select *Frame1* in the **Caption property box** in the Properties window, type **Loan Information**, and press **Enter**.

The text Loan Information: displays at the top of the frame you created.

d. Select the existing value in the **Height property box**, type **84**, and press **Enter**.

You adjusted the height to be the same as the height of the second frame.

e. Select the existing value in the **Left property box**, type **6**, and press **Enter**.

This setting makes sure the frame aligns on the left side with the other two frames that have a Left property value of 6.

f. Scroll down the Properties window, select the existing value in the **Width property box**, type **312**, and press **Enter**.

You adjusted the width to be the same as the width of the first two frames.

g. Click **Save** on the toolbar.

STEP 3 ›› INSERT LABEL AND TEXTBOX CONTROLS

You need to add Label and TextBox controls for the loan amount and interest rate in the top-left corner of the Loan Information frame you just created. As you insert the controls, you will set their properties. Refer to Figure 2.9 as you complete Step 3.

FIGURE 2.9 Label and TextBox Controls ➤

a. Click the border of the Loan Information frame in the form to select it.

b. Click **Label** in the Toolbox and click below the *Loan Information* caption in the frame.

VBA inserts a label within the selected frame.

c. Change the Name property to **lblPrincipal**, change the Caption to **Loan Amount:**, change the Left property to **12**, change the TextAlign to **3 – fmTextAlignRight**, and change the Top property to **10**.

You inserted a Label control. The Left property value specifies the distance from the left side of the form. The Top property value specifies the distance from the top edge of the form.

d. Press and hold **Ctrl**, select the label you just created, and then drag down to create a copy below the original label.

The copied label shows the same caption and has the same TextAlign value, but you need to change the Name, Caption, Left, and Top properties.

e. With the duplicate label selected, change the Name property to **lblRate**, change the Caption to **Interest Rate:**, change the Left property to **12**, and change the Top property to **33**.

You want to make sure the label is the same distance from the left side of the form as the first label; however, this label displays farther down from the top edge of the form.

f. Click the **Loan Information frame** to select it, click **TextBox** in the Toolbox, and click to the right of the *Loan Amount* label.

You inserted a TextBox control to the right of the *Loan Amount* label. The label describes the TextBox because the TextBox does not have a Caption property.

g. Change the Name property to **txtPrincipal**, change the Left property to **90**, and change the Top property to **6**.

h. Insert a Label control below the TextBox control, change the Name property to **lblRateValue**, delete the default Caption text, change the Left property to **90**, change the TextAlign property to **2-fmTextAlignCenter**, and change the Top property to **30**.

You inserted two labels for interest rates. The first displays a descriptive label, and the second displays the calculated interest rate, which is determined by the loan amount, loan term, and whether the applicant has opened or will open an investment account.

i. Insert a Label control to the right of the txtPrincipal control, change the Name property to **lblTerm**, change the Caption to **Term (Years):**, change the Left property to **186**, change the Top property to **6**, and change the Width to **51**.

j. Click **Save** on the toolbar.

STEP 4 ›› INSERT LISTBOX, CHECKBOX, AND BUTTON CONTROLS

To finish the Loan Information frame, you need to insert a ListBox control to list the terms, a CheckBox control for customers to verify they have or plan to open another account with EFS, and a CommandButton to close the form. Refer to Figure 2.10 as you complete Step 4.

Step a: Click the border of the frame

Step d: Click CheckBox

Step b: Click ListBox

Step f: Click CommandButton

Step b: ListBox location

Step d: CheckBox location

Step g: CommandButton properties

Step f: CommandButton location

Step h: Decrease height of the form

FIGURE 2.10 ListBox, CheckBox, and Button Controls ➤

a. Select the outer border of the Loan Information frame in the form.

b. Click the frame, click **ListBox** in the Toolbox and click to the right of the *Term (Years)* label.

You inserted a ListBox control to the right of the Term (Years) label. The label is needed because the ListBox control does not have a Caption property to identify the control.

c. Change the Name property to **lstTerm**, change the Height to **60**, change the Left property to **234**, change the TextAlign to **2-fmTextAlignCenter**, and change the Top property to **6**.

> **TROUBLESHOOTING:** Make sure you type a lowercase *l* in the Name instead of the number *1*.

d. Click the Loan Information frame, click **CheckBox** in the Toolbox and click below the Interest Rate label.

You inserted a CheckBox control below the Interest Rate label.

e. Change the Name property to **chkAccount**, change the Caption property to **I have/will open an Investment Account with EFS.**, change the Left property to **6**, change the Top property to **48**, and change the Width property to **200**.

f. Click the form instead of the frame, click **CommandButton** in the Toolbox, and click in the bottom-right corner of the form.

You inserted a CommandButton in the bottom-right corner of the form.

g. Change the Name property to **cmdClose**, change the Caption property to **Close**, change the Left property to **258**, change the Top property to **312**, and change the Width property to **60**.

h. Click the form to select it and change the Height property to **369.75**.

Previously, you increased the height to make sure you would have enough space to insert the controls. Now that you have inserted the controls, you decreased the height of the form.

i. Click **Save** on the toolbar.

STEP 5 ≫ ADJUST SPECIALIZED PROPERTIES

Now that you have inserted all the controls on the form, you need to set additional properties. The TabStop and TabIndex properties are set in the first two frames; however, you need to set these properties in the third frame to provide a logical flow if the user presses Tab to go from one control to another. In addition, you will set the ControlSource, BackColor, and BorderStyle properties. Refer to Figure 2.11 as you complete Step 5.

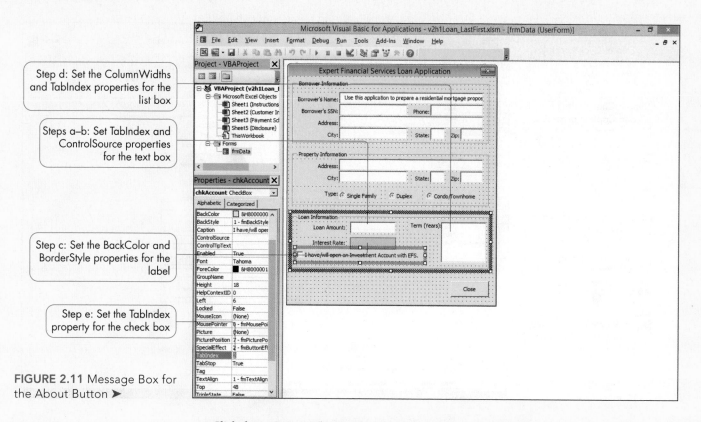

Step d: Set the ColumnWidths and TabIndex properties for the list box

Steps a–b: Set TabIndex and ControlSource properties for the text box

Step c: Set the BackColor and BorderStyle properties for the label

Step e: Set the TabIndex property for the check box

FIGURE 2.11 Message Box for the About Button ➤

a. Click the **txtPrincipal control** in the Loan Information frame.

The TabStop property default setting is True.

b. Change the TabIndex property to **0** and change the ControlSource property to **F6**.

To make sure the txtPrincipal is the first control to receive focus within the selected frame, you set the TabIndex value to 0. Finally, you want to use the value stored in cell F6 of the current worksheet as the source for calculations.

c. Click the **lblRateValue control**, click the **BackColor property arrow**, click the **Palette tab**, and click the **Light Blue color** (third color from the right on the top row). **H00FFFFC0&** should display in the BackColor property setting now. Set the BorderStyle property to **1-fmBorderStyleSingle**.

You selected a different background color so that the interest rate stands out on the form.

d. Click the **lstTerm** control, set the ColumnWidths property to **0.15**, and set the TabIndex property to **1**.

Because labels cannot receive focus, you set the lstTerm control to be the second control (indicated by 1) to receive focus in the selected frame.

e. Click the **chkAccount control** and set the TabIndex property to **2**.

You set the chkAccount control to be the third control (indicated by 2) to receive focus in the selected frame.

f. Click **Save** on the toolbar and close the VB Editor.

The Instructions worksheet displays instructions for entering customer and loan information, calculating and displaying a loan repayment schedule, and displaying the Truth-in-Lending disclosure worksheet. You need to insert three command buttons on the Instructions worksheet. Later, you will write VBA code for each button. Refer to Figure 2.12 as you complete Step 6.

FIGURE 2.12 Controls on a Worksheet ➤

a. Right-click the **Instructions sheet tab** and select **Unprotect Sheet**.

   Excel prevents you from inserting controls on a protected worksheet. You must temporarily unprotect the worksheet to insert a control on it.

b. Click the **DEVELOPER tab** and click **Insert** in the Controls group.

c. Click **Command Button (ActiveX Control)** in the ActiveX Controls section on the palette.

   The mouse pointer looks like a plus sign, indicating you are ready to drag to draw the control on the worksheet.

> **TROUBLESHOOTING:** If you click Button (Form Control) instead of Command Button (ActiveX Control), you will not be able to code the button correctly. You must delete the Button control and click Command Button (ActiveX Control) on the palette to create the correct type of control.

d. Drag to create a command button to approximate the size and location within the top box as shown in Figure 2.12.

e. Click **Properties** in the Controls group.

The Properties window displays so that you can set the properties for the selected command button. You can increase the height and the width of the Properties window, if needed.

f. Change the Name property to **cmdDisplayForm** and change the Caption property to **Enter/Edit Customer Information**.

g. Press **Ctrl+C** to copy the selected button and press **Ctrl+V** twice to paste two copies of the button. Drag the two duplicate buttons to their respective locations (see Figure 2.12).

h. Click the second button to select it. Change the Name property to **cmdCreateSchedule** and change the Caption property to **View the Loan Payment Schedule**.

i. Click the third button to select it. Change the Name property to **cmdDisplayDisclosure** and change the Caption property to **View the Truth-in-Lending Disclosure**.

j. Click **Save** on the toolbar. Close the Properties window. Keep the workbook open if you plan to continue with the next Hands-On Exercise. If not, close the workbook and exit Excel.

Procedures and Functions for Form Controls

After you create a form, insert controls on the form, and set the properties for the controls, you are ready to start writing the code. The code should accept user input, store data into variables, perform calculations if needed, and display output. In Chapter 1, you learned the foundational structures for creating procedures. In this chapter, you will write procedures that are attached to controls.

In this section, you will learn how to write procedures for particular controls on a form and a worksheet. In addition, you will learn how to create and call function procedures.

Adding a Procedure to a Control

The CommandButton control is probably the most common control for which you need to write code. Typically, you write code specifically for a button that executes a procedure when the user clicks the button. The process for writing code is similar to when you created procedures in Chapter 1. The difference is that the procedure name matches the button's name, includes an underscore, and includes the name of the event that triggers the code, such as Click.

STEP 1 To add a procedure to a control that is on a worksheet, do the following:

1. Click Design Mode in the Controls group on the DEVELOPER tab, if necessary, to activate Design mode.
2. Right-click the control and select View Code.

   VBA creates a procedure that handles the button's Click event. The procedure includes the button's name, an underscore, and the event name. For example, if the button's name is cmdDisplayForm, VBA creates the procedure header Private Sub cmdDisplayForm_Click().
3. Type the code for the control's procedure.

After creating the procedure for the control, click Design Mode to deactivate the Design mode and click the button to make sure the procedure runs as you intended.

Use Object Hierarchy

Understanding how objects relate to one another is essential to working with VBA, because VBA statements refer to objects by name and in order according to their position in the object hierarchy.

Assume you are creating a VBA procedure that needs to obtain a value from the Payment worksheet in a workbook named Loan Calculator. The worksheet is a member of the Worksheets collection. Therefore, you specify the Worksheets object with the worksheet object name enclosed in quotation marks within the parentheses. If you are working with two workbooks that both have a worksheet named Payment, you must indicate which worksheet you want to manipulate by specifying the name of the workbook. When you reference multiple objects in a hierarchy, the top-level object is referenced first. A period (dot) separates the object references. To refer to a specific cell or group of cells, use the Range object after the Workbooks and Worksheets objects.

The object highest in the hierarchy is the Application object. To reference every object in the hierarchy to which a specific cell belongs (such as a specific worksheet range), your code must include the Application object. Code Window 2.1 displays four statements that illustrate different levels of depth in referencing objects. To ensure the correct object is being used from the correct worksheet in a specific workbook, you can explicitly or directly state the entire hierarchy.

```
'Only one workbook open with a Payment worksheet
Worksheets ("Payment")

'Two or more workbooks open, each with a Payment worksheet
Workbooks("Loan Calculator.xlsm").Worksheets ("Payment")

'A range in a particular worksheet object
Workbooks("Loan Calculator.xlsm").Worksheets("Payment").Range ("B9")

'Explicit statement showing hierarchy
Application.Workbooks("Loan Calculator.xlsm").Worksheets("Payment").Range ("B9")
```

CODE WINDOW 2.1 ▲

The way you reference an object depends on several factors. First, determine whether other objects in the application have a similar name. For example, referencing a cell range in a worksheet when two workbooks with different names are open and both workbooks have a worksheet with the same name requires an explicit or complete reference that names the workbook, the worksheet, and the range. If your object references omit any part of the hierarchy, Excel uses the active object. For that reason, most programmers do not include a reference to the Application object in code, because by default the application is running. The best principle is to keep your code as simple as possible, while also anticipating how the code will run when multiple workbooks might be open. The more explicit you are by specifying the hierarchy, the less the potential for conflicts, but more coding is required. Therefore, you should explicitly include as many elements in the hierarchy as you think the application will require for typical usage.

Manipulate Object Properties, Methods, and Events

You need to know about the characteristics of objects (properties), the actions that objects can perform (methods), and the actions that cause program statements to act upon objects (events).

A property is an attribute of an object that defines one of the object's characteristics—such as size or color—or an aspect of its behavior—such as whether it is enabled or visible. To change an object's characteristics, you can use an assignment statement to set the value of a property. The object reference and property name are separated by a period, and an equal sign assigns a value to the property.

A method is an action that an object can perform while the application is running. For example, *Worksheet* objects have an *Activate* method, which makes a specified worksheet the active sheet. *Range* objects have a *Clear* method, which clears all the cells in a range.

An event is an action occurring at run time that triggers a program instruction. Recall that VBA is an event-driven language in which program statements execute at run time to process information or perform actions in response to events. The code specifies what the object will do in response to the event. The system triggers some events, such as when a user opens a workbook. Users trigger other events, such as clicking the mouse or pressing a key.

Code Window 2.2 illustrates several statements that manipulate object properties, methods, and events.

```
'Use the Value property to assign 150000 to cell B5 in the active workbook
Workbook("Loan Calculator.xlsm").Worksheets("Payment").Range("B5").Value = 150000

'Move the active cell to the same row (0) and to the right by one cell (1)
ActiveCell.Offset(0, 1).Activate

'Assign a value stored in a variable to the active cell
ActiveCell.FormulaR1C1 = strFirst

'Use the Activate method to make a particular worksheet active
Worksheets("Customer Information").Activate

'Set the RowSource property for a combo box and a list box
cboInvestment.RowSource = "E2:E47"
lstYears.RowSource = "F2:F21"
```

CODE WINDOW 2.2 ▲

The first statement changes the value in a range (cell B5) in a specific worksheet (Payment) in a specific workbook (Loan Calculator).

The second statement uses ActiveCell.Offset to move the active cell to the same row (0) and to the right one cell (1) and use the Activate method to activate that cell.

The third statement uses ActiveCell.FormulaR1C1 to assign the content of the variable strFirst to the active cell.

The fourth statement uses the Activate method to activate a specific worksheet (Customer Information).

The fifth statement populates a combo box by using the values in the range E2:E47 and assigning the range to the RowSource property.

The sixth statement uses the values in the range F2:F21 to populate the lstYears list box through the RowSource property.

At times, you do not want a worksheet to display the values used to populate a list in a ListBox or ComboBox control, because displaying these ranges clutters the user interface. If the list obtains its value from a worksheet range, you can hide the worksheet column containing the range. You can also add items to a list at run time using the AddItem method in a code procedure. For example, a form can include a procedure to initialize the control with a list of items when the application loads the form into memory. Code Window 2.3 contains an example of an initialization procedure.

```
Sub Initialize_InvestmentForm()
'Populate the combo box and list box controls on the form
    cboInvestment.AddItem = "8000"
    cboInvestment.AddItem = "10000"
    cboInvestment.AddItem = "12000"
    cboInvestment.AddItem = "14000"
    cboInvestment.AddItem = "16000"

    lstYears.AddItem = "1"
    lstYears.AddItem = "2"
    lstYears.AddItem = "3"
    lstYears.AddItem = "4"
    lstYears.AddItem = "5"

    lstContribution.AddItem = "25"
    lstContribution.AddItem = "50"
    lstContribution.AddItem = "75"
    lstContribution.AddItem = "100"

End Sub
```

CODE WINDOW 2.3 ➤

Show, Hide, Close, and Unload Forms

When you add custom forms, you decide how to display the form, when to close it, and how to set the initial values when the form opens. In the EFS loan application, you write code procedures to initialize, display, and close the form for entering borrower, property, and loan information. The form displays when the user clicks a button on the Instructions worksheet. The procedure that displays the form also initializes the application by activating the Customer Information worksheet, disabling the worksheet protection, and setting the initial values: $160,000 for the principal, 30 years for the term, and 5.75% as the interest rate. Changing the principal or the term calls a custom procedure that calculates the interest rate and displays the updated rate in the lblRateValue control. Closing the form enables the worksheet protection and activates the Instructions form.

The command button that displays the data entry form handles a click event that opens the form from the Instructions worksheet. The form displays as a modal form. A modal form disables all other worksheet objects until the form is closed. All data entry and editing must be done while the form is open.

STEP 2 >>
The *Show method* displays the form. The *Close method* closes the form and removes it from memory. The *Hide method* closes the form but does not remove it from memory. If you use frmForm.Show again, the form will display with its previous values entered. To unload a form from memory, use the statement *Unload frmForm*, substituting the form's actual name.

If you want to initialize controls on the form when it loads into memory, do the following:

1. Click the Object arrow at the top of the form, and then select UserForm. The Object shows the currently selected object for which you are coding. If you are unsure which arrow is the Object arrow, position the mouse pointer of the arrow to display a ScreenTip, such as Object.

2. Click the Procedures or Methods arrow at the top of the form, and then select Initialize from the Methods list. When you position the mouse pointer over the Methods arrow, the ScreenTip displays *Procedure* or *Method*.

3. Initialize controls. For example, if you want to ensure previously entered data is cleared, you can adapt the following to clear a text box:

```
txtName.Text=[dp][dp]
```

Creating and Calling a Function Procedure

You have used implicit functions in VBA procedures. Implicit functions are predefined VBA functions. For example, the Val function converts a number stored as text into a numeric value for calculations, the Format function formats a value for display, the Input function displays a text box for user input, the MsgBox function displays information in a dialog box, and the IsNumeric function verifies that a value is a number. These are all examples of implicit functions, or functions that are a part of the VBA programming environment. Previously, you created sub procedures to perform actions. For example, you have created sub procedures to display message boxes. Function procedures, on the other hand, perform an action (such as obtaining user input and converting it to values) and return a value (such as calculating the monthly payment).

A function procedure begins with *Function* and ends with *End Function*. A function can receive arguments passed to the function by a procedure that calls the function. A procedure that calls a function is called the **calling procedure**. One advantage of function procedures is that you can create the procedure once and call it from multiple procedures. Code Window 2.4 illustrates a function procedure (LoanPayment) and the calling procedure (Loan_Payment).

```
'Function to calculate the loan payment
Function LoanPayment(Principal, Rate, Term)

    LoanPayment = Principal * (Rate / (1 - (1 + Rate) ^ -Term))

End Function

Sub Loan_Payment()

    'Declare variables
    Dim curPrincipal As Double
    Dim sngRate As Single
    Dim intTerm As Integer
    Dim curPayment As Currency

    'Obtain input and assign to variables
    curPrincipal = Val(InputBox("Please enter the loan principal"))
    sngRate = Val(InputBox("Please enter the annual interest rate")) / 12
    intTerm = Val(InputBox("Please enter the term")) * 12

    'Call the function and pass arguments to it
    curPayment = LoanPayment(curPrincipal, sngRate, intTerm)

    'Format and display the results
    MsgBox ("The monthly payment is: " & Format(curPayment, "Currency"))

End Sub
```

CODE WINDOW 2.4 ▲

Create the Main Procedure with the Calling Statement

STEP 3 ≫   The Loan_Payment procedure is the main procedure. It declares four variables, displays input boxes to obtain the values from the user, and converts the data to values before storing the values in the declared variables. Within two of the InputBox statements, the APR is divided by 12, and the term is multiplied by 12 because the clients make 12 *monthly* payments.

The second-to-the-last statement contains LoanPayment(curPrincipal, sngRate, intTerm), which calls the LoanPayment function and passes the values stored in the curPrincipal, sngRate, and intTerm variables to that function. The function contains code to process the values and returns a value back to the calling procedure, which is then assigned to the curPayment variable.

TIP Calling Procedures

The statement that calls a function always receives a value back from the function. The calling procedure cannot start with the function name. The program must do something with the return value, such as displaying it onscreen or storing the value in a variable. Therefore, the variable or output is typed at the left side, followed by the assignment operator =, and then the calling statement is on the right side of the assignment operator.

Create the Function Procedure

The LoanPayment function procedure receives the three arguments using the alias or similar names Principal, Rate, and Term. Often programmers use similar names for the argument names instead of identical names of the variables being passed to the argument. In this case, the function uses the name Principal instead of the original variable name curPrincipal. The function has one statement to calculate the loan payment. When the term and rate are expressed in monthly payment periods (the years multiplied by 12 months per year for the term and the annual interest divided by 12 months per year), the statement assigns the calculated result to the function name, LoanPayment. The LoanPayment function then returns that value back to the calling procedure in the Loan_Payment sub procedure.

Process the Returned Value from the Function

The calling statement must do something with the returned value. In this case, it assigns the returned value to the curPayment variable. The Loan_Payment sub procedure then displays the formatted monthly payment in a message box.

If a user enters 160000 in the input box when prompted, 0.0645 in the input box that prompts for the interest rate, and 15 in the input box that prompts for the term, the resulting message box will display *The monthly payment is: $1,389.38.*

 TIP | **Passing Arguments by Value and by Reference**

You can pass arguments to procedures in two ways: by reference and by value. The default is by reference, which means that the value is passed by referencing the variable, and the procedure has access to the variable itself, and can potentially change its value. You can also pass arguments to a procedure by value, meaning that the procedure references a copy of the variable, and its value cannot be changed.

Quick **Concepts** ✓

1. Explain the object hierarchy requirements for writing code. *p. 94*

2. What is the different between the Close and Hide methods? *p. 97*

3. What is the purpose of a function? Why does the function calling statement have to have an assignment? *p. 99*

Hands-On Exercises

2 Procedures and Functions for Form Controls

Previously, you inserted controls on the Loan Application form and changed some of the properties. In addition, you inserted a button control directly on a worksheet. You are now ready to start writing the code that displays the form, performs calculations based on input, and closes the form.

Skills covered: Add a Procedure to a Control • Add a Procedure to Close a Form • Create and Call a Function Procedure

STEP 1 ≫ ADD A PROCEDURE TO A CONTROL

You need to write code procedure for the cmdDisplayForm button that you inserted on the Instructions worksheet. The code will activate and unprotect the Customer Information sheet, populate a list box on the form, set initial values in the form, and use worksheet data to complete the form. Refer to Figure 2.13 as you complete Step 1.

Step i: Click to close the form

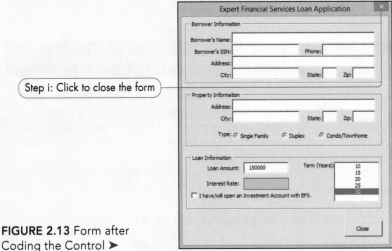

FIGURE 2.13 Form after Coding the Control ➤

a. Open the macro-enabled *v2h1Loan_LastFirst* workbook if you closed it at the end of Hands-On Exercise 1 and save it as **v2h2Loan_LastFirst**, changing *h1* to *h2*.

b. Click the **DEVELOPER tab**, if necessary, and click **Design Mode** in the Controls group to activate Design mode.

c. Right-click the **Enter/Edit Customer Information command button** on the worksheet and select **View Code**.

VBA creates a procedure that handles the button's Click event.

d. Type the code shown in Code Window 2.5.

```
Private Sub cmdDisplayForm_Click()

    'Activate the worksheet
    Worksheets("Customer Information").Activate
    Worksheets("Customer Information").Unprotect

    'Clear and populate the list box
    frmData.lstTerm.Clear
    Dim intItem As Integer
    For intItem = 10 To 30 Step 5
        frmData.lstTerm.AddItem (intItem)
    Next

    'Set the initial values
    If frmData.txtPrincipal.Text = "" Then
        frmData.txtPrincipal.Text = 150000
        Worksheets("Customer Information").Range("F6") = 150000
    End If

    If Worksheets("Customer Information").Range("F10") <> "" Then
        Dim intTerm As Integer
        intTerm = Val(Worksheets("Customer Information").Range("F10"))
    Else
        intTerm = 30
    End If

    Select Case intTerm
        Case 10
            frmData.lstTerm.Selected(0) = True
        Case 15
            frmData.lstTerm.Selected(1) = True
        Case 20
            frmData.lstTerm.Selected(2) = True
        Case 25
            frmData.lstTerm.Selected(3) = True
        Case 30
            frmData.lstTerm.Selected(4) = True
    End Select

    Worksheets("Customer Information").Range("F10") = intTerm
    frmData.txtName.SetFocus

    'Display the form
    frmData.Show

End Sub
```

CODE WINDOW 2.5 ▲

The first two statements activate the Customer Information worksheet and then unprotect it so that the rest of the procedure can add data on the worksheet.

You can use a repetition structure to add items to a list box at run time. In this case, the procedure for initializing a form uses a repetition structure and a selection structure. The For…Next loop populates the list box with a range of values from 10 to 30, at intervals of 5.

The Select Case structure uses the value assigned to the intTerm variable to assign the value of True to the appropriate list box item so that it is selected. The frmData.Show statement displays the form onscreen.

e. Click **Save** on the toolbar and close the VB Editor.

f. Right-click the **View the Truth-in-Lending Disclosure button** and select **View Code**.

g. Press **Enter**, press **Tab**, type **Worksheets("Disclosure").Activate** and press **Enter**. Click **Save** on the toolbar and close the VB Editor.

h. Click **Design Mode** in the Controls group on the DEVELOPER tab in Excel to deactivate Design mode.

i. Click the **Enter/Edit Customer Information button** to view the form. Click the **Close button** in the top-right corner of the form to close it. (The Close command button will not close the form because you have not created the code behind it yet.)

> **TROUBLESHOOTING:** If the form does not open when you click the command button, display the VB Editor, and then check your code carefully. Make any necessary corrections to the code, click Save in VBA, and then repeat step g again.

j. Click the **Instructions sheet tab** and click the **View the Truth-in-Lending Disclosure button** to activate the Disclosure worksheet. Click the **Instructions sheet tab**. Save the workbook.

STEP 2 ➤➤ ADD A PROCEDURE TO CLOSE A FORM

You need to add a procedure to the Close button on the form so that it will close the form. In addition, you need to add a command button on the Customer Information worksheet to return to the Instructions worksheet. Refer to Figure 2.14 as you complete Step 2.

FIGURE 2.14 Customer Information Worksheet ➤

a. Open the VB Editor and display the frmData form.

b. Right-click the **Close button** and select **View Code**.

c. Type the code shown in Code Window 2.6 between the Sub and End Sub statements.

```
Private Sub cmdClose_Click()

    'Determine property type; add to worksheet
    If optSingle.Value = -1 Then
        Worksheets("Customer Information").Range("B17") = "Single Family"
    ElseIf optDuplex.Value = -1 Then
        Worksheets("Customer Information").Range("B17") = "Duplex"
    Else
        Worksheets("Customer Information").Range("B17") = "Condo/Townhome"
    End If

    'Update interest rate, set protection, hide form
    Worksheets("Customer Information").Range("F8") = frmData.lblRateValue.Caption
    Worksheets("Customer Information").Protect
    frmData.Hide

End Sub
```

CODE WINDOW 2.6 ▲

The If...ElseIf statement determines which option button is selected. For each logical test, you compare a specific option button's Value property to –1, which is the value assigned by VBA to the selected option button. When a particular option button's Value property equals –1, a text entry will be entered in cell B17 on the Customer Information worksheet.

Next, the caption value in the lblRateValue control is then copied to cell F8 in the Customer Information worksheet. After the data is copied into cell F8, the procedure protects the Customer Information worksheet from further changes. Finally, the frmData.Hide statement hides the form but does not remove it from memory.

d. Save the code and minimize the VB Editor.

e. Click the **Customer Information sheet tab**, click **Insert** in the Controls group on the DEVELOPER tab, and click **Command Button (ActiveX Control)**.

f. Click to the right side of the Expert Financial Services heading on the left side of the worksheet to create a command button. Refer to Figure 2.14 for placement and size.

g. Click **Properties** in the Controls group. Change the Name property to **cmdReturn** and the Caption property to **Menu**.

h. Close the Properties window, right-click the **Menu button**, and select **View Code**.

VBA creates the Private Sub cmdReturn_Click() and End Sub lines.

i. Press **Enter**, press **Tab**, type **Worksheets ("Instructions"). Activate** and press **Enter**. Save and close the VB Editor.

j. Click **Design Mode** in the Controls group to deactivate Design mode.

k. Click the **Instructions sheet tab** to make it the active sheet. Click the **Enter/Edit Customer Information button** you created earlier. When the form opens, click **Close** in the bottom-right corner.

The form closes now that you have created a procedure for the Click event.

l. Click the **Menu button** you created at the top of the Customer Information worksheet.

The Click event procedure activates the Instructions worksheet again.

m. Save the workbook.

You need to create a function procedure that calculates the interest rate based on the term or principal. If a term is 10 years or if the principal is greater than or equal to $500,000, the interest rate is 4.75%. If the term is 15 years or if the principal is greater than or equal to $400,000, the interest rate is 5%. If the term is 20 years or if the principal is greater than or equal to $300,000, the interest rate is 5.25%. If the term is 25 years or if the principal is greater than or equal to $200,000, the interest rate is 5.5%. All other terms or principal amounts require a 5.75% interest rate. After you create the function procedure, you will create a calling procedure. Refer to Figure 2.15 as you complete Step 3.

FIGURE 2.15 Interest Rate Displayed ➤

a. Display the VB Editor, right-click the **frmData form** in the Project Explorer, and select **View Code**.

b. Press **Ctrl+Home**, type **Option Explicit** and press **Enter** twice.

c. Use Code Window 2.7 to create the Calculate procedure. Remember to type a lowercase l not the number 1 in *lstTerm.Text*. Remember to indent the statements within the If…ElseIf statement block for readability.

```
Sub CalculateRate()
    'Declare variables
    Dim curPrincipal As Currency
    Dim intTerm As Integer

    'Obtain values
    curPrincipal = Val(frmData.txtPrincipal.Text)
    intTerm = Val(lstTerm.Text)

    'Display interest rate
    If intTerm = 10 Or curPrincipal >= 500000 Then
        frmData.lblRateValue.Caption = "4.75%"
    ElseIf intTerm = 15 Or curPrincipal >= 400000 Then
        frmData.lblRateValue.Caption = "5.00%"
    ElseIf intTerm = 20 Or curPrincipal >= 300000 Then
        frmData.lblRateValue.Caption = "5.25%"
    ElseIf intTerm = 25 Or curPrincipal >= 200000 Then
        frmData.lblRateValue.Caption = "5.50%"
    Else
        frmData.lblRateValue.Caption = "5.75%"
    End If

End Sub
```

CODE WINDOW 2.7 ➤

The procedure declares two variables and uses the Text property of the text box and the list box controls to store the current values from the Text properties into the respective variables. You used an If…ElseIf statement block to handle the multiple logical tests. Each If and ElseIf test evaluated to see if either the term was equal to a value or if the principal was greater than or equal to a monetary value.

d. Use the Code Window 2.8 to create the calling procedures immediately after the CalculateRate procedure's End Sub statement.

```
Private Sub lstTerm_Click()

    CalculateRate

End Sub

Private Sub txtPrincipal_AfterUpdate()

    'Declare string variable
    Dim strMessage As String
    strMessage = "Please enter a value between 100000 and 700000"

    'Validate entry
    If Val(frmData.txtPrincipal.Text) < 100000 Or _
       Val(frmData.txtPrincipal.Text) > 700000 Then
            MsgBox strMessage, vbCritical, "Invalid Loan Principal"
    End If

    CalculateRate

End Sub
```

CODE WINDOW 2.8 ➤

The procedure declares a string variable and then assigns text to it to avoid having a lot of extra text in the MsgBox statement. The code then checks to determine if the value entered is either too low or too high. If either condition exists, a message box displays an error to the user. The last statement calls the CalculateRate procedure.

TROUBLESHOOTING: Remember to use the line-continuation (space and underscore) for long statements that carry over to a second line. If you forget the line-continuation character, a VBA error message will appear.

---

e. Click Save on the toolbar and close the VB Editor.

f. Click the **Instructions worksheet tab** and click the **Enter/Edit Customer Information button** in the worksheet.

The Loan Application form displays 5.75% in the Interest Rate label because the term is 30 years.

g. Click the **Close button** on the form. Save the workbook. Keep the workbook open if you plan to continue with the next Hands-On Exercise. If not, close the workbook and exit Excel.

Loan Payment Schedule and Disclosure Worksheets

The loan payment schedule and disclosure worksheets are important to provide additional details about loans to EFS clients. To complete these worksheets, you will incorporate a variety of VBA statements that you have previously learned. For example, you will create procedures that use the object model, declare variables, initialize variables, create a repetition structure, call a custom function procedure, and return a value from a function back to the calling statement.

In this section, you will create a loan payment schedule using variables, If statements, repetition statements, financial functions, and the Excel object model. Furthermore, you will complete a loan disclosure worksheet that includes financial and date functions. Finally, you will complete the entire EFS application by setting workbook options to protect the worksheets against unauthorized data entry.

Creating a List in a Worksheet

You can write VBA code that creates a list in a worksheet. For example, you might want to create an amortization table that lists each monthly payment's details for a particular loan. To create such a list, use a repetition structure (i.e., loop) where through each iteration, data is entered on the next blank row in the worksheet.

A loan payment schedule provides information for each monthly payment until a loan is paid in full. When you make a residential mortgage payment, you pay the same amount each month, but the portion of the payment that applies to the loan principal varies each month. For the initial payments, a greater portion of each payment applies to the interest charged for the loan, but as the payments continue, a greater portion of the monthly payment applies to the outstanding loan principal. A loan repayment schedule is useful for displaying the details of each monthly payment and determining the outstanding balance at any time during the loan.

The EFS workbook includes the Payment Schedule worksheet to display the loan principal, term, rate, monthly payment, and closing costs. It also displays the following details for each monthly payment: the payment number, the amount of the monthly payment that applies to the loan principal, the amount of the monthly payment that applies to the loan interest, the principal paid to date, the interest paid to date, the total principal and interest paid to date, and the outstanding loan balance.

Prepare the Worksheet and Obtain Input

Before writing code to populate a list on a worksheet, you need to prepare the worksheet. This process may include creating a control that will run the code, declaring variables, and obtaining input from a data-entry section on a worksheet or from a form.

STEP 1 To prepare the worksheet and obtain input, use the following general steps:

1. Insert a Command Button (ActiveX Control) on a worksheet. The button will be used to execute the VBA code.
2. View the code for the control.
3. Write the code to unprotect a worksheet and clear an existing range from a previous list, if needed.
4. Declare variables to store data obtained from a worksheet, calculated values, a counter variable to store the current row number of the list, and a counter variable to control the iterations.

   Code Window 2.9 declares intCurrentRow, a counter variable to store the value of the current row number where you want to enter data in the list. This value will change during each iteration of the loop.

The intCounter is a counter variable that controls the number of times the loop iterates. For example, if a user takes out a 5-year loan with monthly payments, the intCounter variable will be set to 60 (5 years with 12 months each).

CODE WINDOW 2.9 ➤

```
'Current row number for entering data in the list
Dim intCurrentRow As Integer

'Counter variable to control loop iterations
Dim intCounter As Integer
```

5. Use the Worksheets.Range code to obtain values from appropriate cells in a worksheet and assign the values to variables.
6. Perform any calculations that will be needed before the loop begins.

Write Code to Create a List

After preparing a worksheet, declaring variables, and obtaining input, you are ready to write the code to create a list. The code should include a statement that primes the loop; that is, you should set the value of the variable that will control which row the data will be entered in the worksheet. Then, create a loop that will iterate the number of times needed to populate the list.

STEP 2 ❯❯   To write code to create a list, use the following general steps:

1. Assign a value of the first row for which you want to enter data. This variable will increment each iteration so that data will be entered on the next empty row in the list.
2. Create the loop header using a For statement. Specify the starting value of the counter variable, such as 1, and specify its termination value using a variable to iterate enough times based on the data. For example, if you are making monthly payments on an automobile loan for 5 years, the loop needs to iterate 60 times. Do not hard-code 60 because the number of monthly payments will vary based on whether the user takes out a 4-, 5-, or 6-year loan.
3. Create the body of the loop to enter data on the current row. For the first iteration, the current row should be the starting row of the list.
4. Write the code for the last line of the loop before the Next statement to increment the row number. The counter variable controlling the iterations should automatically increment because of the For header.

Code Window 2.10 illustrates a loop to enter data on a worksheet. The statement before loop, intCurrentRow = 10 makes sure the first data is entered on row 10 in the worksheet. The header starts the intCounter variable at 1. During each iteration, the value increases until it reaches the total of payment periods, indicated by the value stored in intTerm.

```
'Specify starting row number for the list
intCurrentRow = 10

'Loop through each monthly payment to calculate & display values
For intCounter = 1 To intTerm
    'Enter current payment number in Column A of current row
    Worksheets("Payment Schedule").Range("A" & intCurrentRow) = intCounter

    'Calculate monthly payment and enter it in Column B of current row
    curPpmt = PPmt(dblRate, intCounter, intTerm, -curPrincipal)
    Worksheets("Payment Schedule").Range("B" & intCurrentRow) = curPpmt

    'Calculate current interest and enter it in Column C of current row
    curIpmt = IPmt(dblRate, intCounter, intTerm, -curPrincipal)
    Worksheets("Payment Schedule").Range("C" & intCurrentRow) = curIpmt

    'Increment the row number for the next row in the worksheet
    intCurrentRow = intCurrentRow + 1

Next
```

CODE WINDOW 2.10 ⮝

To make sure the data gets entered in the correct cells, the Range argument specifies the column letter in quotation marks. For example, to enter the payment number in the first column, use Range("A" & intCurrentRow). The & concatenates the column letter A with the value in the intCurrentRow variable. During the first iteration, the data starts in cell A10. The comments explain the calculations and what data is entered in columns B and C. The last statement increments the intCurrentRow by 1 and saves that value back to the intCurrentRow variable. At the end of the first iteration, intCurrentRow contains the value 11 so that during the next iteration, data will be placed on row 11.

Understand Other Sections on the Payment Schedule Worksheet

The range B4:B7 summarizes the loan details. Because some of this information is already displayed on the Customer Information worksheet, you can use 3-D references to display the same information on this worksheet and the Pmt function to calculate the monthly payment.

The range G5:G7 summarizes the closing costs, which include the loan origination fee (2% of the loan principal) and the loan points (which range from 1% to 3% of the loan principal) based upon the loan term. In addition, customers who currently have or plan to open an investment account with EFS receive a 1% discount on the loan points. The total closing cost is the sum of the origination fee and the points. These values can be calculated from the loan information displayed in cells B4 and B6 of the Payment Schedule worksheet, and cell F4 of the Customer Information worksheet, which displays TRUE if the customer has opened or will open an investment account and FALSE if the customer does not have an account.

Preparing an Application for Distribution

When you create a custom application you should test its functionality before you distribute it. However, before testing the application, you should prepare the application for distribution. In the EFS application, the Instructions worksheet provides menu options for opening the data entry form, generating and displaying the payment schedule, and displaying the Truth-in-Lending disclosure.

Create Code to Activate the Instructions Worksheet

All data entry is through the form; therefore, all the worksheets need to have protection set to prevent accidental data entry within the worksheet. The Payment Schedule worksheet will contain the loan amortizations schedule. However, you want to create an easy way for a user to go back to the Instructions worksheet. Therefore, you will add a button that when clicked will display the Instructions worksheet again.

STEP 3 »

To create a control that will return to the Instructions worksheet, do the following:

1. Right-click the button and select View Code.
2. Enter the code *Worksheets("Instructions").Activate* and press Enter. The Activate method will activate or display the worksheet specified. In this case, it will display the Instructions worksheet.
3. Deactivate Design mode and protect the Payment Schedule worksheet.

Add Formulas to the Disclosure Worksheet

The Disclosures worksheet summarizes the amount to be financed, the total finance charges, the total payments, the interest rate, the term, and the dates the first and last payments are due. You can create formulas that refer to values stored in other worksheets to display on this summary worksheet. In addition, you can insert functions to perform other summary calculations:

STEP 4 »

- CUMIPMT function: calculates the cumulative interest, which represents the total finance charges on the loan.
- PMT function: calculates the monthly payment, including principal and interest.
- DATE function: determines the last payment date, when nesting YEAR, MONTH, and DAY functions and their respective arguments.

Users have two methods of navigating the application interface: using the buttons to open and display the various application components or using the sheet tabs. Although the sheet tabs can be hidden, many Excel users prefer the sheet tabs to navigate through a workbook. The sheet tabs display the worksheets; to make changes to the loan scenario or customer information, users need to use the buttons on the Instructions worksheet. After you make the final changes to each worksheet, you can set worksheet protection and then test the worksheet.

TIP Hiding Excel Window Elements

When you create your own applications, you can hide the Formula Bar and row and column headings on an unprotected worksheet. To do this, click the File tab, and then click Options. Click Advanced, and then deselect the Show formula bar and the Show row and column headers check boxes. Click OK, and then protect the appropriate worksheets.

Quick Concepts

1. Why is a counter variable needed when using code to create a list on a worksheet? ***p. 106***
2. What statement would ensure the intThisRow variable starts on row 15? What would be the last line of code within a loop to make sure the variable starts on the next blank row in the worksheet? ***p. 108***

Hands-On Exercises

3 Loan Payment Schedule and Disclosure Worksheets

You need to write the code behind the View the Loan Payment Schedule button to populate and view the loan payment schedule. You will also add a button to the Payment Schedule worksheet to return to the Instruction worksheet. In addition, you need to add formulas to provide summary data about the loan on the Truth-in-Lending worksheet.

Skills covered: Prepare the Worksheet and Obtain Input • Write Code to Create a List • Create Code to Activate the Instructions Worksheet • Add Formulas to the Disclosure Worksheet

STEP 1 >> PREPARE THE WORKSHEET AND OBTAIN INPUT

You need to write the initial code for the cmdCreateSchedule button. When the user clicks the button, the VBA code will unprotect the Payment Schedule worksheet so that the worksheet can be altered. The code will clear the existing range containing the loan payment schedule, declare variables, and perform some calculations. Refer to Figure 2.16 as you complete Step 1.

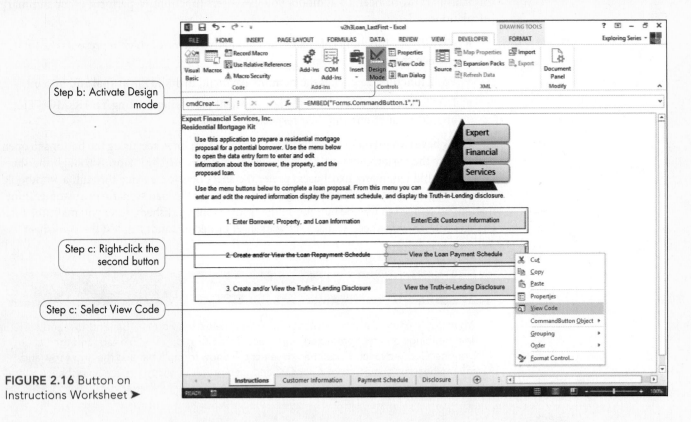

FIGURE 2.16 Button on Instructions Worksheet ➤

a. Open the *v2h2Loan_LasteFirst* macro-enabled workbook if you closed it at the end of Hands-On Exercise 2 and save it as **v2h3Loan_LastFirst**, changing *h2* to *h3*.

> **TROUBLESHOOTING:** The Instructions worksheet should still be unprotected. If not, right-click the Instructions sheet tab and select Unprotect Sheet.

b. Click the **Instructions sheet tab** if necessary, click the **DEVELOPER tab**, and then click **Design Mode** in the Controls group to enable Design mode.

c. Right-click the **View the Loan Payment Schedule command button** and select **View Code**.

> **TROUBLESHOOTING:** If you click View Code in the Controls group on the Developer tab, the VB Editor shows existing code. It does not create a sub procedure for the button. If this happens, close the VB Editor, right-click the button, and select View Code.

VBA creates the Private Sub cmdCreateSchedule_Click() and End Sub lines.

d. Type the code shown in Code Window 2.11 and click **Save** on the toolbar.

CODE WINDOW 2.11 ➤

```
Private Sub cmdCreateSchedule_Click()

    'Disable worksheet protection
    Worksheets("Payment Schedule").Unprotect

    'Clear any previous schedules
    Worksheets("Payment Schedule").Range("A10:G369").Clear

    'Declare variables for input and calculated values
    Dim curPrincipal As Currency
    Dim dblRate As Double
    Dim intTerm As Integer
    Dim curPpmt As Currency
    Dim curIpmt As Currency

    'Current row number for entering data in the list
    Dim intCurrentRow As Integer

    'Counter variable to control loop iterations
    Dim intCounter As Integer

    'Obtain worksheet values to calculate and store other values
    intTerm = Worksheets("Payment Schedule").Range("B6") * 12
    curPrincipal = Worksheets("Payment Schedule").Range("B4")
    dblRate = Worksheets("Payment Schedule").Range("B5") / 12
```

When a user clicks the Create Schedule command button, the Payment Schedule worksheet is unprotected so that it can clear a range of data. The procedure declares variables, and uses data on the worksheet to store in variables intPayments, curPrincipal, and dblRate. You will add to the cmdCreateSchedule procedure in the next step.

STEP 2 ≫ WRITE CODE TO CREATE A LIST

Your next task is to complete the code for the cmdCreateSchedule button. You will use the For...Next repetition structure to iterate enough times to enter data in a list on the Payment Schedule worksheet. Refer to Figure 2.17 as you complete Step 2.

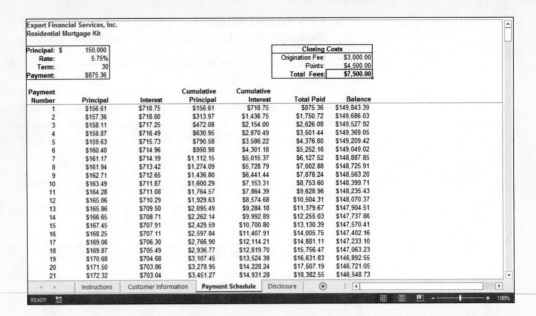

FIGURE 2.17 Payment Schedule Created from VBA Procedure ➤

a. Make sure the insertion point is on the blank line after the dblRate = Worksheets… statement that you just typed. Press **Enter** and type the code shown in Code Window 2.12.

```vba
'Specify starting row number for the list
intCurrentRow = 10

'Loop through each monthly payment to calculate & display values
For intCounter = 1 To intTerm
    'Enter current payment number in Column A of current row
    Worksheets("Payment Schedule").Range("A" & intCurrentRow) = intCounter

    'Calculate monthly payment and enter it in Column B of current row
    curPpmt = PPmt(dblRate, intCounter, intTerm, -curPrincipal)
    Worksheets("Payment Schedule").Range("B" & intCurrentRow) = curPpmt

    'Calculate current interest and enter it in Column C of current row
    curIpmt = IPmt(dblRate, intCounter, intTerm, -curPrincipal)
    Worksheets("Payment Schedule").Range("C" & intCurrentRow) = curIpmt

    'Calculate the cumulative interest and cumulative principal
    'Enter values in Columns D and E of current row
    Worksheets("Payment Schedule").Range("D" & intCurrentRow) = curPpmt _
        + Val(Worksheets("Payment Schedule").Range("D" & intCurrentRow - 1))
    Worksheets("Payment Schedule").Range("E" & intCurrentRow) = curIpmt _
        + Val(Worksheets("Payment Schedule").Range("E" & intCurrentRow - 1))

    'Calculate the total paid to date from Columns D and E of current row
    'Enter total paid in Column F of current row
    Worksheets("Payment Schedule").Range("F" & intCurrentRow) = _
    Worksheets("Payment Schedule").Range("D" & intCurrentRow) + _
    Worksheets("Payment Schedule").Range("E" & intCurrentRow)

    'Calculate the outstanding balance and enter it in Column G of current row
    Worksheets("Payment Schedule").Range("G" & intCurrentRow) = _
    curPrincipal - Val(Worksheets("Payment Schedule").Range("D" & intCurrentRow))

    'Increment the row number for the next row in the worksheet
    intCurrentRow = intCurrentRow + 1

Next

'Enable worksheet protection
Worksheets("Payment Schedule").Protect
Worksheets("Payment Schedule").Activate

End Sub
```

CODE WINDOW 2.12 ➤

The procedure you started in Step 1 sets the intTerm variable equal to the value in the intPayments variable that was obtained from a calculation from cell B6. The first statement sets the intStartRow value to 10 so that the procedure will start entering data on row 10 of the worksheet.

The repetition statement loops through each monthly payment (based on the intCounter variable's value) to calculate and display values on the respective row. During each iteration, the loop places data on the next available row in the worksheet. Finally, the procedure protects the Payment Schedule worksheet again and then activates it because the Click event occurred on the Instructions worksheet.

b. Save the code, close the VB Editor, and click **Design Mode** in the Controls group to deactivate Design mode.

c. Click the **View the Loan Payment Schedule button**. Save the workbook. Figure 2.17 shows the results.

> **TROUBLESHOOTING:** If a Compiler Error message box or a Debugging window displays, review each line of code to determine where the error exists. Fix the error, save the code, and then click the Create Schedule command button again to execute the sub procedure.

STEP 3 ➤➤ CREATE CODE TO ACTIVATE THE INSTRUCTIONS WORKSHEET

You want users to be able to quickly go back to the Instructions worksheet after viewing the results in the Payment Schedule worksheet. Therefore, you need to insert a button with VBA code on the Payment Schedule worksheet to make the Instructions worksheet active again. Refer to Figure 2.18 as you complete Step 3.

FIGURE 2.18 Menu Button on Payment Schedule Worksheet ➤

a. Right-click the **Payment Schedule sheet tab** and select **Unprotect Sheet**.

b. Click **Insert** in the Controls group on the DEVELOPER tab and click **Command Button (ActiveX Control)**.

c. Drag to create a command button to the right of the Expert Financial Services heading in the top-left corner (see Figure 2.18).

d. Click **Properties** in the Controls group, type **cmdReturn** in the **Name property box**, and type **Menu** in the **Caption property box**. Adjust the height and width to be similar to the button you created on the Customer Information worksheet in Hands-On Exercise 1. Close the Properties window.

e. Right-click the **Menu button** and select **View Code**.

VBA creates the Private Sub cmdReturn_Click() and End Sub lines.

f. Press **Enter**, press **Tab**, type **Worksheets("Instructions").Activate** and press **Enter**.

g. Save and close VBA. Click **Design Mode** in the Controls group to deactivate it.

h. Right-click the **Payment Schedule sheet tab**, select **Protect Sheet**, and click **OK** in the **Protect Sheet dialog box**.

After inserting the command button and coding it, you protect the worksheet again.

i. Click the **Menu button** you just created on the Payment Schedule worksheet to return to the Instructions worksheet. Save the workbook.

STEP 4 ›› ADD FORMULAS TO THE DISCLOSURE WORKSHEET

The Disclosure worksheet needs formulas that get data from other worksheets and perform calculations, such as the cumulative interest payment and the last payment date. In addition, you need to insert a command button on the Disclosure worksheet to return to the Instructions worksheet again. Refer to Figure 2.19 as you complete Step 4.

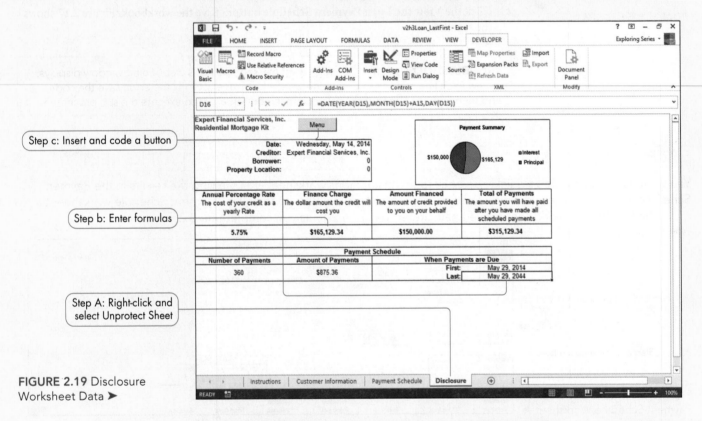

FIGURE 2.19 Disclosure Worksheet Data ➤

a. Right-click the **Disclosure sheet tab**, and then select **Unprotect Sheet**.

b. Use the Go To feature to go to the respective cells, and then enter the following formulas in the worksheet:

- Cell B4: **=NOW()**
- Cell B6: **='Customer Information'!$B$4**
- Cell B7: **='Customer Information'!$B$13**
- Cell A11: **='Customer Information'!$F$8**
- Cell A15: **='Customer Information'!F10*12**
- Cell B11: **=-CUMIPMT(A11/12,A15,C11,1,A15,0)**

Make sure you type the minus sign after the equal sign so that the result will be converted to a positive number.

> **TROUBLESHOOTING:** The cell will display #NUM! error here because cell A11 currently contains 0. The error message will disappear when you enter real values later.

- Cell B15: =PMT('Customer Information'!F8/12, 'Customer Information'!F10*12, -'Customer Information'!F6)
- Cell C11: ='Customer Information'!F6
- Cell D11: =B11+C11
- Cell D15: =B4+15
- Cell D16: =DATE(YEAR(D15),MONTH(D15)+A15,DAY(D15))

Cells B6 and B7 display zeroes. This is because the cells referenced by the formulas do not contain any values yet. After you add information about the borrower and the property, these cells display the name of the borrower and the location of the property.

c. Repeat steps 3b–g to insert a command button on the Disclosure worksheet.

d. Right-click the **Disclosure sheet tab**, select **Protect Sheet**, and click **OK** in the **Protect Sheet dialog box**.

After inserting the command button and coding it, you need to protect the worksheet again.

e. Click the **Menu button** you just created on the Disclosure worksheet to return to the Instructions worksheet.

f. Click the **View the Truth-in-Lending Disclosure button** to ensure it works, and click the **Menu button** in the Disclosure worksheet to return to the Instructions worksheet.

g. Click each button on each worksheet to test the functionality of each button again. If errors exist, view the code, identify the error, save the code, and then click the buttons again.

h. Make sure each worksheet is protected.

i. Save and close the workbook.

Chapter Objectives Review

After reading this chapter, you have accomplished the following objectives:

1. Create forms.

- To create a form in VBA, click Insert on the menu bar and select UserForm.
- After creating the form, set the Name property so that you can reference it in code. Type descriptive text in the Caption property to display on the form's title bar.

2. Add controls to forms.

- The Toolbox contains controls that you can add to a form. Each control provides specific functionality.
- Name the controls after inserting them on a form.
- Insert a frame control to enclose related controls in a border. The frame's caption appears at the top of the frame.
- Insert Label and TextBox controls to provide descriptions and data entry, respectively.
- Insert ListBox, CheckBox, and CommandButton controls so that users can select items from a list, select one or more options, and click to execute the code, respectively.

3. Add specialized properties.

- Set the Enabled, TabStop, and TabIndex properties. The Enabled property determines if a control can receive focus. Focus is the ability for a control to be able to be interacted with by the user. The TabStop property determines if a control can receive focus when the user presses Tab. The TabIndex property determines the order in which a control receives focus.
- Use bound and unbound controls. Use a bound control to connect the control to a data source, such as a range in a worksheet. The ControlSource and RowSource properties can be used to specify the location of the data.
- Set properties for the loan application form. It is a good practice to list the names of the controls, their properties, and the desired settings before creating a form.

4. Insert controls on a worksheet.

- You can use the DEVELOPER tab in Excel to insert controls directly on a worksheet.
- Use Design mode to insert and design the controls. Disable Design mode when you are ready to use the controls.
- Click Properties in the Control group on the DEVELOPER tab to adjust the properties of controls on a worksheet.
- The prompt argument specifies the text that appears within the message box. The title argument specifies the text that appears on the title bar.

5. Add a procedure to a control.

- Right-click a control and select View Code to display the Code window. VBA will create the procedure header and End statement for that control.
- Use object hierarchy to specify the level of objects.
- Manipulate object properties, methods, and events. Use the Properties window to set the settings for a control's properties. After typing the period, VBA will prompt with suggested methods that apply for that control.
- Show, hide, close, and unload forms. Use the Show method to show a form or a worksheet, Hide method to hide a form or worksheet but keep it in memory, Close to close a form or a worksheet, and Unload to close a form or a worksheet and unload it from memory.

6. Create and call a function procedure.

- A function is a procedure that contains code that can be called from any procedure.
- Create the main procedure with the calling statement. Any procedure can call a function that is created within the same workbook. From within the main procedure, create a statement that calls or invokes the function. You can pass variables to the function that the function can then manipulate.
- Create the function procedure. The function can receive variables passed from the main procedure. The parameters must be the same data type and quantity. When the function completes its task, it returns a value back to the calling statement and returns control back to the calling statement.
- Process the returned value from the function. The function returns a value. The calling statement then assigns that value to a variable or does some other action with the variable, such as displaying it onscreen.

7. Create a list in a worksheet.

- You can use VBA code to create a list within a worksheet where data is entered on individual rows.
- Prepare the worksheet and obtain input. The VBA code often unprotects a worksheet so that data can be entered to create the list. Variables are declared, and statements perform any necessary calculations.
- Write code to create a list. Use a repetition structure, such as a For...Next loop to iterate enough times to add data to create the list in a worksheet. The statement before the loop primes the loop by specifying the starting row number with a variable. The body of the loop must include specific column letters that will concatenate with the current row number to populate the list. The last statement of the loop typically increments the row counter so that data will be entered on the next row during the next iteration of the loop.

8. Prepare an application for distribution.

- Create code to active a worksheet. Right-click a button to write the code behind it.
- Add formulas to a worksheet. Complete any formulas needed in the workbook.
- Protect worksheets where users should not change data directly.

Key Terms Matching

Match the key terms with their definitions. Write the key term letter by the appropriate numbered definition.

a. Bound control
b. Calling procedure
c. Caption property
d. CheckBox control
e. CommandButton control
f. Control
g. ControlSource property
h. Enabled property
i. Frame control
j. Label control
k. ListBox control

l. Name property
m. Object
n. RowSource property
o. TabIndex property
p. TabStop property
q. TextAlign property
r. TextBox control
s. Toolbox
t. Unbound control

1. _____ A text string, such as frmClient, that identifies an object; this attribute may be used in VBA code to manipulate the object. **p. 75**

2. _____ A control that enables the user to select one or more options at the same time. **p. 80**

3. _____ A window that contains the standard controls that can be added to a form. **p. 76**

4. _____ An attribute of True or False that determines whether a control can receive focus and respond to the user. **p. 81**

5. _____ A control that is connected to a data source in the host application. **p. 81**

6. _____ An attribute that defines the cell to which a control is bound. **p. 82**

7. _____ A property that specifies items through an Excel worksheet range that will appear in a list box or combo box at run time. **p. 82**

8. _____ A control that is not connected to a data source in the host application. **p. 81**

9. _____ A statement within a procedure that calls or executes a function. **p. 97**

10. _____ A property that specifies the horizontal alignment of a caption appearing in a label. **p. 79**

11. _____ An object that displays a frame or border around selected controls on a form. **p. 78**

12. _____ An object or controls' attribute that displays onscreen, such as the text that appears onscreen for a form's title bar. **p. 75**

13. _____ A property that has an attribute of True or False that determines whether a control receives focus when the Tab key is pressed. **p. 81**

14. _____ An element, such as a worksheet cell, within a host application. **p. 74**

15. _____ An object, such as a text box, that enables interaction with the user. **p. 76**

16. _____ An object that displays text onscreen, usually to describe other controls that do not have captions. **p. 79**

17. _____ A property that determines the order in which a control receives the focus. **p. 81**

18. _____ An object that enables the user to click it; usually triggers VBA code to complete an algorithm of steps. **p. 80**

19. _____ An object that enables the user to type data on a form. **p. 79**

20. _____ An object that displays a list of items from which the user may select. **p. 80**

Multiple Choice

1. What are the steps to creating a user form in Excel?

   (a) Click the DEVELOPER tab, click Insert in the Controls group, and select Form.

   (b) Click the DEVELOPER tab, click Visual Basic in the Controls group, click Insert on the VBA menu, and select UserForm.

   (c) Click the INSERT tab, click Visual Basic in the Charts group, click Insert on the VBA menu, and select Form.

   (d) Click the INSERT tab, click Reports in the Visual Basic group, click Insert on the VBA menu, and select UserForm.

2. Which statement makes cell E5 the active cell in the Salary worksheet?

   (a) Worksheet(Salary).Cell(E5)

   (b) Worksheets("Salary").Range("E5")

   (c) Cell("E5").Worksheet("Salary")

   (d) Cell(E5).Worksheet(Salary)

3. What property displays text onscreen for a Label control?

   (a) Name

   (b) ControlSource

   (c) TextAlign

   (d) Caption

4. Which control is the least likely to need to have the programmer enter a specific value for the TabIndex property?

   (a) TextBox

   (b) CommandButton

   (c) Label

   (d) OptionButton

5. What type of control is used to organize other controls on a form?

   (a) Frame control

   (b) ComboBox control

   (c) TextBox control

   (d) BorderStyle control

6. Which statement displays a worksheet named Payments within a workbook named Finances?

   (a) Workbook.Payments.Display

   (b) Finances.Payments.Display

   (c) Payments.Finances.Show

   (d) Worksheets("Payments").Activate

7. Which statement clears existing text within the txtCity text box?

   (a) txtCity.Clear

   (b) txtCity = 0

   (c) txtCity.Text = [dp][dp]

   (d) txtCity.Text(Clear)

8. Which of the following statements is NOT true about a function calling statement?

   (a) The return value may be assigned to a variable.

   (b) The calling statement starts with the name of the function.

   (c) The returned value may be displayed as output on screen.

   (d) The calling statement passes variables to the function to process.

9. Study the following function that calculates net pay.

   Function NetPay(GrossPay, FederalTaxes, StateTaxes, LocalTaxes)

       NetPay = GrossPay – (FederalTaxes + StateTaxes + LocalTaxes)

   End Function

   Given the values curGrossPay = 800, curFedTaxes = 75, curStateTaxes = 20, and curLocalTaxes = 10, what is the value returned by the function?

   (a) 855

   (b) 905

   (c) 105

   (d) 695

10. To create a list of data in rows using VBA code, which of the following is not necessary?

    (a) A Select Case statement

    (b) A counter variable

    (c) A repetition structure

    (d) A variable to indicate the current row

Practice Exercises

1 Sports Grill Receipt Calculator

Matt Claw owns Matt's Sports Grill, a small restaurant in Salt Lake City. The servers have handheld devices that are synchronized to a printer and that use Excel to enter customer orders and calculate totals. Matt wants you to create an application so that the servers can enter the total food and beverage costs and allow customers to enter a tip percentage. The program will then calculate the total taxes, tips, and grand total and display a receipt that can be printed. You started a workbook with two worksheets: Start and Receipt. The Start worksheet will contain a welcome screen and a button to click to display an input form. The input form will enable servers to enter the food and beverage total and the customers to enter a tip percentage. When users click a Calculate button, the VBA code unprotects the Receipts worksheet, calculates and enters values in that worksheet, and then protects the worksheet again. The form needs to have a Clear button and a Close button as well. This exercise follows the same set of skills as used in Hands-On Exercises 1–3 in the chapter. Refer to Figure 2.20 as you complete this exercise.

FIGURE 2.20 Receipt Worksheet and Form ➤

a. Open the macro-enabled *v2p1Grill* and save it as **v2p1Grill_LastFirst**. Click each worksheet tab to see what work has been done and what work you will do. Try typing in the Receipt worksheet, and notice that it is protected.

b. Click the **DEVELOPER tab** and click **Visual Basic** in the Code group. Click **Insert** on the VBA menu bar, select **UserForm**, display the Properties window, and set these form properties:
   - Name: **frmDataEntry**
   - Caption: **Matt's Sports Grill**
   - Height: **132.75**
   - Width: **185.25**

c. Click the form to display the Toolbox, click **Label** in the Toolbox, drag a label to the top-left corner of the form, and set its properties as the following:
   - Name: **lblFoodBeverage**
   - Caption: **Food & Beverages:**
   - Left: **12**
   - Top: **15**
   - Width: **72**

d. Insert other controls as shown in Figure 2.20 and set their properties as indicated in Table 2.7. Make sure the TabStop values are set to **True** for the two text boxes and the three command buttons.

TABLE 2.7 Controls and Properties

Control	Property	Setting
TextBox	Name	txtMeal
	Height	18
	Left	84
	TabIndex	0
	TextAlign	2 – fmTextAlignCenter
	Top	12
	Width	72
Label	Name	lblTipPercent
	Caption	Tip Percent:
	Left	12
	Top	45
	Width	72
TextBox	Name	txtTip
	Left	84
	TabIndex	1
	Top	42
	Width	36
Label	Name	lblPercent
	Caption	%
	Left	120
	Top	45
	Width	15
CommandButton	Name	cmdCalculate
	Caption	Calculate
	Left	12
	TabIndex	2
	Top	72
	Width	45
CommandButton	Name	cmdClear
	Caption	Clear
	Left	69
	Top	72
CommandButton	Name	cmdClose
	Caption	Close
	Left	126
	Top	72

e. Press and hold **Ctrl** as you click all three buttons to select them, click **Format** on the menu bar, point to **Make Same Size**, and select **Both** to make all three buttons the same height and width.

f. Select **Format** on the menu bar, point to **Horizontal Spacing**, and select **Make Equal** to equalize the space between buttons.

g. Deselect the three buttons. Right-click the **Calculate button**, select **View Code**, and enter the code shown in Code Window 2.13.

```
Private Sub cmdCalculate_Click()

    'Declare variables
    Dim dblMeal As Double
    Dim dblTip As Double
    Dim dblTotal As Double
    Dim dblTaxAmount As Double
    Dim dblAmountDue As Double

    'Get cost of meal from text box
    dblMeal = txtMeal.Text

    'Function call to perform calculations
    dblAmountDue = TotalBill(dblMeal, dblTip, dblTotal, dblTaxAmount)

    'Complete the receipt
    Worksheets("Receipt").Unprotect
    Worksheets("Receipt").Range("B5") = dblMeal
    Worksheets("Receipt").Range("B6") = dblTaxAmount
    Worksheets("Receipt").Range("B7") = dblTotal
    Worksheets("Receipt").Range("B8") = dblTip
    Worksheets("Receipt").Range("B9") = dblAmountDue

    Worksheets("Receipt").Protect
    Worksheets("Receipt").Activate

End Sub
```

CODE WINDOW 2.13 ▲

The code declares variables, obtains text entered in the txtMeal text box and assigns it to a variable, calls the TotalBill function and assigns the returned value to a variable. Then, the sub procedure unprotects the Receipt worksheet and then uses the values stored in the variables to enter into five cells in the Receipt worksheet. Finally, the procedure protects and activates the Receipt worksheet.

h. Press **Enter** twice after the End Sub statement and create the function that will accept variables, perform calculations, and return the total amount due shown in Code Window 2.14.

```
Function TotalBill(dblMeal, dblTip, dblTotal, dblTax)

    'Declare constant and variable
    Const dblTaxRate As Double = 0.065
    Dim dblTipRate As Double

    'Calculate the tax and subtotal
    dblTax = Round(dblMeal * dblTaxRate, 2)
    dblTotal = dblMeal + dblTax

    'Calculate the tip and grand total
    dblTipRate = Val(txtTip.Text) / 100
    dblTip = Round(dblTotal * dblTipRate, 2)
    TotalBill = dblTotal + dblTip

End Function
```

CODE WINDOW 2.14 ➤

The function uses the Round function to round taxes and tips to the nearest cent. Because the user types the tip percent as a whole number, such as 18, the code must convert that to a decimal equivalent, such as .18.

The code declares a constant and variables. Then, it calculates the tax, subtotal, tip, and total bill. It returns the value of the total bill to the calling statement.

i. Create the event procedures for the Clear and Close buttons as shown in Code Window 2.15.

CODE WINDOW 2.15 ➤

```
Private Sub cmdClear_Click()

    'Clear data entry form
    txtMeal.Text = ""
    txtTip.Text = ""
    txtMeal.SetFocus

End Sub

Private Sub cmdClose_Click()

    'Close the form
    frmDataEntry.Hide
    Worksheets("Start").Activate

End Sub
```

The cmdClear procedure clears the data entry form and sets the focus to the txtMeal box. The cmdClose procedure hides the data entry form and then activates the Start worksheet.

j. Save and close the VB Editor and click the **Start sheet tab**.

k. Click the **DEVELOPER tab** if necessary, make sure **Design mode** is enabled, click **Insert** in the Controls group, select **Command Button (ActiveX Control)**, and drag to create a button below the server information in the **range B7:B8**. Then do the following:

- Click **Properties** in the Controls group, select the existing text in the Name property box, and type cmdStart.
- Select the existing text in the Caption property box, and type **Click to Start**.
- Change the **Height property** to **35.25**. Change the **Width property** to **191.25**.

l. Close the Properties window, right-click the **Click to Start button**, and select **View Code**. Press **Enter**, press **Tab**, type frmDataEntry.Show and press **Enter**. This line of code will display the form you created when a user clicks the button. Save and close the VB Editor. Click **Design Mode** in the Controls group on the DEVELOPER tab to turn it off.

m. Click the **FILE tab**, click **Options**, click **Advanced**, scroll down to the *Display options for this worksheet* section, deselect the **Show row and column headers check box**. Click the **Start arrow**, select **Receipt**, deselect the **Show row and column headers check box**, and click **OK**.

n. Click the **Click to Start button** on the Start worksheet, enter **25** in the Food & Beverages box, press **Tab**, type **20**, and click **Calculate**. Refer to Figure 2.20.

o. Click **Clear** and click **Close** within the form.

p. Save and close the workbook, and then submit based on your instructor's directions.

Janelle Mayer is a financial consultant. She works with people who are considering investment opportunities. Because of your extensive work with Excel and interest in VBA coding, you volunteered to help create an application in which Janelle can enter data for a potential investment, click a button, and then display a summary of results and a list of month-by-month data to show how much interest is made. This exercise follows the same set of skills as used in Hands-On Exercises 1–3 in the chapter. Refer to Figure 2.21 as you complete this exercise.

FIGURE 2.21 Monthly Investment Schedule ➤

a. Open the macro-enabled *v2p2Invest* and save it as **v2p2Invest_LastFirst**. Enable the content, if necessary.

b. Click the **DEVELOPER tab**, click **Design Mode** in the Controls group to enable it, click **Insert** in the Controls group, click **Command Button (ActiveX Control)**, and draw a command button in the **range A10:A11** on the Inputs sheet. Click **Properties** in the Controls group, type **cmdDisplayResults** in the Name property box, type **Display the Results** in the Caption property box, change the **Height property** to **26.25**, change the **Width property** to **145.5**, and close the Properties window.

c. Right-click the **Display the Results command button** and select **View Code**. Type the variable declarations shown in Code Window 2.16.

These variables will store data the user enters in the Inputs worksheet, calculations to display in the Investment worksheet, and variables needed for the VBA code. You will continue adding to the procedure in the next step.

```
Private Sub cmdDisplayResults_Click()

    'Declare variables for input from worksheet cells
    Dim dblAPR As Double
    Dim intYears As Integer
    Dim dblAmountInvest As Double
    Dim dteStartDate As Date

    'Declare variables for calculated output
    Dim dteLastPeriod As Date
    Dim dteMaturityDate As Date
    Dim dblFutureValue As Double

    'Declare variables for calculations and loop
    Dim intCounter As Integer
    Dim dteCurrentDate As Date
    Dim dblBegBalance As Double
    Dim dblBalance As Double
    Dim dblInterest As Double
    Dim intPrevRow As Integer
    Dim intStartRow As Integer
```

CODE WINDOW 2.16 ➤

d. Position the insertion point two blank lines below the code you just typed and type the code shown in Code Window 2.17. You will continue adding to the procedure in the next step.

This code unprotects the Investment worksheet so that the VBA procedure can clear existing data in the month-by-month list and enter new data in the worksheet.

The second block of code obtains values from the Inputs and Investment worksheets and stores the values in the variables you declared.

The third block of code uses the Excel EDate function to determine the ending or maturity date of the investment. Its arguments are the starting investment date and the total number of investment periods (months). Because monthly payments are made, the argument must multiply the number of investment years by 12 months in a year.

The final block of code calculates the interest and balance for the first investment period and then displays formatted results in the first row (row 12) of the month-by-month list. That block of code uses the Format function to display the contents of a variable in a specific way. The date format Short Date and the monetary values $##,##0.00 are enclosed in quotation marks.

```
'Clear any previous schedules
Worksheets("Investment").Unprotect
Worksheets("Investment").Range("A12:E373").Clear

'Get inputs from worksheets
dblAPR = Worksheets("Inputs").Range("B4")
intYears = Worksheets("Inputs").Range("B5")
dblAmountInvest = Worksheets("Inputs").Range("B6")
dteStartDate = Worksheets("Inputs").Range("B7")
dteLastPeriod = Worksheets("Investment").Range("B7")

'Calculate and verify maturity date (should be equal to B8 in Investments)
dteMaturityDate = Application.WorksheetFunction.EDate(dteStartDate, intYears * 12)

'Calculate and display first period's interest and balance
dblInterest = dblAmountInvest * dblAPR / 12
dblBalance = dblAmountInvest + dblInterest
Worksheets("Investment").Range("A12") = Format(dteStartDate, "Short Date")
Worksheets("Investment").Range("C12") = Format(dblAmountInvest, "$##,##0.00")
Worksheets("Investment").Range("D12") = Format(dblInterest, "$##,##0.00")
Worksheets("Investment").Range("E12") = Format(dblBalance, "$#,##0.00")
```

CODE WINDOW 2.17 ▲

e. Position the insertion point two blank lines below the code you just typed and type the code shown in Code Window 2.18.

This code uses the intStartRow variable to designate row 13 as the row to start the rest of the table. Prior to the loop, the code populated the first month's data. The loop takes over starting with the second investment period because it must identify the previous month's balance and add this month's investment to calculate the interest earned.

The code then formats and displays output for the current month during each iteration of the loop and then increments the intStartRow variable so that the next iteration of the loop places data on the next available row in the worksheet.

After the loop terminates, the code provides a cross-check to determine if the future value is almost identical (excluding a little rounding in cents) with what is produced by the Excel FV function and with the final ending investment value produced by the loop.

Finally, the procedure protects the Investment worksheet and displays it to the user.

```
      'Initialize row to start the loop
      intStartRow = 13

      'Loop through each monthly period to calculate and display values
      For intCounter = 1 To (intYears * 12 - 1)
          intPrevRow = intStartRow - 1

          'Calculate beginning balance, balance after deposit, and interest
          dteCurrentDate = Application.WorksheetFunction.EDate(dteStartDate, intCounter)
          dblBegBalance = Val(Worksheets("Investment").Range("E" & intPrevRow))
          dblBalance = dblBegBalance + dblAmountInvest
          dblInterest = dblBalance * dblAPR / 12

          'Display formatted values in the list
          Worksheets("Investment").Range("A" & intStartRow) = _
                    Format(dteCurrentDate, "Short Date")
          Worksheets("Investment").Range("B" & intStartRow) = _
                    Format(dblBegBalance, "$##,##0.00")
          Worksheets("Investment").Range("C" & intStartRow) = _
                    Format(dblAmountInvest, "$##,##0.00")
          Worksheets("Investment").Range("D" & intStartRow) = _
                    Format(dblInterest, "$##,##0.00")
          Worksheets("Investment").Range("E" & intStartRow) = _
                    Format(dblBalance + dblInterest, "$##,##0.00")

          'Increment the row number
          intStartRow = intStartRow + 1
      Next

      'Calculate and display a cross check to compare with last cell in list
      dblFutureValue = FV(dblAPR / 12, intYears * 12, -dblAmountInvest, , 1)
      Worksheets("Investment").Range("E9") = Format(dblFutureValue, "$##,##0.00")

      'Finalize worksheet
      Worksheets("Investment").Protect
      Worksheets("Investment").Activate

End Sub
```

CODE WINDOW 2.18 ▲

f. Save and close the VB Editor. Turn off the **Design Mode** on the DEVELOPER tab.

g. Click the **Inputs sheet tab** if necessary, select the **range B4:B7**, display the Format Cells dialog box, click the **Protection tab**, deselect the **Locked check box**, and click **OK**.

h. Right-click the **Inputs sheet tab**, select **Protect Sheet**, and click **OK** in the Protect Sheet dialog box. Steps g and h ensure that the user can enter values only in the input cells on the Inputs worksheet.

i. Type **6, 4, 100,** and **1/1/2016** in the respective input cells in the Inputs worksheet. Click the **Display the Results button**. After the VBA code executes, the Investment worksheet is active and displays the data. Scroll through the list to review the monthly start date, beginning balance, investment, interest earned, and ending balance.

The Start of Last Period date stored in cell B7 matches the last date in the list. The Maturity Date value stored in cell B8 is one month after that. Note the final ending value may be a few cents different from the FV function results stored in cell B9 and the VBA FV function results stored in cell E9 due to rounding.

j. Save and close the workbook, and then submit based on your instructor's directions.

Mid-Level Exercises

1 Test Scores

You are a teaching assistant for one of your professors, Dr. Patti Rosequist. You created a small grade-book with student IDs, first names, and three test scores to create a prototype application that you can modify for other classes. Dr. Rosequist would like a program that prompts her for a student's ID and test number and then displays the student's name, test score, and letter grade. You will use VBA to create an easy-to-use form within Excel. In addition, you need to create a command button that Dr. Rosequist can click to open the form. Refer to Figure 2.22 as you complete this exercise.

FIGURE 2.22 Gradebook with Student IDs ➤

a. Open the macro-enabled *v2m1Grades* workbook and save it as **v2m1Grades_LastFirst**.

b. Use VBA to create a form named frmStudent with the labels, text boxes, list box, and command buttons shown in Figure 2.22. Set these properties for the controls:
- Name: Use standard prefixes and descriptive names.
- Caption: Use captions as shown in the figure.
- Left: Align common controls on the left side.
- BackColor: Use a light blue background color for the output labels as shown.

c. Adjust the widths, heights, and vertical spacing as needed to ensure balance and consistency.

d. Write the VBA procedure for the **Clear button** to do the following
- Clear the text box where the user types a student's ID.
- Set the list box value to −1 (to avoid selecting a test number by default)
- Clear the three output labels, such as **lblName = [dp][dp]**
- Set the focus back to the input text box, such as **txtID.SetFocus**.

e. Write the VBA procedure for the **Close button** to hide the form, such as **frmStudent.Hide**.

f. Write the VBA procedure for the **Display Grade button**:
- Declare integer variables for the ID, test number, and test score. Declare a string variable for the student's name.
- Assign the values in the form's text box and list box to appropriate variables. Convert the list box selected test number to a value before assigning it to a variable.
- Create a function call to a GetName function in which you pass the ID variable. The returned value should be the student's name, which you assign to the string variable you declared.
- Use a Select Case statement that uses the selected test number to move the active cell to the right on the same row by the correct number of columns. Each Case statement uses the ActiveCell. Offset method to offset the active cell on the same row and over the appropriate number of columns (1 through 3, respectively), such as **ActiveCell.Offset(0, 1).Select**.
- Store the active cell's respective test score in a variable using ActiveCell.Value, such as **intScore = ActiveCell.Value**.
- Display the string variable and test score variable contents in respective output labels within the form.
- Create a function call to a GetGrade function in which you pass the test score variable and then display the respective returned letter grade in an output label on the form.

g. Create a **GetName function** shown in Code Window 2.19 to go to cell A1, find the ID and make that the active cell, select the current student's name, and assign the text string to the GetName function name so that it will be returned to the calling statement.

```
Function GetName(intID)

    'Make cell A1 active
    Application.Goto Reference:="R1C1"

    'Use the Find dialog box to locate ID within the list
    Cells.Find(What:=intID, After:=ActiveCell, LookIn:=xlFormulas, LookAt:= _
        xlWhole, SearchOrder:=xlByColumns, SearchDirection:=xlNext, MatchCase:=False _
        , SearchFormat:=False).Activate

    'Get student's name for respective ID
    ActiveCell.Offset(0, 1).Select
    GetName = ActiveCell.Value

End Function
```

CODE WINDOW 2.19 ▲

h. Create a GetGrade function that receives the integer test score from the calling statement and uses a Select Case statement block to do the following:
   - If the score is greater than or equal to 90, assign an A to the function name. The code should look similar to this:

     Case Is >= 90

     GetGrade = "A"
   - If the score is greater than or equal to 80, assign a B to the function name.
   - If the score is greater than or equal to 70, assign a C to the function name.
   - If the score is greater than or equal to 60, assign a D to the function name.
   - For all other scores, assign an F to the function name.

DISCOVER

i. Change the Object from **General** to **UserForm** at the top of the code window and select the **Initialize procedure**. Delete any other empty procedures that might be created as you get to this one. This procedure will populate the list box and set the focus when the form first loads each time.
   - Enter three lines of code to populate the list box with 1, 2, and 3. For example, to populate the list box with the first item, the code looks like this: **lstTest.AddItem ("1")**
   - Set the focus to the first text box in the form.

j. Save and close the VB Editor. Enable the Design mode. Create a **Find Student button** and write the code so that when a user clicks it, the Student Data form displays.

k. Deactivate the Design mode. Click the **Find Student button** you created on the worksheet, type **343** in the text box, select **3** in the list box, and click the **Display Grade button** on the form. See Figure 2.22. Clear the form and try out several other combinations to ensure the program selects the right data.

l. Test the **Close button** to make sure it works.

m. Save and close the workbook, and then submit based on your instructor's directions.

2 Financial Functions

You want to compare the results of Excel financial functions with the results of VBA financial functions. You will use a workbook that contains two worksheets. You will write the code for three command buttons on the Inputs worksheet that, when clicked, will execute respective procedures. Each procedure will call functions that can be used by multiple procedures that get user input via input boxes. The results will display on the Output worksheet, along with the results from direct financial functions in that worksheet. Refer to Figures 2.23 and 2.24 as you complete this exercise.

FIGURE 2.23 Input Sheet with Command Buttons ➤

FIGURE 2.24 Output Sheet with Results ➤

DISCOVER

a. Open the macro-enabled *v2m2Finance* workbook and save it as **v2m2Finance_LastFirst**.

b. Enter the following finance functions on the Output worksheet:

- PV function in cell B8. Use cell references in column B as the three arguments.
- FV function in cell E9. Use cell references in column E as the four arguments. Make sure the result is a positive value.
- RATE function with formula to convert to APR in cell H8. Use cell references in column H as the three arguments.

c. Display the VB Editor, change the Object to **(General)** and change the Procedure to **(Declarations)**. Type **Option Explicit** then declare the following variables: **dblPV**, **dblAPR**, **dblYears**, **dblRate**, **dblNPER**, **dblPMT**, and **dblFV**. You declare these at this level so that they are available throughout all procedures.

d. Create these four functions with each function displaying an input box asking for the appropriate data and storing it in the function name. Make sure the functions are Public not Private so that the functions can be accessed from any given module or procedure.

- **GetAPR function.** Display the prompt **Enter the annual rate, such as 0.06 instead of 6%:**. The input box title bar should display **Rate**. The data entered by the user should be converted to a value and then saved to the function name so that the value gets returned back to the calling statement in the main procedure. The body of the code should look like this, including the line-continuation character:

  GetAPR = Val(InputBox("Enter the annual rate, such as 0.06 instead of 6%: ", _"Rate"))

- **GetYears function.** Display the prompt **Enter the number of years for the annuity:**. The input box title bar should display **Term in Years**. The data entered by the user should be converted to a value and then saved to the function name so that the value gets returned back to the calling statement in the main procedure.

- **GetPMT function.** Request the monthly payment with an appropriate prompt and title for the input box. Convert the value, and then save it to the function name.

- **GetPV function.** Request the present value of the annuity with an appropriate prompt and title for the input box. Convert the value and save it to the function name.

e. Create the procedure for the **cmdPresentValue button** with these requirements. Refer to Code Window 2.20 to complete this procedure.

- Include function calls for the APR, years, and monthly payment, and then store each returning value in the appropriate variable. The calling statements do not pass any variables to the functions you created.
- Calculate the periodic rate, the NPER, and the present value. Store each calculated result in the respective variable.
- Unprotect the Output worksheet.
- Display the results in cells B2 through B7 for the APR, rate, years, NPER, payment, and present value. Format the percentages and monetary values appropriately within the VBA code.
- Protect the Output worksheet again and activate the Output worksheet.

```
Private Sub cmdPresentValue_Click()

    'Function calls to get and assign values
    dblAPR = GetAPR()
    dblYears = GetYears()
    dblPMT = GetPMT()

    'Calculations
    dblRate = dblAPR / 12
    dblNPER = dblYears * 12
    dblPV = PV(dblRate, dblNPER, -dblPMT)

    'Display output
    Worksheets("Output").Unprotect
    Worksheets("Output").Range("B2") = Format(dblAPR, "#0.00#%")
    Worksheets("Output").Range("B3") = Format(dblRate, "#0.00#%")
    Worksheets("Output").Range("B4") = dblYears
    Worksheets("Output").Range("B5") = dblNPER
    Worksheets("Output").Range("B6") = Format(dblPMT, "$###,##0.00")
    Worksheets("Output").Range("B7") = Format(dblPV, "$###,##0.00")

    'Protect and activate the worksheet
    Worksheets("Output").Protect
    Worksheets("Output").Activate

End Sub
```

CODE WINDOW 2.20 ➤

f. Create the procedure for the **cmdFutureValue button** with these requirements:

- Include function calls for the APR, years, monthly payment, and present value, and then store each returning value in the appropriate variable. The calling statements do not pass any variables to the functions you created.
- Calculate the periodic rate, the NPER, and the future value. Store each calculated result in the respective variable. The code for the future value looks like this:

  dblFV = -FV(dblRate, dblNPER, dblPMT, dblPV)

- Unprotect the Output worksheet. Display the results in cells E2 through E8 for the APR, rate, years, NPER, payment, present value, and future value. Format the percentages and monetary values appropriately within the VBA code.
- Protect the Output worksheet again and activate the Output worksheet.

g. Create the procedure for the **cmdAPR button** with these requirements:

- Include function calls for the years, monthly payment, and present value, and then store each returning value in the appropriate variable. The calling statements do not pass any variables to the functions you created.
- Calculate the NPER, the periodic rate, and the APR. Store each calculated result in the respective variable. The code that calculates the periodic rate looks like this:

  dblRate = Rate(dblNPER, dblPMT, -dblPV)

- Unprotect the Output worksheet. Display the results in cells H3 through H7 for the present value, years, NPER, payment, and APR. Format the percentages and monetary values appropriately within the VBA code.
- Protect the Output worksheet again, and then activate the Output worksheet.

h. Save the code and close the VB Editor.

i. Protect the Input worksheet in Excel (not VBA code).

j. Click the **Present Value button** on the Input worksheet and type these values when prompted: **0.05** (APR), **15** (years), and **125.35** (payment). Compare your answers with Figure 2.24 and click the **Go Back button** on the Output worksheet.

k. Click the **Future Value button** on the Input worksheet and type these values when prompted: **0.075** (APR), **25** (years), **125.50** (payment), and **50000** (present value). Compare your answers with Figure 2.24 and click the **Go Back button** on the Output worksheet.

l. Click the **APR button** on the Input worksheet and type these values when prompted: **20** (years), **965.02** (payment), and **100000** (present value). Compare your answers with Figure 2.24, and click the **Go Back button** on the Output worksheet.

m. Save and close the workbook, and then submit based on your instructor's directions.

Beyond the Classroom

Valentine's Day Dance

GENERAL CASE ✓

Victoria Johnson is a party organizer for a student organization that is sponsoring a Valentine's Day Ball at your university. She has identified income and expenses and started an Excel workbook. However, she does not want people to directly enter data in the worksheet. As the IT developer for the student organization, you volunteer to create forms and write VBA code that provide prompts for users to enter information and store it in the protected worksheet. Open the macro-enabled *v2b1Dance* workbook and save it as **v2b1Dance_LastFirst**. Open *v2b1Dance.docx* in Word to read more details about the program, what buttons are needed, what event procedures are needed, and so on. Use this document to guide you as you design the form and create VBA procedures in the workbook.

The Instructions worksheet should have four buttons. The first button displays an input box to ask the user for the number of attendees, the second button displays a form to enter income sources, the third button displays a form to enter expenses, and the fourth button displays the results on the protected worksheet. The Budget worksheet contains some formulas, but clicking the OK button on the Expenses form performs two calculations.

Save and close the workbook, and then submit based on your instructor's directions.

Apartment Rentals

RESEARCH CASE →

You want to create an Excel application for apartment managers. The program should prompt the manager to enter the number of complexes managed. A repetition statement should ask the user to enter the name of each complex, how many one-bedroom apartments are located there, how many one-bedroom apartments are rented, how many two-bedroom apartments are located there, and how many two-bedroom apartments are rented. The procedure calculates the occupancy rate of each apartment type. For example, if 10 one-bedroom apartments are located in a complex and 9 are rented, the occupancy rate is 90%. Open the macro-enabled *v2b2Apartments* workbook and save it as **v2b2Apartments_LastFirst**. Open **v2b2Apartments.docx** in Word to read more details about the program and what functions are needed and to see screenshots to help you code the program. Use this document to guide you as you design the form and create VBA procedures in the workbook. You will start adding code beginning after the *Get # of complexes managed* comment.

The workbook contains variable declarations. Research in Help how to convert an integer to a double within an expression. If you do not convert the integers to doubles, the resulting percentages will not be stored. In the chapter, you learned how to create a function calling statement and assign the returned value to a variable. Use Help to research how to create another procedure with a calling statement to the procedure without having a return value. Review the use of loops, input boxes, and message boxes.

Save and close the workbook, and then submit based on your instructor's directions.

Studio Equipment Loan

DISASTER RECOVERY

You work for a company that sells studio equipment. Most customers make a down payment and obtain a short-term loan to pay off the balance for the equipment they purchase. To help them determine how much their monthly payment will be and to see the portion of each payment that goes toward the principal and the interest, you developed a workbook that contains a list of inputs and a place for the monthly payment information. Open the macro-enabled *v2b3Equipment* workbook and save it as **v2b3Equipment_LastFirst**.

You created a VBA form to accept input and then to store the values obtained in the top-left corner of the worksheet. However, the form does not populate the list box correctly, and several financial functions are producing incorrect results. Furthermore, the output is often incorrect or not formatted correctly. Review the VBA code carefully and make all necessary corrections. Save and close the workbook, and then submit based on your instructor's directions.

Capstone Exercise

You manage a small temp agency in your town. You hire up to 25 college students to perform a variety of jobs. Instead of investing in a payroll system, you started an Excel workbook that contains two worksheets: StartPage and Payroll. You will create forms and write VBA code to obtain information and calculate gross pay.

Get the Number of Employees

You want to click the # of Employees button on the StartPage worksheet to display an input box to enter that week's number of employees. The result should store the value in a publicly declared variable that is accessible from all procedures. The sub procedure should then disable the # of Employees button until the user clicks the Reset button.

a. Open the macro-enabled *v2c1Payroll* and save it as **v2c1Payroll_LastFirst**. Enable the content, if necessary.

b. Open the VB Editor. Type the **Option Explicit** statement at the top of the General Declarations section of the code window for the StartPage worksheet. Create a public integer variable to store the number of employees.

c. Create a sub procedure for the # of Employees button's Click event.

- Display an input box to ask the user how many employees worked that week. Include an appropriate title for the input box title bar.

- Assign the value entered by the user to the appropriate public variable you declared in step b.

- Change the # of Employees button's Enabled property to **False**.

d. Save the VBA code.

Display the Payroll Worksheet

Although users will click the Display Payroll button third, you want to program it now because it will be easier to code. When users click the Display Payroll button, the sub procedure should activate the Payroll worksheet and then change the Display Payroll button's Enabled property to False.

a. Create a sub procedure for the Display Payroll button's Click event.

- Activate the Payroll worksheet.

- Change the Display Payroll button's Enabled property to **False**.

b. Save the VBA code.

Reset the Command Buttons

As users click each button, the respective button is disabled so that users will not accidentally click a button and empty the Payroll worksheet too soon. You now need to code the Reset button so that it will enable the first three buttons when clicked.

a. Create a sub procedure for the Reset button's Click event.

b. Type three statements, one to change each of the first three buttons' Enabled property to **True**.

c. Save the VBA code.

Design Employee Input Form

You want an easy-to-use interface to enter each employee's name, pay rate, and hours worked each weekday.

a. Create a user form named **frmEmployee**, type Employee Data for the Caption property, set **285.75** for the Height, and set **171** for the Width.

b. Create and format eight labels for **Last Name**, **First Name**, **Pay Rate**, **Monday Hours**, **Tuesday Hours**, **Wednesday Hours**, **Thursday Hours**, and **Friday Hours**. Align these labels on the left side, and then ensure consistent heights, widths, and vertical spacing.

c. Insert eight text boxes to the right of the eight labels. Assign descriptive names for the text boxes, such as txtLast and txtFirst. Align the text boxes on the left side, and then ensure consistent height and consistent vertical spacing.

d. Insert a command button in the bottom-right corner named **cmdSave**. Set its Caption property to **Save**.

e. Set the TabIndex property for the text boxes and command button in proper sequence with the txtLast control with a value of 0 and the cmdSave control with a value of **8**.

f. Make any necessary adjustments to the properties for the labels, text boxes, or command button.

Code the Form's Initialize Method

The form will display several times during execution, once for each employee. To ensure the form is cleared of previously entered data, you need to create an Initialize method for the UserForm.

a. Select the form, display the code window for the **UserForm** and select the UserForm object and the Initialize method.

b. Type statements to clear each text box on the form, such as **txtLast.Text = ""**, substituting the actual text box names you assigned.

c. Type a statement to set the focus back to the txtLast box on the form.

d. Save the VBA code.

Write a GetHours Function

You need to write a public function that you can call from the Save button's sub procedure. You will create the function before creating the button's sub procedure. The GetHours function will not accept any arguments. It declares a variable to hold the cumulative hours worked. It should obtain the hours worked from the respective text boxes, convert the data to values, and then add to the cumulative weekly hours. For example, the Monday hours are added to 0 hours to start. The Tuesday hours are added to the Monday hours, and so on. For example, if an employee worked 8 hours on Monday, 8 is added to the initial cumulative variable value of 0 for a total of 8 hours so far. If the employee worked 7 hours on Tuesday, those 7 hours are added to the cumulative 8 hours previously for a total of 15 hours. The function returns the total hours to the calling statement.

a. Type the function header **Public Function GetHours()** outside any other sub procedure, and then press Enter twice.

b. Declare a local variable named **dblHours** to store the cumulative hours worked for the current employee.

c. Write five statements, one for each weekday's text box (such as txtMonday.Text), to obtain the value in the respective text box, and convert it to a value and add it to the dblHours variable. The last statement should store the result in the GetHours function name, which will return the total hours worked to the calling statement you will create later.

d. Save the VBA code.

Write a GetPay Function

You need to write a public function that you can call from the Save button's sub procedure. You will create the function before creating the button's sub procedure. The GetPay function will accept six arguments. Use alias names for the received argument variables. The function does not declare any other variables. The function should determine how many of the total hours are regular and how many are overtime hours. It should then calculate the regular pay (pay rate * regular hours), overtime pay (pay rate * 1.5 * overtime hours), and gross pay, which will be returned to the calling statement.

a. Type the function header **Public Function GetPay(Hours, RegHours, OTHours, PayRate, RegPay, OTPay)** outside any other sub procedure, and press **Enter** twice.

b. Create an If…Else statement to determine how many hours are regular hours. Regular hours are up to 40 hours worked. For example, if a person works 36 hours, the total regular hours are 36. If a person works 45 hours, the regular hours are 40. Assign the correct number of hours to the RegHours variable.

c. Calculate the number of overtime hours (any hours over 40). For example, if a person worked 45 hours, the number of overtime hours is 5. You do not need an If statement for this calculation. Assign the correct number of overtime hours to the OTHours variable.

d. Calculate the regular pay as a product of the regular hours worked and the pay rate.

e. Calculate the overtime pay as a product of the overtime hours, pay rate, and 1.5.

f. Calculate the gross pay and assign its value to the GetPay function name, which will then return that value to the calling statement.

g. Save the VBA code.

Code the Form's Save Button

When the form displays, the user enters data into the text boxes and then clicks the Save button. You need to write the sub procedure to obtain the data in the text boxes, call functions, and then display formatted output into the Payroll worksheet (pay rate * 1.5 * overtime hours), and gross pay, which will be returned to the calling statement.

a. Create a sub procedure for the Save button.

b. Declare nine variables of appropriate data types: last name, first name, pay rate, hours, regular hours, overtime hours, regular pay, overtime pay, and gross pay.

c. Assign the value 0 to the hours, regular hours, and overtime hours variables.

d. Write statements to obtain the last name, first name, and pay rate from the respective text boxes on the form and assign the data to the appropriate variables.

e. Call the GetHours function and return its accumulated total hours to the hours variable.

f. Type the statement **ActiveCell.FormulaR1C1 = strLast**, substituting the name of the last name variable you declared. This statement will enter the last name in the active cell in the Payroll worksheet (which is cell A2 for the first person).

g. Type the statement **ActiveCell.Offset(0, 1).Select** to move the active cell one cell to the right on the same row.

h. Type the statement to assign the first name variable contents to the active cell, similar to step f.

i. Type another statement with the Offset method statements to move over one cell for total hours worked. Use the Format function to format hours in this format "#0.0".

j. Type a function call statement for the GetPay function. Pass the hours, regular hours, overtime hours, pay rate, regular pay, and overtime pay variables to the function (which you created earlier). The function will assign values to these variables and calculate the gross pay, which gets returned through the GetPay function name. Assign the result to the gross pay variable.

k. Continue typing the ActiveCell.Offset statements with each of those statements followed by the ActiveCell. FormulaR1C1 statements. Format the regular hours and overtime hours in the "#0.0" format. Format the pay rate, regular pay, overtime pay, and gross pay with the "Currency" format.

l. Type the statement **ActiveCell.Offset(1, -8).Select** to go down one row and to the left eight cells so that the active cell in the next blank row is ready to enter data for the next employee.

m. Type the statement **Unload frmEmployee** to unload the form from memory. You do not want to simply hide the form or it will preserve the previously entered data.

n. Save the VBA code.

Code the Employee Data Button

You need to code the Employee Data button. When the user clicks this button, the sub procedure should unprotect the Payroll worksheet, clear existing payroll data, make cell A2 the active cell, and then loop through to display the Employee Data form once for each employee. After the data is gathered and displayed using the form's Save button and the two functions you previously created, the Employee Data button's sub procedure should then protect the Payroll worksheet, activate the StartPage worksheet, and then display the Employee Data button.

a. Create a sub procedure for the Employee Data button.

b. Declare **intCount** as a counter variable for a loop. Assign the value of **1** to the variable.

c. Write statements that do the following tasks. Type the bold statements exactly as shown below:

- Unprotect the Payroll worksheet.
- **Worksheets("Payroll").Select**
- Select the **range A2:I26**.
- **Selection.ClearContents**
- **Worksheets("Payroll").Application.Goto Reference:="R2C1"**

d. Write a For…Next loop to iterate as many times as the number of employees. The first statement in the body of the loop should load the frmEmployee form, and the second statement should show the form. No other statements should be in the body of the loop. The form's Save button's sub procedure takes over when the user clicks Save each time.

e. Write statements to protect the Payroll worksheet, activate the StartPage worksheet, and then change the Employee Data button's Enabled property to **False**.

f. Save the VBA code. Close the VB Editor.

Test the Buttons

You need to test the buttons to ensure the application works.

a. Click the **Payroll sheet tab** and try to type in an empty cell. The worksheet should be protected.

b. Click the **StartPage sheet tab**.

c. Click the **# of Employees button** to display the input box. Type **3** and click **OK** in the input box. The # of Employees button should now be disabled so that you cannot click it.

d. Click the **Employee Data button** to display the form. Enter your name, a pay rate without the $, and **10** hours each day. Click the **Save button**, and the data is entered on row 2 of the Payroll worksheet. An empty form displays.

e. Enter data for a second employee. Enter **7** hours each day. Click the **Save button**, and data is entered on row 3 of the Payroll worksheet. An empty form displays.

f. Enter data for a third employee. Enter **8** hours each day. Click the **Save button**, and data is entered on row 4 of the Payroll worksheet. No more forms display because you specified 3 employees in the input box earlier. The Payroll worksheet should be protected again, the StartPage worksheet is activated, and the Employee Data button should now be disabled so that you cannot click it.

g. Click the **Display Payroll button** to display the Payroll form. Try typing in the Payroll worksheet and notice it is disabled. Click **OK** to close the message box.

h. Click the **StartPage sheet tab** and click the **Reset button**. The first three buttons are now enabled again.

i. Save and close the workbook, and then submit based on your instructor's directions.

VBA

Customizing Access with VBA

OBJECTIVES | AFTER YOU READ THIS CHAPTER, YOU WILL BE ABLE TO:

CASE STUDY | Croton Sporting Goods

Croton Sporting Goods is a locally owned sporting goods store that specializes in outdoor adventure sports. After 20 years of business, the owner of Croton, Randy Barnes, has decided to update his business processes by incorporating a Microsoft Access database into his company's everyday business functions. The current database manages customers, inventory, suppliers, and transactions.

Randy has decided to add you to his management team as an IT intern. As part of your job responsibilities, you have been asked to add new features to the database including data validation, data entry, shortcuts, and the ability to search all records easily based on multiple search criteria. After researching the requests, you have decided to use VBA to accomplish your goals.

VBA in Access

When working in database design, the first steps require the creation of objects such as tables or reports. Once these objects are created, Access includes some basic macro actions that can add additional functionality in the way the objects interact. While these included actions can be manipulated using the Access Macro Builder, they are only a small portion of what can be achieved using VBA. By using VBA in Access you will gain the ability to perform tasks that could not be accomplished any other way. As you work with VBA in Access, you will need to open the Visual Basic Editor (VB Editor) and then determine which type of module to create. Because the VB Editor is a separate program from Access, the program will always open in a new window. Once the VB Editor is open, you may be unsure about which type of module to create. This section will explore a variety of methods for creating code and modules so that you can determine how to create the correct procedure in the correct module.

In this section, you will use the VB Editor to learn how to create procedures in modules, write code for forms and reports, work with objects, and create functions.

Writing Code in Modules

STEP 1 ▷
When you create VBA code in Access, you can create the code using one of three modules: a standard module, a class module, or an Access object module. A standard module stores procedures that are available to any event in the application and an Access object module stores procedures that are available to a specific form or report. Class modules are advanced programs that are used to create custom objects similar to the preexisting objects that are included in Microsoft Office. You can create a class module to group related actions into one location. To specify the module type, follow one of the steps listed next.

Insert a Standard Module:

1. With Access open, press Alt + F11 to open the VB Editor, as shown in Figure 3.1. Open the VB Editor, as shown in Figure 3.1.
2. Click Insert on the menu bar and select Module.

    The VB Editor appears with the statement Option Compare Database at the top of the Code window; Module1 appears in the Project Explorer on the left.
3. Begin the procedure by typing Sub followed by the Name of the procedure, such as Sub TotalShipping (). Note that the Sub name cannot contain spaces. The editor will add End Sub automatically after you press Enter, as shown in Figure 3.2. Continue typing the rest of the code until the procedure is completed.

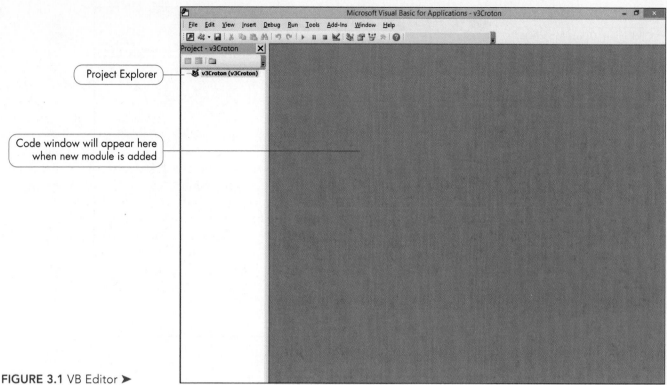

FIGURE 3.1 VB Editor ➤

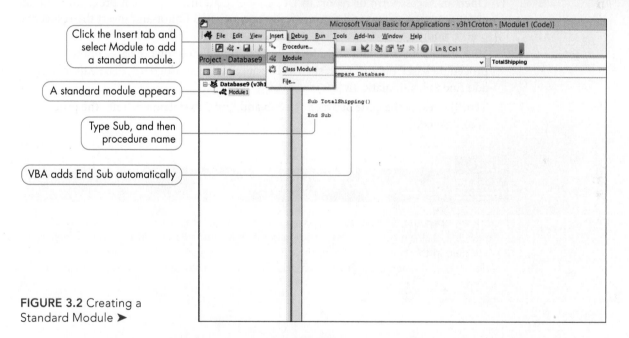

FIGURE 3.2 Creating a Standard Module ➤

Insert a Class Module:

1. Click Insert on the menu bar and select Class Module.

   The Code window appears with the statement Option Compare Database at the top; Class1 appears in the Project Explorer on the left.

2. Begin the procedure by typing Public Sub followed by the Name of the procedure, such as Public Sub AddVendor(). The editor will add End Sub automatically after you press Enter, as shown in Figure 3.3.

3. Continue typing the rest of the code until the procedure is completed.

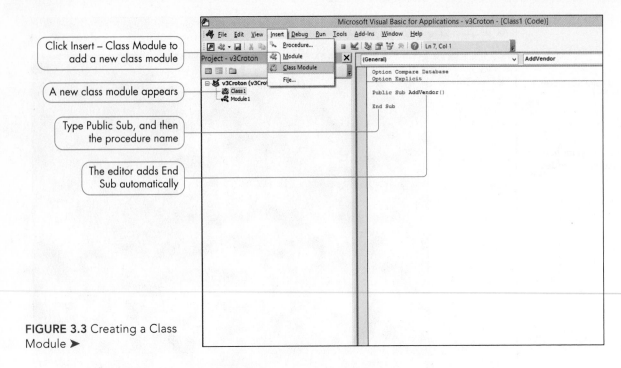

- Click Insert – Class Module to add a new class module
- A new class module appears
- Type Public Sub, and then the procedure name
- The editor adds End Sub automatically

FIGURE 3.3 Creating a Class Module ➤

Create an Access object module:

1. Open an Access form or report in Design view and insert an event procedure into an event property. Access will automatically open the VB Editor and insert the respective object module.

   VBA begins the procedure by adding Private Sub followed by the name of the procedure based on the event, such as Private Sub Form_Current(). The editor will add End Sub automatically.

2. Type the rest of the code between the Sub and End Sub statements until the procedure is completed.

TIP Shortcuts to the VB Editor

You can open the VB Editor by pressing Alt+F11. Another way to open the VB Editor is to double-click a module or class module in the Navigation Pane. When you double-click a module in the Navigation Pane, the VB Editor opens that module so you can view or edit the code immediately. Note the modules will not appear until they have been initially saved.

Writing Code for Forms and Reports

STEP 2 ≫ Forms and reports are two pivotal objects that appear within Access databases. Reports provide clean business-oriented and -formatted information. Forms provide the ability to review and enter information into the database without the need to access a data table. Access contains many tools to allow the customization of forms and reports; however, you can use VBA to add functionality that can surpass what is achievable with built-in features.

Create VBA code for a form or a report following the steps listed next:

1. Open the object in Design view and click Property Sheet in the Tools group within the DESIGN tab from within Form Design Tools.

2. Select an event from the Event tab (e.g., On Load) and click Build on the right side of the property cell. The Choose Builder dialog box, as shown in Figure 3.4, appears with three options—Macro Builder, Expression Builder, and Code Builder.
3. Select the Code Builder and click OK to open the VB Editor.

Property Sheet

Form in Design view

Select Code Builder, and then click OK to open the VB Editor

Click the Build button to create VBA code for an event

FIGURE 3.4 Opening the VB Editor from Inside a Form ➤

When the VB Editor opens, a new form module is created to store the VBA code for the selected form. Notice the Private Sub statement is automatically inserted into the Code window by the editor along with the End Sub statement. The Option Compare Database and Option Explicit declarations also appear at the top of the code by default. The **Option Compare Database** statement is used in a module to declare that string comparisons are not case sensitive when data is compared. The **Option Explicit** statement is used in a module to require that all variables be declared before they are used. This is a best practice that is often used by programmers and can be set as a default setting in the VB Editor options menu.

At this point, you (the programmer) probably have a reason for wanting to add a procedure to the On Load event of the form. For example, you may want to remind the user where the supplier of a warehouse item is located. Add the remaining code to your procedure, as shown in Figure 3.5, and then save the code. When you close the VB Editor, the original Access form is available.

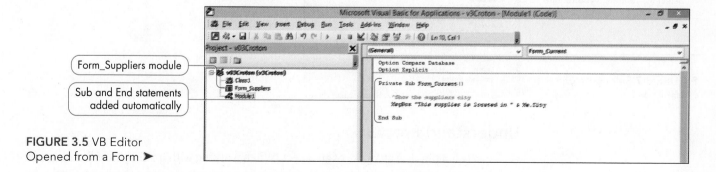

Form_Suppliers module

Sub and End statements added automatically

FIGURE 3.5 VB Editor Opened from a Form ➤

Verify this item is selected

FIGURE 3.6 Set Require Variable Declaration to Yes ➤

Working with Objects

VBA works with the objects in the various *object libraries* that are available in the applications that support VBA. You can use objects in the object libraries along with their resources to accomplish the programming tasks. These object libraries include Access and Excel, which are the two most popular applications that support VBA. Word, PowerPoint, and Outlook can also be automated using VBA.

In addition to the Office applications, you can also set references to other object libraries such as Adobe Acrobat, Skype, and Yahoo! Messenger if the programs are installed on your system. All of these libraries require you to set a reference in the VB Editor. Click Tools on the menu bar, click References, and then select the check boxes for the references (or libraries) that you need in the References dialog box, as shown in Figure 3.7; click OK when finished. By default, some of the references you need may already be selected. Knowing which references to select will take practice and some trial and error.

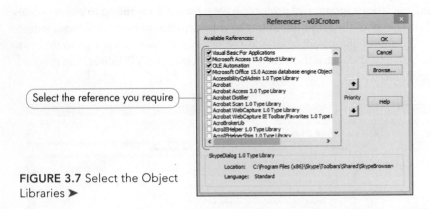

Select the reference you require

FIGURE 3.7 Select the Object Libraries ➤

Understand Properties

A property is a physical attribute of an object. When working with forms, you will notice they each have a size, a type of border, a back color, and various bound and unbound controls. All of these represent properties of the form except for the bound and unbound controls, which are objects themselves. As a rule, any form property you can change in Design view can also be changed using VBA code. If you can change the back color property of a label or textbox to Text 2, Lighter 80%, you can also change the same property using VBA. When using VBA to designate the back color, you must use the numerical equivalent. For example, if you create a form based on the Office Theme, you can set the back color to yellow in VBA using the RGB number 255,255,0 (see Code Window 3.1).

Change the background color of a form using VBA

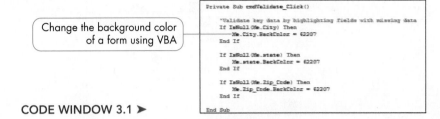

```
Private Sub cmdValidate_Click()

    "Validate key data by highlighting fields with missing data
    If IsNull(Me.City) Then
        Me.City.BackColor = 62207
    End If

    If IsNull(Me.state) Then
        Me.state.BackColor = 62207
    End If

    If IsNull(Me.Zip_Code) Then
        Me.Zip_Code.BackColor = 62207
    End If

End Sub
```

CODE WINDOW 3.1 ➤

TIP | Assigning Color Properties Using VBA

There are several standardized ways to identify colors when programming. Two of the most popular are HEX (#FFFF00) and RGB (255,255,0), both of which are supported in VBA. By using these standards you ensure the same color is produced across applications. This allows for thematic continuity when programming multiple applications. To learn more explore the following link: http://www.w3schools.com/html/html_colors.asp

If you are a VBA programmer, you have to ask yourself the question, "Why would I want to change the background color of a form?" Programmers usually think of the reason first and the action second. For example, you might want to convey a message to the user, as he or she is entering the data into the fields. When the user successfully fills in the required fields, the form could change color to notify the user the required fields have been filled in. Another technique is to simply display a message to tell the user whether or not they are successful when the record is saved.

Understand Methods

A method is an action that is performed by an object. A few examples of form methods are .Open, .Close, .RefreshAll, and .GoToRecord. You can accomplish all of these actions manually in Form view by using the Ribbon and the Record Navigation bar. Many actions that you can perform in Form view can also be performed automatically using VBA code. For example, to refresh the form to give the user the most up-to-date information, you could create a command button and attach a procedure, as shown in Figure 3.8. The VBA code to refresh a form is Me.Refresh.

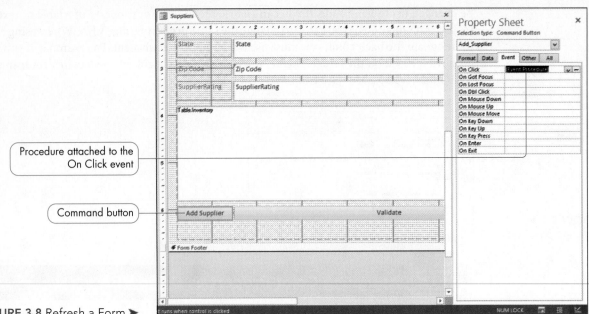

FIGURE 3.8 Refresh a Form ➤

At first, you may find it difficult to differentiate between methods and properties. You may want to change a property or use a method only to discover that VBA reports an error. VBA provides some visual help when adding code to a procedure using the Me prefix. Me refers to the current instance of the object you are in. When you type the Me keyword and then type a period, the editor will provide a list of available items and indicate which items are properties and which are methods using a unique icon. This list is helpful because you do not have to memorize all the properties and methods on a form or report. If you are still unsure and use a property or method improperly, VBA will correct you. As a rule, methods are more difficult to use and master.

Understand Events

An event is what happens when a user takes an action. For example, users can take the following actions when working in a form—change a record, open a form, close a form, and filter the records in a form. The corresponding events that are triggered are shown in Table 3.1, Event Examples.

TABLE 3.1   Event Examples

User Action	How Access Responds	Event Triggered
Change and save a record in a form	Saves the record	Before Update
Click a button to open a form	Opens the form	On Click
Click the Close button to close a form	Closes the form	On Close
Find records in a form with certain criteria	Filters the record source	On Filter

Events are extremely useful to programmers because they can interrupt user actions and verify that the user really wants to take the action they requested. The first example in Table 3.1, change and save a record in a form, may need confirmation from the user. Did the user intentionally change the data? Adding a message that asks, "Do you want to save your changes?" helps to eliminate inadvertent changes. You can intercept the save process with the Before Update event and then ask the user to confirm; this gives the user a chance to discard the changes. The message would appear to the user, as shown in Figure 3.9.

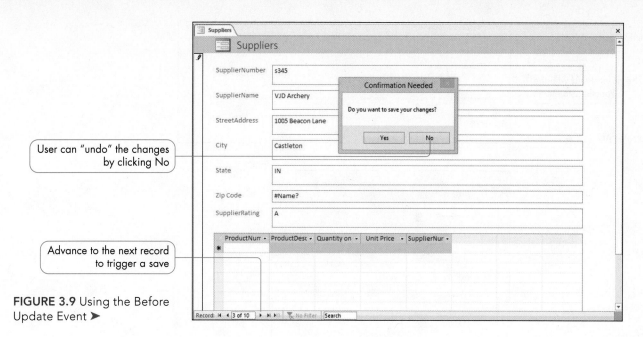

User can "undo" the changes by clicking No

Advance to the next record to trigger a save

FIGURE 3.9 Using the Before Update Event ➤

Creating Functions

STEP 4➤ As discussed earlier, a function is a procedure that performs an action and returns a value. Many functions are predefined in VBA and ready to use. To use a predefined function, simply add the function to your procedure and insert the required arguments; when the procedure runs, the function will assign the value to the function name.

When no preexisting function will fit your needs you have the ability to author calculations directly into procedures; however, a custom function allows cleaner design. To create a custom function, open a module, and then type a statement into the Code window with the format:

Function NameOfFunction(Argument As Data Type) As Data Type

End Function

The VB Editor automatically adds the statement End Function after you press Enter. An argument is the value that the procedure passes to the function; arguments can be assigned a specific data type. The data type at the end of the first statement refers to the type of data the function returns to the procedure. Add the remaining lines of code to complete the function, save, and then test the function. When a procedure encounters a function, the procedure takes the following steps:

1. The procedure runs and encounters the function.
2. The procedure calls the function and passes one or more values to it.
3. The function receives the values and processes them according to the function code.
4. The function returns a different value (with possibly a different data type) to the calling procedure by assigning the result to the function name.

For example you could create a custom function to calculate the total value of inventory in the warehouse. This function would multiply the quantity on hand by the sale price. The value could then be returned to a field in the current form. The function would contain the lines of code, as shown in Code Window 3.2. The end result is shown in Figure 3.10.

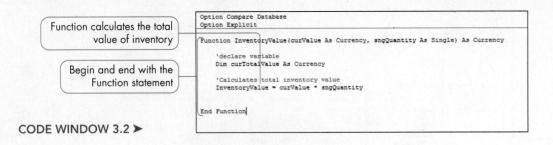

Function calculates the total value of inventory

Begin and end with the Function statement

```
Option Compare Database
Option Explicit

Function InventoryValue(curValue As Currency, sngQuantity As Single) As Currency

    'declare variable
    Dim curTotalValue As Currency

    'Calculates total inventory value
    InventoryValue = curValue * sngQuantity

End Function
```

CODE WINDOW 3.2 ➤

FIGURE 3.10 Function Calculation Displayed in Form ➤

Quick Concepts ✓

1. What is the difference between a standard module and a class module? *p. 138*

2. What does the statement Option Explicit mean and when is it used? *pp. 141–142*

3. Why would you create a custom function? *p. 145*

Hands-On Exercises

1 VBA in Access

After reviewing the current needs of the database you have decided to add a welcome message box indicating the current date and company name, as well as add data validation to identify and highlight required fields that are missing data in the suppliers form. Your last step will be to create a custom function to allow for automatic calculation of inventory value.

Skills covered: Write Code In Modules • Write Code to Test for Key Data in A Form • Work with Objects • Create a Function That Calculates Inventory Value

---

STEP 1 >> WRITE CODE IN MODULES

You open the VB Editor and then verify that the Require Variable Declaration check box is set to Yes. You write a simple procedure to practice creating and running a procedure. Refer to Figure 3.11 as you complete Step 1.

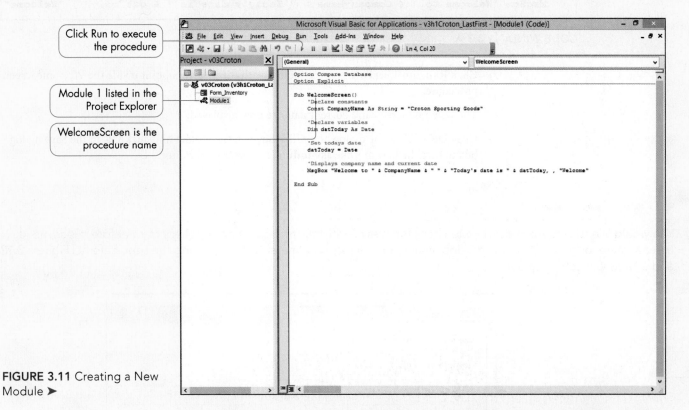

FIGURE 3.11 Creating a New Module ➤

a. Start Access, open *v3h1Croton.accdb* and save it as **v3H1Croton_LastFirst.accdb**.

> **TROUBLESHOOTING:** If you make any major mistakes in this exercise, you can close the file, open *v3H1Croton* again, and then start this exercise over.

b. Click the **Database Tools tab** and click **Visual Basic** in the Macro group.

The VB Editor opens.

c. Click **Tools** on the menu bar and select **Options**.

The Options dialog box opens.

d. Click the **Require Variable Declaration check box,** if necessary, to select it.

This option requires that all variables be declared prior to being introduced.

e. Click **OK** to close the Options dialog box.

f. Click **Insert** on the menu bar and select **Module.**

g. If necessary, place your insertion point on line 4 and create a new procedure by typing the code shown in Code Window 3.3.

```
Sub WelcomeScreen()
    'Declare constants
    Const CompanyName As String = "Croton Sporting Goods"

    'Declare variables
    Dim datToday As Date

    'Set today's date
    datToday = Date

    'Displays company name and current date
    MsgBox "Welcome to " & CompanyName & " Today's date is " & datToday, , "Welcome"
```

CODE WINDOW 3.3 ▲

h. Click **Run Sub/UserForm** on the toolbar with the insertion point inside the WelcomeScreen procedure.

The welcome screen and current date are now displayed.

i. Click **OK** to close the dialog box. Click **Save** on the toolbar and click **OK** in the Save dialog box to save the new module as **Module1.** Close the VB Editor.

STEP 2 ≫ WRITE CODE TO TEST FOR KEY DATA IN A FORM

You would like to create a procedure to check for missing city information in the supplier's form before it is saved. If the city, state, or zip code data is missing, your code will display a message box warning the user. Refer to Figures 3.12 and 3.13 as you complete Step 2.

FIGURE 3.12 Use VBA to Validate Data on a Form ➤

a. From the Navigation Pane, open the Suppliers form in Design view.

b. Click **Property Sheet** in the Tools group of the Design tab to open the Property Sheet, if necessary. If not already selected, select the **Form** using the Selection type box at the top of the Property Sheet. Click the **Before Update event** on the Event tab.

c. Click **Build,** select **Code Builder** in the Choose Builder dialog box and click **OK.**

The VB Editor opens with Suppliers form added to the Project Explorer. A new procedure is started in the Code window.

d. Add the code to the procedure, as shown in the Code Window 3.4.

CODE WINDOW 3.4 ➤

```
Private Sub Form_BeforeUpdate(Cancel As Integer)
    'Verify City, State, and Zip code are not blank
    If IsNull(Me.City) Then
        MsgBox "City is blank.", vbCritical, "Key Data Missing"
        Cancel = True
        Exit Sub
    End If

End Sub
```

This section of code verifies that the city is not blank. If it is, the user is notified and the record cannot be saved, because the statement Cancel = True cancels the update. Exit Sub stops the procedure from executing the rest of the code.

e. **Save** the procedure, and then minimize the VB Editor. Display the Suppliers form in Form view.

f. Delete the City in the first record of the Suppliers form. Press **Tab** until the focus reaches the State. Continue to press **Tab** until the message box appears. When the message appears, click **OK** and press **Esc** to restore the city.

g. Return to the VB Editor. Place the insertion point at the end of the existing code and add the additional code to the Form_BeforeUpdate procedure, as shown in Code Window 3.5.

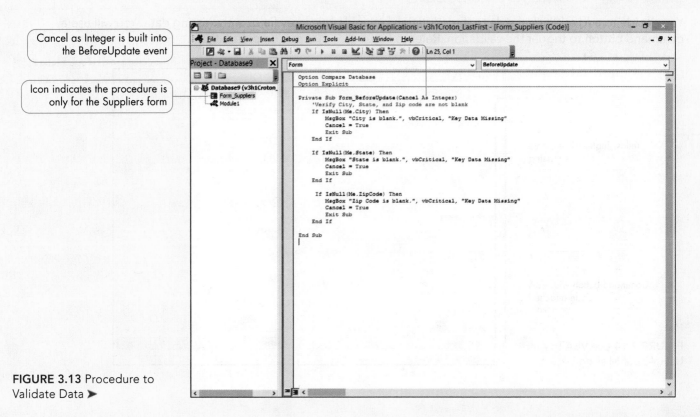

Cancel as Integer is built into the BeforeUpdate event

Icon indicates the procedure is only for the Suppliers form

FIGURE 3.13 Procedure to Validate Data ➤

```
If IsNull(Me.State) Then
    MsgBox "State is blank.", vbCritical, "Key Data Missing"
    Cancel = True
    Exit Sub
End If


 If IsNull(Me.ZipCode) Then
    MsgBox "Zip Code is blank.", vbCritical, "Key Data Missing"
    Cancel = True
    Exit Sub
End If
```

CODE WINDOW 3.5 ➤

This section of code verifies that the state and zip code are not blank. If either is, the user is notified and the record cannot be saved, because the statement Cancel = True cancels the update.

h. Save the procedure and minimize the VB Editor.

i. Delete the State in the first record of the Suppliers form. Press **Tab** until the focus reaches the zip code. Press **Tab** twice. When the message appears, click **OK** and press **Esc** to restore the state.

j. Delete the zip code in the first record of the Suppliers form. Press **Tab** until the focus reaches the Supplier Rating. Press **Tab** again. When the message appears, click **OK** and press **Esc** to restore the zip code.

TROUBLESHOOTING: If you receive a run time error, return to the VB Editor and match your code against the completed code in Figure 3.13.

---

k. Save the changes to the Suppliers form.

STEP 3 ≫ WORK WITH OBJECTS

You decide to add additional style to the validation by highlighting key fields with missing data. You will use a command button to trigger the validation. Refer to Figure 3.14 as you complete Step 4.

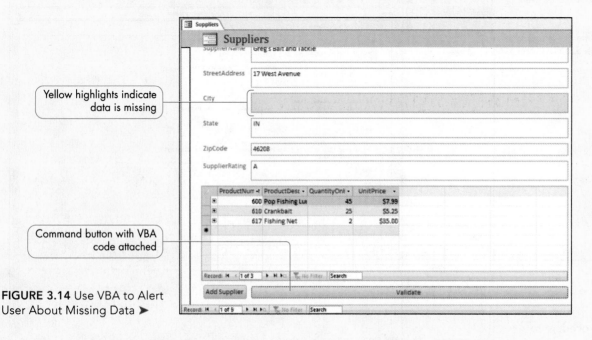

Yellow highlights indicate data is missing

Command button with VBA code attached

FIGURE 3.14 Use VBA to Alert User About Missing Data ➤

a. Display the Suppliers form in Design view.

b. If necessary, scroll down, select the validate button, click the **All tab** in the Property Sheet and modify the name property to display **cmdValidate**.

c. Click the **Event tab** in the Property Sheet, if necessary click **On Click event**. Next click **Build**, click **Code Builder** in the Choose Builder dialog box and click **OK**.

The VB Editor opens and a new procedure, Sub cmdValidate_Click(), is added to the Code window above the Form_BeforeUpdate procedure.

d. Type the code shown in Code Window 3.6 into the Sub cmdValidate_Click() procedure.

This section of code verifies that the zip code is not blank. If it is, the field is highlighted in yellow (RGB code 255,255,0) to alert the user; if it does contain information, the backcolor will be set to white (RGB code 255,255,255).

CODE WINDOW 3.6 ➤

```
Private Sub cmdValidate_Click()
    'Validate key data by highlighting fields with missing data.
    If IsNull(Me.City) Then
        Me.City.BackColor = RGB(255, 255, 0)
    Else
        Me.City.BackColor = RGB(255, 255, 255)
    End If

End Sub
```

e. Save the procedure, and then minimize the VB Editor. Display the Suppliers form in Form view.

f. Delete the city in the first record of the Suppliers form. Click the **Validate button**.

The background color of the city field is highlighted in yellow, alerting you that the city field is blank.

g. Retype the city name in the city field and press the **Validate button**. Note the box color changes back to white. Return to the VB Editor and add additional code to the cmdValidate_Click() procedure, as shown in Code Window 3.7.

CODE WINDOW 3.7 ➤

```
    If IsNull(Me.State) Then
        Me.State.BackColor = RGB(255, 255, 0)
    Else
        Me.State.BackColor = RGB(255, 255, 255)
    End If

    If IsNull(Me.ZipCode) Then
        Me.ZipCode.BackColor = RGB(255, 255, 0)
    Else
        Me.ZipCode.BackColor = RGB(255, 255, 255)
    End If
```

This section of code verifies that the state and zip code are not blank. If either is, the user is alerted with a yellow background, the same as in the city field. This code also returns the background color to white if the correct information is entered into the fields.

h. Save the procedure and minimize the VB Editor.

i. Delete the state in the first record of the Suppliers form. Click the **Validate button**.

The state field is highlighted with a yellow background.

j. Press **Esc** to restore the deleted state. Delete the zip code in the first record of the suppliers form. Click the **Validate button**.

The zip code field is highlighted with a yellow background.

k. Retype the deleted Zip code and press **Validate**. Note the yellow color returns to white. Close the VB Editor and save the changes to the Suppliers form. Close the form.

STEP 4 ➤ CREATE A FUNCTION THAT CALCULATES INVENTORY VALUE

After adding validation to the suppliers form you have decided to add functionality to the Inventory form. You would like to create a custom function that will determine the amount of product to order based on the maximum desired amount in stock of 125 per item. When called not only will it return the quantity to order from the vendor, it will also calculate the total value of inventory in the warehouse. Refer to Figure 3.15 as you complete Step 4.

Message box displays the return value

Click to calculate inventory value

FIGURE 3.15 Function Calculates Units to Order ➤

a. Click **Visual Basic** in the Macro group.

b. Click **Insert** on the menu bar and select **Module**.

The Module2 appears in the Project Explorer.

c. Type the code as shown in Code Window 3.8 into the Code window:

```
Function InventoryOrder(intCurrentInventory As Integer) As Integer
    'Declare constant maximum inventory per item
    Const intMaxInventory As Integer = 125

    InventoryOrder = intMaxInventory - intCurrentInventory

End Function
```

CODE WINDOW 3.8 ➤

This code creates a function that calculates the total amount of product to order by finding the difference between the current stock in the warehouse and the declared constant maximum inventory of 125 units.

d. Save the Module with the name **Functions** and press Alt+F11 to exit the VB Editor.

Now you will add a procedure to the InventoryToOrder text box on the bottom of the form, as well as to the Inventory Value button to call the function and display a message box that displays the total inventory value as well as the quantity to order.

e. Open the Inventory form in Design View, click the InventoryToOrder text box located at the bottom of the form. Type the following function into the text box =**InventoryOrder**([**QuantityOnHand**]).

This uses the function created in Step c. to return the amount of inventory to order. Because a text box was used, this will display for every record that is displayed and does not need to be activated with a button.

> **TROUBLESHOOTING:** If you experience difficulties entering the function directly into the text box, you can also enter the function as a control source within the properties menu.

f. Select the Inventory Value button in the Inventory form and, if necessary, click Property Sheet in the Tools group within the Design tab of the Ribbon to display its Property Sheet. Click **On Click event** in the Event tab, click the Build button, click **Code Builder** in the Choose Builder dialog box and click **OK**. Add the code shown in Code Window 3.9 starting in line 5 of the Code window.

```
Private Sub cmdTotalInventoryValue_Click()
    'Displays quantity to order and inventory value text box
    If Me.InventoryToOrder = 0 Then
        MsgBox ("Current Inventory Value is : " & Me.QuantityOnHand * Me.UnitPrice)
    Else
        MsgBox ("Current Inventory Value is :" & " " & Format _
        (Me.QuantityOnHand * Me.UnitPrice, "Currency") & " " & vbNewLine & _
        "Place Next Order For : " & Me.InventoryToOrder & " " & "Units")
    End If

End Sub
```

CODE WINDOW 3.9 ▲

Code Window 3.7 calls the InventoryOrder function and adds the value to a message box if the quantity on hand is less than the maximum quantity of 125. It then displays the value of the amount in the warehouse based on the quantity on hand and the unit price.

g. Save the procedure and minimize the VB Editor.

h. Return to the Inventory form, and then switch to Form view. Click **Next Record** in the Navigation bar of the form and click the **Inventory Value button**.

The total value of the inventory is now displayed.

i. Click **OK** to close the dialog box. Close the Inventory form. Save the form if necessary.

j. Save the database. Keep the database onscreen if you plan to continue with Hands-On Exercise 2. If not, close the database, and then exit Access.

Working with Recordsets

A *recordset* is a set of records selected from a table or query loaded in the random access memory of your computer. A recordset is similar to a table or a query; the same data source would be represented in all three cases. For example, if you were working with a database that contained supplier data, the same results would be achieved with any of the three methods shown in Table 3.2.

TABLE 3.2 Table Data Achieved with Three Methods	
Method	**Results**
Open Suppliers table	All columns and all records are displayed
Create a query based on the Suppliers table	All columns and all records are displayed (as long as all columns are added to the design grid)
Create a Recordset using VBA based on the Suppliers table	All columns and all records are stored in memory (as long as all columns are selected in the OpenRecordset statement)

The Suppliers table would display all the columns and all the records in Datasheet view, but could then be filtered into groups and sorted based on multiple criteria. A query based on the Supplier table could limit the number of columns (by selecting a subset of fields); the query could also limit the number of records by entering criteria in one or more fields. A recordset could limit the number of columns and fields, evaluate each record in the recordset individually, and then take action based on the logic of the procedure.

The benefit of the recordset is the versatility of working with records and data programmatically. Although you can manipulate records and data using an action query, only recordsets enable you to update records using decision structures.

In this section, you will learn how to manipulate recordsets using DAO (Data Access Objects) and ADO (ActiveX Data Objects).

Using DAO to Access Data

DAO (Data Access Objects) refers to an object library specifically created to work with Access databases. The DAO object library was first released in 1992 along with Access 1.0. Needless to say, it has evolved and improved with all the versions of Access released since, including Access 2013. Although newer database object libraries have been created, DAO remains the object library of choice for many Access developers.

Create Recordsets

STEP 1 ≫ As stated earlier, a recordset is a set of records in memory. To create the recordset, you first write a procedure using VBA that extracts data from one or more tables in an Access database and then places the results in memory. Once the recordset has been placed in memory, you can then logically examine the records and make decisions and changes based on your own criteria.

To create a recordset in DAO, you must first explicitly connect to a database, usually the database that is currently opened. Next, you create a recordset object based on a table, a query, or an SQL statement. Then, you can loop through the records in the recordset and count the total number of records, count only the records that meet a certain criteria, or modify field data of all records that meet a certain criteria.

An outline for a procedure that creates a DAO recordset is shown in Figure 3.16.

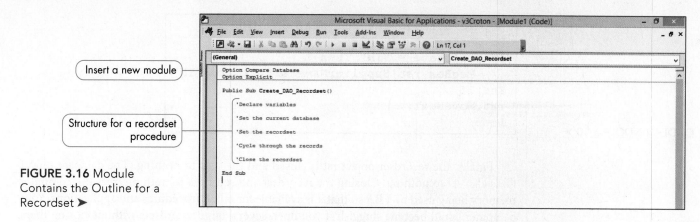

Insert a new module

Structure for a recordset procedure

FIGURE 3.16 Module Contains the Outline for a Recordset ➤

Find Records in a Recordset

STEP 2 ➤ To create a recordset and then search for records that meet certain criteria, you must first identify the table or query that contains the initial recordset. For example, if you need to find all the suppliers who live in Indiana, you could create a recordset based on the Suppliers table. After the recordset has been set, you could use the *MoveNext* method to advance through the records of the recordset. Stopping at each record, you could test the suppliers' State to see if it equals IN. If a supplier resides in IN, the procedure would then take the appropriate action to update one or more field values in the matching records. Figure 3.17 shows a sample procedure that creates a DAO recordset and then advances through the records looking for suppliers who live in IN.

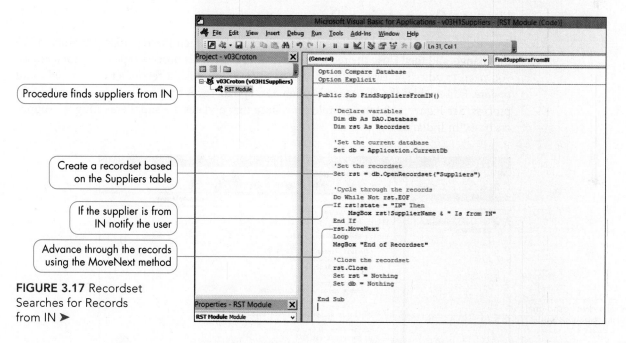

Procedure finds suppliers from IN

Create a recordset based on the Suppliers table

If the supplier is from IN notify the user

Advance through the records using the MoveNext method

FIGURE 3.17 Recordset Searches for Records from IN ➤

The line of code Set rst = db.OpenRecordset("Suppliers"), establishes the recordset using the OpenRecordset method of the db object. Our example opens the Supplier table and sets the rst object equal to it. At this point, the recordset object (rst) exists in memory. The procedure can now cycle through the records looking for a match to the code's criteria.

The Do Loop is used in combination with the MoveNext method to cycle through the supplier records. The While clause is used to end the loop when the End of File (EOF) is reached. As each new record is visited, the state value is compared to IN. If it matches, then a predefined action is performed. In our example, the user is notified that a supplier is from IN. This Do Loop statement, shown in Code Window 3.10, is very common when working with recordsets; you will repeat these statements for almost every recordset you create:

```
'Cycle through the records
Do While Not rst.EOF
If rst!state = "IN" Then
    MsgBox rst!SupplierName & " Is from IN"
End If
rst.MoveNext
Loop
```

CODE WINDOW 3.10 ➤

Finally, the recordset object rst is closed and then set to nothing. The database object db is also set to nothing. Closing the recordset and setting it to nothing frees the computer memory being used by VBA so that it is available for other procedures and applications. Your computer could become sluggish if you open several large recordsets without closing them because they tie up memory resources.

 TIP · Working with Recordset Fields

When you create a recordset procedure in VBA, you refer to the fields in the recordset using the rst! prefix. When you create a recordset object, refer to the field names as rst!SupplierName, rst!SupplierRating, and rst!SupplierAddress. If you omit the object rst or the ! delimiter, the fields will not be recognized by VBA.

Update Records in a Recordset

STEP 3 ➤ To update the field values in a recordset, you must first open the recordset for edits, make the change, and then close the recordset to further edits. This process repeats for each record you need to edit. The two methods you need to accomplish a recordset edit are *edit* and *update*. Edit enables the change to happen and update saves the changes and closes the edit process. See Figure 3.18 for a sample procedure that updates the suppliers rating for suppliers based in Indiana.

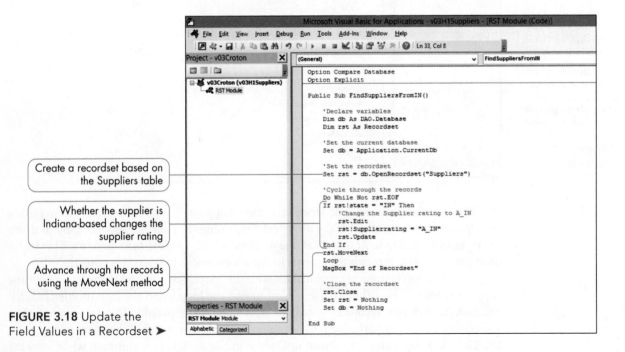

Create a recordset based on the Suppliers table

Whether the supplier is Indiana-based changes the supplier rating

Advance through the records using the MoveNext method

FIGURE 3.18 Update the Field Values in a Recordset ➤

Because VBA updates to a recordset are not easily reversible, you should back up your database before you run an update procedure. The first time you create an update procedure, you must be prepared for errors and unexpected results. Always check the results by opening the affected table(s); if there are problems, revert to the backup version of the database.

Delete Records in a Recordset

STEP 4 »

Sometimes, you may need to delete records from a recordset, for the same reason you need to delete records from a table. Instead of scanning the records in the table and then pausing to delete the records that you want to remove, you can create a VBA procedure to cycle through the records and delete only the records that meet your predefined criteria. Using VBA to perform this action is much more efficient. See Figure 3.19 for a sample procedure that deletes all suppliers from the suppliers table who have a C rating.

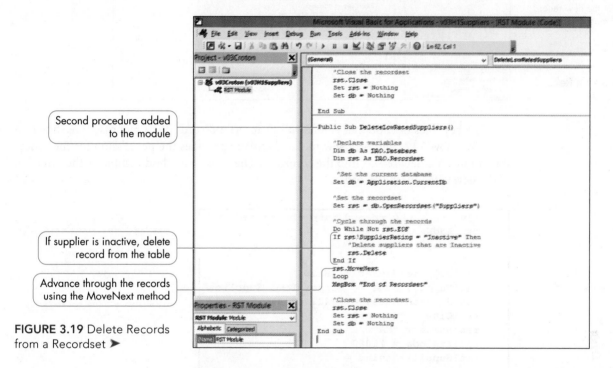

Second procedure added to the module

If supplier is inactive, delete record from the table

Advance through the records using the MoveNext method

FIGURE 3.19 Delete Records from a Recordset ➤

The key lines of code that enable you to delete records from a recordset are shown in Code Window 3.11. The Delete method actually provides the delete as the Do Loop cycles through the records in the table.

```
'Cycle through the records
Do While Not rst.EOF
If rst!SupplierRating = "Inactive" Then
    'Delete suppliers that are Inactive
    rst.Delete
End If
rst.MoveNext
Loop
```

CODE WINDOW 3.11 ➤

Insert Records in a Recordset

STEP 5 »

Sometimes, you may want to insert records into a recordset, the same way you need to insert records into a table. The difference is that you can create a VBA procedure to insert a record when a certain event takes place in your database. For example, if a customer enters data into an application form for processing, you may want to insert the data into another table only after the application is approved. See Figure 3.20 for a sample procedure that inserts a record into the Suppliers table.

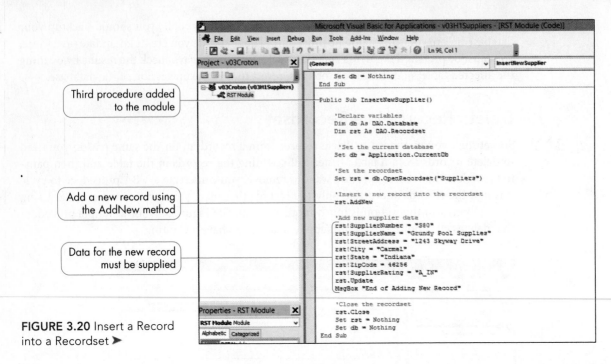

FIGURE 3.20 Insert a Record into a Recordset ➤

Third procedure added to the module

Add a new record using the AddNew method

Data for the new record must be supplied

The key lines of code that enable you to insert a record into a recordset are shown in Code Window 3.12. The AddNew method actually provides the permission for the procedure to insert a new record into the recordset. The Update method completes the insertion of the new data into the recordset.

```
'Insert a new record into the recordset
rst.AddNew

'Add new supplier data
rst!SupplierNumber = "S110"
rst!SupplierName = "Popper Pool Supplies"
rst!StreetAddress = "3421 Bigsky Drive"
rst!City = "Boston"
rst!State = "MA"
rst!ZipCode = 21080
rst!SupplierRating = "B"
rst.Update
MsgBox "End of Adding New Record"

'Close the recordset
rst.Close
Set rst = Nothing
Set db = Nothing

End Sub
```

CODE WINDOW 3.12 ➤

Using ADO to Access Data

Prior to the release of Microsoft Access 2000, DAO was used to obtain data from local Access databases and Remote Data Objects, (RDO), was used to access larger databases such as SQL. Microsoft introduced ADO, **ADO (ActiveX Data Objects)** as a replacement for the older DAO and RDO. While RDO has lost popularity to the newer ADO, there are still many who opt for DAO in certain situations. ADO was designed with the functionality to connect to a wide range of external data sources. Although DAO was designed to work with your local Access database, ADO was designed and excels when connecting to relational databases, ISAM data sources, disk files, and so on. Whereas DAO uses the db = CurrentDb statement to connect to the current database, ADO uses the CurrentProject.Connection argument, as shown in Figure 3.21.

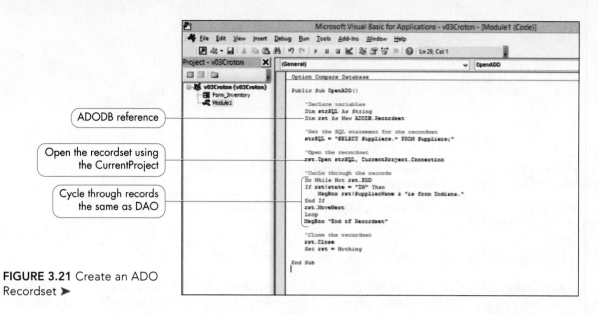

FIGURE 3.21 Create an ADO Recordset ➤

In ADO (as in DAO), it is important to declare database variables with the object library prefix. For example, when declaring the rst variable, use *Dim rst As ADODB.Recordset*. After the variable is declared, you can open the recordset using the rst.Open statement. Cycle through the records in the recordset using the Do Loop (the same as the DAO recordset).

Before you can use the ADO object library, you must create a link to the library by clicking Tools on the menu bar, and then selecting References. Figure 3.22 shows the references dialog box for a typical Access database, including a link to the ADO library.

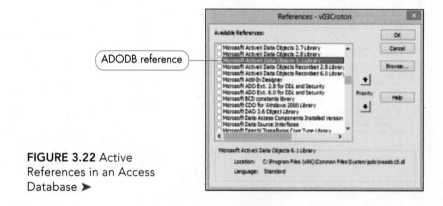

FIGURE 3.22 Active References in an Access Database ➤

TIP Make a Copy Before Changing References

Changing the references in a database can cause serious problems. Always make a copy of your database before changing references. If anything goes wrong, you can revert to the original database. Even if your database contains no VBA code, the built-in functions that are probably in use in various places will stop working if you disconnect one of the references.

In Hands-On Exercise 2, you will create recordsets, find records in a recordset, update records in a recordset, delete records from a recordset, and insert records in a recordset.

Quick Concepts

1. What is DAO, and how is it used? *p. 154*

2. What is a recordset, and how does it compare to a query? *p. 154*

3. What is ADO, and how is it used? *p. 158*

Hands-On Exercises

2 Working with Recordsets

Randy would like you to add the ability to locate, review, update, and if necessary delete selected records within the company's database. You have decided to use VBA to create recordsets to reach his goal.

Skills covered: Create a Recordset Using DAO • Find Records in a Recordset • Update Records in a Recordset • Delete Records in a Recordset • Insert Records in a Recordset

STEP 1 ≫ CREATE A RECORDSET USING DAO

You need to create a recordset using the Suppliers table in the Croton database. You will make sure to add comments for each section so you can easily diagnose problems or make changes later. You will add additional lines of code as you complete the remaining steps in this activity. Refer to Figure 3.23 as you complete Step 1.

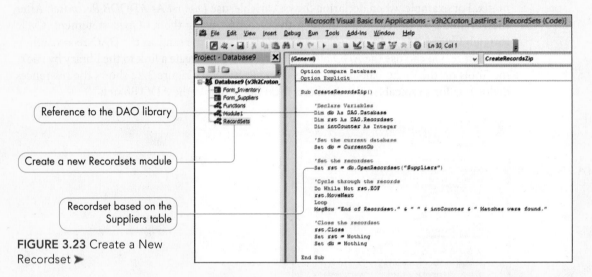

Reference to the DAO library

Create a new Recordsets module

Recordset based on the Suppliers table

FIGURE 3.23 Create a New Recordset ➤

a. Open the *v3h2Croton*, and then save it as **v3h2Croton_LastFirst**.

> **TROUBLESHOOTING:** If the Security Warning toolbar displays, click Enable Content.

b. Click the **DATABASE TOOLS tab** and click **Visual Basic** in the Macro group.

The VB Editor opens.

c. Click **Insert** on the menu bar and select **Module**.

The Option Compare Database and Option Explicit statements appear at the top of the Code window.

d. Click **Save As** on the toolbar, type **RecordSets** in the **Save dialog box** as the module name and click **OK**.

The Recordsets module appears in the Project Explorer.

e. Type the lines of code shown in Code Window 3.13.

```
Sub CreateRecordsZip()

    'Declare Variables
    Dim db As DAO.Database
    Dim rst As DAO.Recordset
    Dim intCounter As Integer

    'Set the current database
    Set db = CurrentDb

    'Set the recordset
    Set rst = db.OpenRecordset("Suppliers")

    'Cycle through the records
    Do While Not rst.EOF
    rst.MoveNext
    Loop
    MsgBox "End of Recordset." & " " & intCounter & " matches were found."

    'Close the recordset
    rst.Close
    Set rst = Nothing
    Set db = Nothing

End Sub
```

CODE WINDOW 3.13 ▲

f. Click **Run Sub/Userform** on the toolbar, with the insertion point inside the CreateRecordsetZip procedure. Click **OK** when the message appears.

The procedure runs, and returns zero records found. This occurs because there is no criteria specified for the recordset. In the next step you will specify a zip code to locate and count within the record set.

> **TROUBLESHOOTING:** If the VB Editor reports an error, check the highlighted line for errors, correct the error, and then try again.

g. Save the Recordsets module.

STEP 2 ›› FIND RECORDS IN A RECORDSET

You need to revise the Suppliers recordset to find records with a certain zip code. Because this step does not alter the data, you do not have to save a backup of the database. You will display the matching records using the message box function. Refer to Figure 3.24 as you complete Step 2.

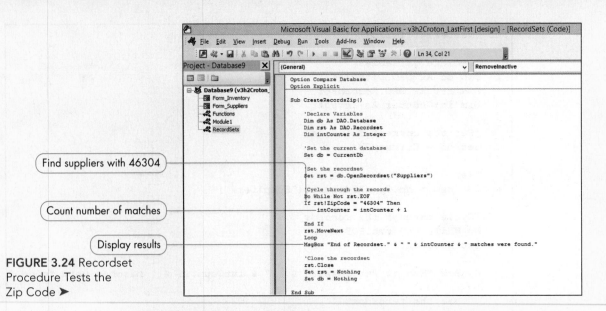

Find suppliers with 46304

Count number of matches

Display results

FIGURE 3.24 Recordset
Procedure Tests the
Zip Code ➤

a. On a new line underneath the *Do While Not rst.EOF* code type the three lines of code shown in Code Window 3.14 into the procedure.

This code will add one to the counter if the ZipCode is 46304.

```
'Cycle through the records
Do While Not rst.EOF
If rst!ZipCode = "46304" Then
    intCounter = intCounter + 1

End If
```

CODE WINDOW 3.14 ▲

b. With the insertion point inside the CreateRecordsZip procedure and click **Run Sub/ Userform** on the toolbar.

Now when this procedure runs it will count the one occurrence of zip code 46304.

Click **OK**.

> **TROUBLESHOOTING:** If the VB Editor reports an error, stop the procedure and press F8 to step into the code. Continue to press F8 until a portion of the code is highlighted in yellow. This is the erroneous code. Check your work against Code Window 12; then make the appropriate corrections.

c. Press Alt + F11 to exit the VB Editor. Open the Suppliers table and click the filter drop down menu for the ZipCode data. Deselect all zip codes except 46304 and click OK. Note there is one occurrence of 46304 in the database. The VBA code entered in Step d. will automate this process.

d. Press Alt + F11 to return to the VB Editor. Locate the zip code 46304 in the code. As shown in Code Window 3.15, you will alter the zip code to the new location 46208 and rerun the sub to verify its functionality.

The box sub identifies the new criteria and returns a count of 3 occurrences.

CODE WINDOW 3.15 ➤

```
'Cycle through the records
Do While Not rst.EOF
If rst!ZipCode = "46208" Then
    intCounter = intCounter + 1
```

e. Click **OK** and minimize the VB Editor. Open the Suppliers table and filter the table for zip code 46208. Verify there are three suppliers within the 46208 zip code. Close the table without saving.

STEP 3 ≫ UPDATE RECORDS IN A RECORDSET

Due to the frequency of shipments from your Indiana supplier, it has been suggested you modify all Indiana zip codes to add -9999 to each corresponding code to conform to the post office's more specific ZIP+4 notation, and then you display the matching records using the message box function. Because this step alters the data, you save a backup copy of the database. Refer to Figure 3.25 as you complete Step 3.

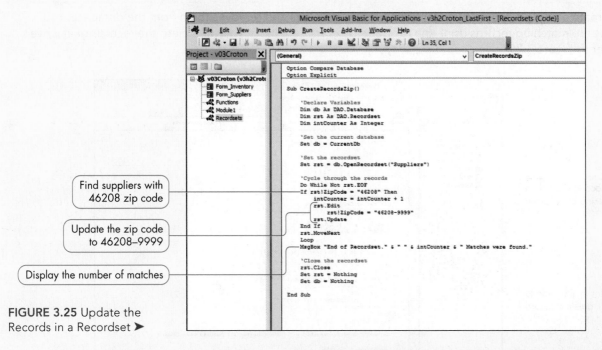

Find suppliers with 46208 zip code

Update the zip code to 46208–9999

Display the number of matches

FIGURE 3.25 Update the Records in a Recordset ➤

a. Click the **FILE tab**, click **Save As**, click **Save Database As**, click **Back Up Database** and click **Save As**. Accept the default file name (e.g., *v3H2Croton_LastFirst_2014-03-20*), and then click **Save**.

The following steps will alter the data within the database. To safeguard against data lost when you are crafting the updated code, you created a backup of the database. Verify that the original *v3h2Croton_LastFirst* database is still open.

b. Open the VB Editor and revise the procedure by adding three lines of code into the Code window below intCounter = intCounter + 1 on line 21, as shown in Code Window 3.16.

```
'Cycle through the records
Do While Not rst.EOF
If rst!ZipCode = "46208" Then
    intCounter = intCounter + 1
    rst.Edit
        rst!ZipCode = "46208-9999"
    rst.Update
End If
rst.MoveNext
Loop
MsgBox "End of Recordset." & " " & intCounter & " Matches were found."
```

CODE WINDOW 3.16 ➤

   c. Run the procedure.

       The procedure runs and then displays the number of supplier records that were effected.

   d. Minimize the VB Editor. Open the Suppliers table, and filter the table for zip code 46208-9999. Verify that the table contains three records with the new zip code. Close the table without saving.

   e. Maximize the VB Editor and save the module.

STEP 4 ›› DELETE RECORDS IN A RECORDSET

You need to create a new procedure that identifies inactive suppliers and removes them from the database. You will first display the matching records using the message box function. Next, you will delete the records of inactive suppliers. Refer to Figure 3.26 as you complete Step 4.

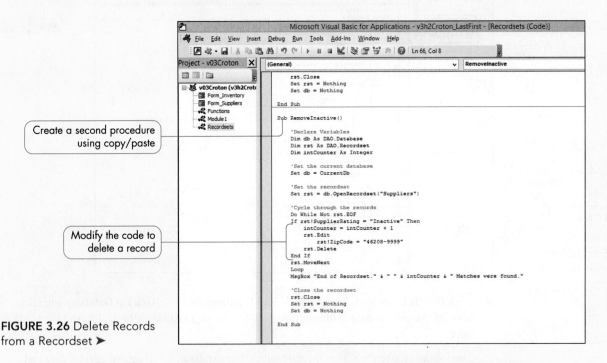

FIGURE 3.26 Delete Records from a Recordset ➤

   a. Copy the entire CreateRecordsZip procedure excluding Option Compare Database and Option Explicit, and paste it below the End Sub statement starting at line 36.

   b. Change the name of the Sub CreateRecordsZip to **Sub RemoveInactive**.

   c. Modify the procedure by changing the *Do While Not* section of the code, as noted in Code Window 3.17. (Note that some lines need to be deleted.)

```
'Cycle through the records
Do While Not rst.EOF
If rst!SupplierRating = "Inactive" Then
    intCounter = intCounter + 1
    'rst.Delete
End If
rst.MoveNext
Loop
MsgBox "End of Recordset." & " " & intCounter & " Matches were found."
```

d. Run the procedure.

The procedure runs, and then displays the End of Recordset message notifying one match is found.

e. Remove the comment (') in front of the rst.Delete statement. Run the procedure again.

VBA deletes the inactive supplier.

f. Minimize the VB Editor. Open the Suppliers table and sort the table by supplier rating. Verify that the table contains no records with inactive suppliers. Close the Suppliers table.

> **TROUBLESHOOTING:** If the suppliers table is not closed when the code is run it will not update. If this scenario takes place, close and reopen the table to view the changes.

g. Return to the VB Editor and save the module.

STEP 5 》 INSERT RECORDS IN A RECORDSET

You need to create a new procedure that inserts a new supplier into the Suppliers table. You will supply the key field data in the procedure, and then insert the data into the table. You will verify that the record was added by opening the table. Refer to Figure 3.27 as you complete Step 5.

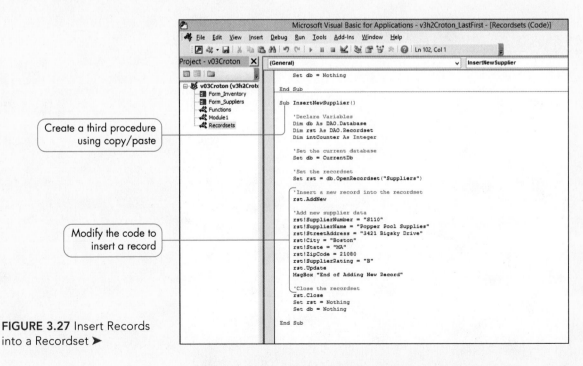

FIGURE 3.27 Insert Records into a Recordset ➤

a. If necessary, open the VB Editor, copy the entire CreateRecordsZip procedure and paste it below the last End Sub statement in the Code window starting at line 66.

b. Change the name CreateRecordsZip to **InsertNewSupplier**.

c. Modify the procedure by removing the *'Cycle through records'* section of the code and adding the Insert section as noted below in Code Window 3.18. (Note that some lines will need to be deleted.)

CODE WINDOW 3.18 ➤

```
'Insert a new record into the recordset
rst.AddNew

'Add new supplier data
rst!SupplierNumber = "S110"
rst!SupplierName = "Popper Pool Supplies"
rst!StreetAddress = "3421 Bigsky Drive"
rst!City = "Boston"
rst!State = "MA"
rst!ZipCode = 21080
rst!SupplierRating = "B"
rst.Update
MsgBox "End of Adding New Record"
```

d. Run the procedure.

The procedure runs and then inserts the new supplier into the Suppliers table.

e. Minimize the VB Editor. Open the Suppliers table, and then sort the table by descending Supplier number. Verify that the table contains the new record. Close the Suppliers table, and don't save the sort.

f. Return to the VB Editor, save the module, and then close the VB Editor.

g. Save the database. Keep the database open if you plan to continue with Hands-On Exercise 3. If not, close the database, and then exit Access.

Forms, Reports, and Errors in VBA

Enhancing the functionality of forms and reports is one of the most common uses of VBA. By themselves, Access forms and reports work well most of the time. However, sometimes, you may need the programming power of VBA to add functionality to a form or report. When a user opens a form and begins to enter data, VBA can monitor the data entry process and warn the user when invalid data is entered. VBA can also increase the versatility of a report by allowing the user to choose from a list of parameters. For example, a user may want to see a report based on the previous fiscal year as opposed to the current fiscal year. VBA can help accomplish this.

When you add VBA code to your application, you should include error trapping in your procedures. Errors are a common occurrence whenever you add VBA code to a database; *error trapping* is the process of intercepting and handling errors at run time. Errors are part of any software application and it is important to account for them. As a VBA programmer, your job is to test and find the logical and syntax errors before the code runs; once the code runs, you must also account for run time errors. These run time errors can be addressed with VBA's error trapping techniques. The VB Editor also enables error debugging as part of the built-in tools; these tools enable you to pinpoint the cause of an error and hopefully help you find a solution.

In this section, you will learn how to enhance forms and reports using VBA. You will also learn how to handle run time errors that appear in VBA code.

Using VBA to Add Events to Forms

Almost all of the VBA code added to a form is triggered by an event. Common events include On Open, On Click, On Enter, On Exit, Before Update, and After Update. As you learned earlier, events are what happen when a user takes action. In order for the On Open event to occur, the user must open a form (see Table 1 for more examples). All of the available events are found on the Event tab on the Property Sheet, as shown in Figure 3.28.

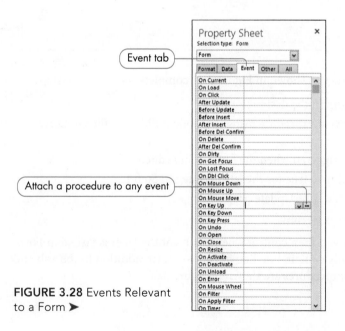

FIGURE 3.28 Events Relevant to a Form ➤

A form or report has one set of events and each object on a form or report has another set of events. Many events overlap between a form and the objects on a form. For example, a form and a text box on a form both have the On Click event. They also both contain the Before Update and After Update events. However, although a form contains the On Current event, a text box does not. *After Update* is an event that is triggered after a record is saved.

On Current is the event that is triggered by a record being loaded into a form. A text box is needed to display the data in a record, but it is not responsible for loading the data.

A text box can trigger the On Enter event, a form does not. *On Enter* refers to the act of placing the insertion point in a text box (using the mouse or pressing Tab or Enter). However, a form is opened rather than entered.

Add an Event Procedure to a Form

While you are editing a record in a form, the pencil appears in the record selector on the left. When the pencil disappears, the record has been saved. A user may miss the pencil (or the pencil may be missing if the record selector is turned off). To notify the user when a record is being changed, you could add a hidden message to the top of the form and then make the message visible while a user is changing a record (see Figure 3.29). After the record is saved, the message could be hidden again.

FIGURE 3.29 Display a Message While Editing a Record ➤

STEP 1 »

To add the additional message as shown in Figure 3.31 complete the following steps:

1. Add a label control to a form in the desired location.
2. In Design view create an event procedure using the Code Builder for the On Dirty property.
   The *On Dirty* property is triggered when the file is being edited.
3. In the VB Editor set visibility to true for the label created in Step 1.
4. Create a second event for the AfterUpdate property.
5. In the VB Editor set visibility to False.

The two event procedures will then control whether or not the label is visible in Form view. The procedures would only contain one line of code each (in addition to the Sub and End Sub statements). The two procedures are shown in Figure 3.30.

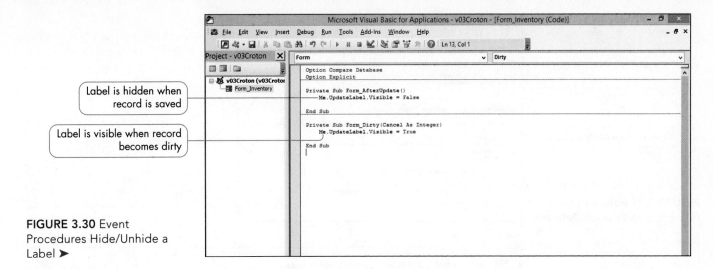

Label is hidden when record is saved

Label is visible when record becomes dirty

FIGURE 3.30 Event Procedures Hide/Unhide a Label ➤

Validate Data Before an Update

The Before Update event is used to intercept the saving of a record if any key fields are blank or if any fields contain data outside the acceptable boundaries. *Before Update* is triggered before a record is saved. Notifying a user that fields are blank or that data is outside normal boundaries can greatly improve the reliability of the data. Retrieving the data later, running reports, and analyzing data with queries will be much more effective if the data is reliable.

To create a procedure that will validate a record before saving it, start an event procedure attached to the Before Update event. When the VB Editor opens, add a comment in the Code window that explains what each statement is validating, and then add the appropriate conditional statements. For example, if you were working with the Inventory form, you could verify that the following conditions were not violated:

- Quantity on hand is between 0 and 125
- Unit Price must be greater than 0

Open the Inventory form in Design view, open the Property Sheet, and then click the Before Update procedure. Click Build, select the Code Builder from the Choose Builder dialog box, and then click OK. The Visual Basic window opens and the Sub BeforeUpdate() procedure has been started. Add one section for each type of validation; each section should contain a comment, a conditional statement (If...Then), and a message to the user if the condition is violated. If a condition is violated, exit from the procedure; this will give the user a chance to correct the first problem before notifying him or her of the next issue. See Figure 3.31 for a sample Before Update procedure that checks the two conditions mentioned earlier. The alert message when data is entered outside of the acceptable range is shown in Figure 3.32.

TIP Shortcut: Add a Procedure to an Event

To quickly add a procedure to an event, double-click the event name. [Event Procedure] appears in the event property box. Next, click Build and you are immediately taken to the VB Editor.

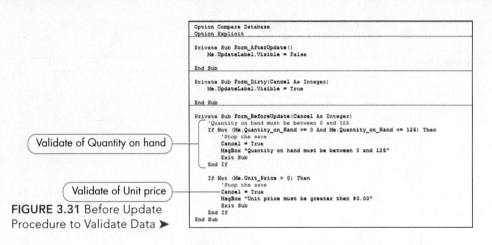

```
Option Compare Database
Option Explicit

Private Sub Form_AfterUpdate()
    Me.UpdateLabel.Visible = False

End Sub

Private Sub Form_Dirty(Cancel As Integer)
    Me.UpdateLabel.Visible = True

End Sub

Private Sub Form_BeforeUpdate(Cancel As Integer)
    'Quantity on hand must be between 0 and 125
    If Not (Me.Quantity_on_Hand >= 0 And Me.Quantity_on_Hand <= 125) Then
        'Stop the save
        Cancel = True
        MsgBox "Quantity on hand must be between 0 and 125"
        Exit Sub
    End If

    If Not (Me.Unit_Price > 0) Then
        'Stop the save
        Cancel = True
        MsgBox "Unit price must be greater then $0.00"
        Exit Sub
    End If
End Sub
```

Validate of Quantity on hand

Validate of Unit price

FIGURE 3.31 Before Update Procedure to Validate Data ➤

Validate of Quantity on hand

Validate of Unit price

FIGURE 3.32 Message Box Warning – Invalid Data ➤

Adding VBA to Reports

Sometimes, you may want to modify the layout of a report before the report prints. For example, a report that contains multiple sections may have one or more sections that you want to hide, even though they contain data. Access does not have an option for hiding a section at run time. You can use VBA to test if a section matches a certain criteria and then tell Access how to respond when the condition is met. One option is to simply tell Access to hide the matching sections and show all other sections. The procedure would be similar to the code in Figure 3.33.

```
Private Sub ReportHeader_Print(Cancel As Integer, PrintCount As Integer)

    If Me.State <> "IN" Then
        Me.GroupHeader1.Visible = False
        Me.Detail.Visible = False
    Else
        Me.GroupHeader1.Visible = True
        Me.Detail.Visible = True
    End If

End Sub
```

If the state is not IN the header is hidden

FIGURE 3.33 Procedure to Hide One Section of a Report ➤

Understand Report Events

Report events are similar to form events; however, once a report runs, most of the events happen in succession with very little intervention by the user. When you run a report, the On Open, On Load, and On Activate events fire in succession. A user cannot change the order of events; the order is predefined by Access. An explanation of these three events is listed in Table 3.3.

TABLE 3.3	Explanation of Common Report Events
Event	**Explanation**
On Open	This event is triggered when the report is open but before the first record is displayed. If there are no records, you can add Cancel = True to the procedure to cancel the opening of the report.
On Load	This event occurs when the report is open and its record(s) are displayed. Here, you can set the values of controls or do calculations with records displayed on the report.
On Activate	This occurs when the window of your report becomes the active window.

Set the Record Source Based on Form Properties

STEP 3 A report is more versatile if you let the user set one or more parameters before you open it. Setting parameters can be done using a blank form that contains no record source. The form would contain all the parameters that affect the report and a method for selecting the parameters. For example, if an inventory report contained a list of suppliers, a combo box containing all the suppliers could be created. The user could select a supplier before running the inventory report. Figure 3.34 shows a sample parameter form with a supplier combo box and a button to preview the inventory report.

User selects a Supplier Name

Preview the report based on Supplier Name

FIGURE 3.34 Create a Parameter Form for a Report ➤

When the report opens, a procedure (triggered by the On Open event) looks at the selected parameter (e.g., supplier Vong's Kayaks) and then creates the record source, as shown in Figure 3.35. Because the On Open event is triggered before the report contains any records, the record source can be created using the selected supplier. Next, the On Load event is triggered and the record source has been set. The report is displayed for supplier Vong's Kayaks only, as shown in Figure 3.36.

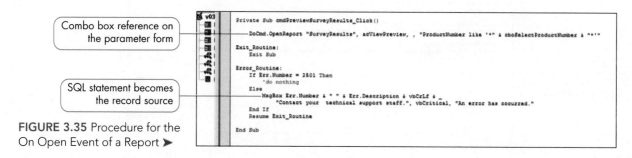

Combo box reference on the parameter form

SQL statement becomes the record source

FIGURE 3.35 Procedure for the On Open Event of a Report ➤

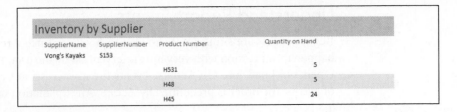

FIGURE 3.36 Supplier Report for Supplier Number S153 ➤

Handling Errors in VBA

STEP 4 ≫ Two types of errors exist in VBA—handled and unhandled. If you create procedures and functions without error handling, when VBA reports an error message, the code will stop working and the user will be presented with a confusing list of options. On the other hand, if you create a procedure with a built-in error handling routine, you can intercept errors and tell VBA to display a friendly message to the user, with options that make sense.

As an example, the procedure in Figure 3.37 illustrates how to assign the record source to a report after the user selects a supplier. If the user did not choose a supplier—and the combo box was left blank on the parameter form—the report would produce an error, as shown in Figure 3.37. Some users might understand the problem immediately and know how to fix it; but, the message contains perplexing choices: Continue, End, Debug, and Help. Continue is unavailable, and clicking Debug or Help may cause additional confusion. Clicking End would be the only choice that would enable the user to select another region, and then try again.

VBA reports an error when the report opens

FIGURE 3.37 Unhandled Error Message in VBA ➤

Add an Error Handling Routine

Error messages generated from VB can be quite confusing and frustrating to a novice user. To help relieve some of the ambiguity caused by error codes, you can produce a more user-friendly error message using an error routine. A typical error routine has been added to the procedure shown in Code Window 3.19. In this procedure, when an error occurs, the *On Error statement* directs the code to skip to a particular line in the procedure (usually at the bottom) where the appropriate message is displayed and any corrective action can be taken.

On Error statement added

Exit routine added

Error routine added

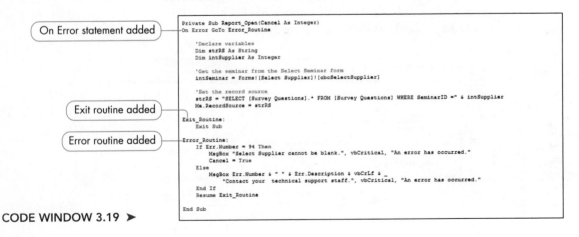

CODE WINDOW 3.19 ➤

When using an error routine in a procedure, when an error occurs, a custom message is displayed and the user only has the option to click OK. See Figure 3.38. This message replaces the confusing message shown previously in Figure 3.37. If another occurs, the procedure will still display a revised message but not a custom message. If another error appears, a second custom error message could be added using the Else...If statement.

> ## TIP | Where Do Error Numbers Come From?
>
> Error numbers, such as 94, are generated by Microsoft Access. Error numbers range from 3 to 746 with gaps between some numbers. Errors can also fall between 31001 and 31037. Once an error number is known, you can use VBA's error handling techniques to trap the error and give the user a helpful message.

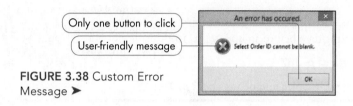

FIGURE 3.38 Custom Error Message ➤

The ***Resume Exit_Routine statement*** directs the code to jump to the exit routine. The exit routine will then exit the procedure. If the Resume Exit_Routine statement did not exist, then the error routine would exit at the End Sub statement. The reason why the resume statement is used is to enable the procedure to execute a number of cleanup statements.

Test and Debug Code

In addition to error handling, programmers also need to debug code that is not working. Errors indicate that an obvious change is needed; but, the lack of an error does not mean a procedure is working correctly. A VBA procedure must be tested thoroughly to verify it is working as expected. The more options and the more complex a procedure, the more difficult it will be to test the logic.

In addition to error messages, VBA also provides a tool to debug a procedure that is not working properly. When an error appears and it is not evident what is causing the error, you can use the debugger. The ***VBA debugger*** enables the programmer to momentarily suspend the execution of VBA code so that the following debug tasks can be done:

- Check the value of a variable in its current state.
- Enter VBA code in the Immediate window to view the results.
- Execute each line of code one at a time.
- Continue execution of the code.
- Halt execution of the code.

To use the debugger, set a breakpoint by clicking in the left margin next to any line of executable code, as shown in Figure 3.39. When the procedure is triggered (e.g., when a report is opened in Print Preview), the debugger pauses at the breakpoint and waits for the user to take action. The current line appears highlighted in yellow, as shown in Figure 3.40. To watch the procedure run one line at a time, press F8 or click Step Over in the Debug toolbar. To open the Debug toolbar, right-click any toolbar, and then select Debug from the list.

FIGURE 3.39 Set a Breakpoint in the Code Window ➤

Current line shown in yellow

FIGURE 3.40 Debugger Stops at the First Breakpoint ➤

As the debugger steps through each line of code, you can determine where the error(s) occur. Once you determine where the errors occur, you can stop the debugger and correct the code. To stop the debugger, click Reset on the Debug toolbar. After the code is fixed, remove the breakpoint by clicking the dot in the margin, and then run the procedure again.

In Hands-On Exercise 3, you will add VBA code to forms and reports and practice handling errors, testing, and debugging.

Quick Concepts ✓

1. What is the benefit of validating data before an update? *p. 169*

2. Why is error trapping important? *p. 167*

3. Why is it important to thoroughly check and debug code? *p. 173*

Hands-On Exercises

3 Forms, Reports, and Errors in VBA

Your manager would like to add additional functionality to better manage orders. To accomplish this, you will use the existing Orders form. You need to add code to the form to notify the user that a record is being modified; then you will add code to verify billing information. You also decide to add user form to allow your manager to choose the order that is reported in the preexisting order history report. You will add an error routine so future users of the database will not have to deal with any unexpected errors later.

Skills covered: Add an Event Procedure • Validate Data Before an Update • Set a Report Record Source Based on Form Properties • Add Error Handling to the Survey Results On Open Event

---

STEP 1 >> ADD AN EVENT PROCEDURE

You would like to use a VBA procedure that displays text notification to alert the user that a record is being edited. Refer to Figure 3.41 as you complete Step 1.

FIGURE 3.41 Orders Form ➤

a. Open the *v3h2Croton_LastFirst* database if you closed it at the end of Hands-On Exercise 2 and then save it as **v3h3Croton_ LastFirst**

b. Open the **Orders Form** in Design View.

c. Add a text box to the top of the form that contains the following text. ="***Data is being edited.***" Delete the label that was created with the text box and format the box with a yellow fill color and red text as shown in Figure 3.42. Use Figure 3.42 as a guide for color and format.

d. Select the newly created text box and on the Other tab of the Property Sheet name it **EditAlert.**

e. Click the Event tab in the Property Sheet and choose **Form** from the drop down menu. Click the event *On Dirty* and click **Build.**

   This will open the VB Editor and create a new procedure that is activated when the file is being edited.

f. Place your insertion point on line 5, press Tab and enter the comment '**Activates the edit alert text box when the form is being edited.**

g. Press Enter and enter the following code under the comment created in the prior step. **Me.EditAlert.Visible = True**

   This makes the visibility property of the edit notice text box true when the file is being edited.

h. Press Alt+F11 to return to the form in Design view. Click **After Update** on the Event tab of the Property Sheet, click **Build** and select Code Builder from the Choose Builder dialog box.

i. Place the insertion point on line 5 and press Tab. Next type the following comment. **'Deactivates the edit alert text box when editing is complete.**

j. Press Enter and then type **Me.EditAlert.Visible = False**

This makes the visibility property of the edit notice text box false after the file is updated.

k. Press Alt+F11 to return to the form. Click View in the Views group of the Home tab in the Ribbon to switch to Form view and save the form. Next type **your name** into the **CustomerName** field to test your work. Once the work is verified, replace your name with the original customers name **Tyler Lewis** and save but do not close the form.

STEP 2 ≫ VALIDATE DATA BEFORE AN UPDATE

You notice that the bill type is missing for the first order listed on the orders form. You need to add a Before Update procedure to validate billing information. Refer to Figure 3.42 as you complete Step 2.

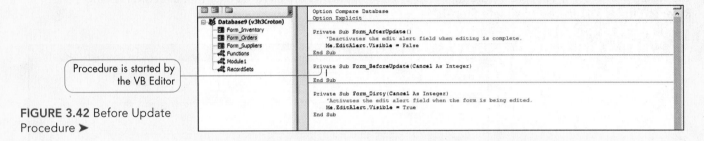

Procedure is started by the VB Editor

FIGURE 3.42 Before Update Procedure ➤

a. Click the View tab from the Views group in the Ribbon to display the Orders form in Design view.

b. If not already selected, select **Form** from the Selection type box at the top of the Property Sheet. Click the **Event tab**, click **Before Update event,** and click **Build**.

The VB Editor opens and a new subroutine is started in the code window, as shown in Figure 3.45.

c. Place your insertion point below the **Form_BeforeUpdate** Private Sub and add the code as shown in Code Window 3.20.

```
Private Sub Form_BeforeUpdate(Cancel As Integer)
    If IsNull(Me.BillType) Then
        MsgBox "Bill type cannot be blank"
        Cancel = True
    Else
        'Do nothing
    End If
End Sub
```

CODE WINDOW 3.20 ➤

This section of code verifies that a billing type has been entered in the form. The user is notified and the record cannot be saved because of the statement Cancel = True.

d. Minimize the VB Editor, switch to Form view of the Orders form, type **9** in the CustomerID field and then press Tab four times. Note the responses from Step 1 trigger the Before Update event. Take note how the code responds to the missing data as well.

e. Press OK when the message box appears, type **1** in the CustomerID field and **Credit** in the BillType field.

f. Maximize the VB Editor and save the procedure. Close the VB Editor and close the Orders form.

> **TROUBLESHOOTING:** If the newly created code does not work on the first attempt, return to the VB Editor and verify the code against Code Window 3.19. Next press the Reset button in the menu of the VB Editor, return to the form, save and reopen.

STEP 3 ≫ SET A REPORT RECORD SOURCE BASED ON FORM PROPERTIES

Randy would like to add functionality to the pre-created OrderHistory report without the need for additional querying. You will use the pre-created report, Orders table, and create a Select Order Number form to make it easy for him to isolate one order. Refer to Figures 3.43 and 3.44 as you complete Step 3.

Order history by month

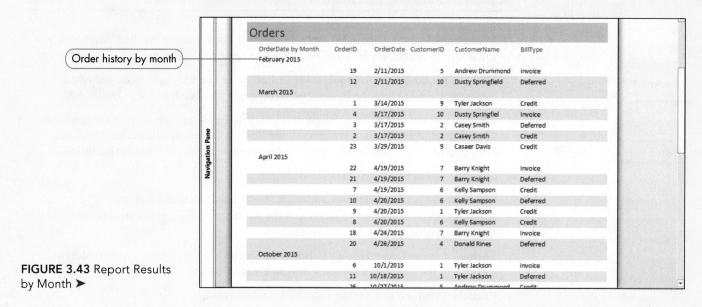

FIGURE 3.43 Report Results by Month ➤

Combo box contains all supplier names

FIGURE 3.44 Select Order Number ➤

a. If open from prior steps, close all database objects. Click the **Create tab** and click **Form Design** in the Forms group.

A blank form is displayed.

b. Click the **Combo Box control** from the gallery in the Controls group and click in the middle of the form. Provide the Combo Box wizard with the following answers, and then click **Finish**:

Combo Box Wizard Question	Action
The wizard creates a combo box, which displays a list of values you can choose from. How do you want your combo box to get its values?	Select **Option 1** (I want the combo box to get the values from another table or query.).
Which table or query should provide the values for your combo box?	Select Table: **Orders**
Which fields contain the values you want included in your combo box?	Select **OrderID.**
What sort order do you want for the items in your list box?	Skip.
How wide would you like the columns in your combo box?	Keep default.
What label would you like for your combo box?	OrderID.

After completing the steps in the table click **Finish**. After completing the Combo Box, you will return to the Orders form in Design view to begin the next step.

c. Click the **Rectangle control tool** on the Design tab of Form Design Tools, and add a rectangle around the combo box created in the prior step. As depicted in Figure 3.47.

d. Add a Command Button from the control group in the Design tab of Form Design Tools. Click **Cancel** without making changes in the Command Button Wizard. Use the Label control to add a label that reads **Select Order Number** above the OrderID combo box.

e. Save the form as **SelectOrderID**.

f. Display the SelectOrderID form in Design view. Click the **combo box**, and if necessary open the Property Sheet. Click the **All tab** and change the Name property to **cboOrderHistory**.

g. Click the **Review Order History button**. Change the Name property to **cmdOrderHistory** and change the Caption property to **Review Order History**.

h. Click the **Event tab** and double-click the **On Click event**.

i. Click **Build** to open the VB Editor and type the following code under the cmdOrderHistory Private Sub. **DoCmd.OpenReport "OrderHistory", acViewPreview**

The VB Editor opens and a new procedure is started in the Code window. The code entered will use the Do Command to open the preexisting OrderHistory report when activated. You will add the code shown in Figure 3.48 to allow the user to select the OrderID featured in the report.

j. Press **Alt+F11** to exit the VB Editor. Open the OrderHistory report in Design view and add a new **On Open event**. Type the following code as shown in Figure 3.45 into the procedure and save the code.

Procedure sets the record source based on the form input

FIGURE 3.45 On Open Event of Report ➤

k. Minimize the VB Editor, display SelectOrderID form in Form view and click the **Review Order History button**.

STEP 4 ≫ ADD ERROR HANDLING TO THE SURVEY RESULTS ON OPEN EVENT

If the user attempts to run the Order History report without first selecting an OrderID from the combo box, an error will occur. You will add error handling to the VBA procedure to trap run time errors. Refer to Figure 3.46 as you complete Step 5.

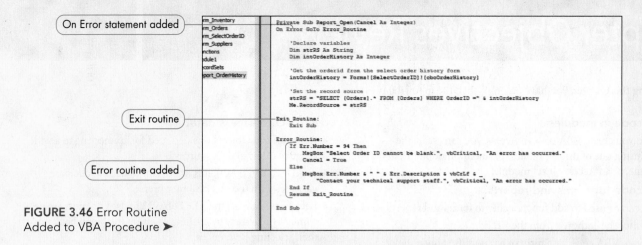

On Error statement added

Exit routine

Error routine added

FIGURE 3.46 Error Routine
Added to VBA Procedure ➤

a. Return to the VB Editor and locate Report_Open procedure for the OrderHistory report.

b. Add the *On Error GoTo, Exit_Routine, and the Error_Routine* sections, as shown in Figure 3.49.

   One line of code is added above the existing procedure; the rest of the code is added below the existing procedure.

c. Save the code.

d. Exit the VB Editor and open the SelectOrderID form in Form view. Delete the contents of the Select ProductNumber combo box and click the **Review Order History button**.

   A message box appears that says *Select Order ID cannot be blank.*

e. Click **OK** the message box to open the second message box and click **End.**

   To clear the second message, an error routine must be added to the cmdPreviewSurveyResults_Click() procedure in the Select ProductNumber form.

f. Revise the cmdOrderHistory_Click() procedure by adding the code shown in Code Window 3.21.

```
Private Sub cmdOrderHistory_Click()
On Error GoTo Error_Routine

    DoCmd.OpenReport "OrderHistory", acViewPreview

Exit_Routine:
    Exit Sub

Error_Routine:
    If Err.Number = 2501 Then
        'Do Nothing
    Else
        MsgBox Err.Number & " " & Err.Description & vbCrLf & _
            "Contact your technical support staff.", vbCritical, "An Error has occured."
    End If
    Resume Exit_Routine

End Sub
```

CODE WINDOW 3.21 ▲

g. Save the code and minimize the VB Editor. Click the **Review Order History button**.

   Only the first message appears. The second message was intercepted by the error routine.

h. Close the VB Editor and close the form and report.

i. Save and close the database. Submit it based on your instructor's directions, and then exit.

Chapter Objectives Review

After reading this chapter, you have accomplished the following objectives:

1. **Write code in modules.**
   - When you create VBA code in Access, you can create the code using one of three modules: a standard module, a class module, or an Access object module.

2. **Write code for forms and reports.**
   - VBA can be used to add functionality to forms and reports.
   - VBA must be authored from the VB Editor.
   - To create VBA code for a form or a report, first open the object in Design view, and then click Property Sheet in the Tools group. Next, select an event, and then click Build on the right side of the property cell. The Choose Builder dialog box appears with three options—Macro Builder, Expression Builder, and Code Builder on the Event tab. Select the Code Builder, and then click OK.

3. **Work with objects.**
   - VBA works with the objects in the various object libraries that are available in the applications that support VBA.
   - You can use objects in the object libraries along with their resources to accomplish the programming tasks.
   - In addition to the Office applications, you can also set references to other object libraries such as Adobe Acrobat, Skype, and Yahoo! Messenger.

4. **Create functions.**
   - A function is a procedure that performs an action and returns a value.
   - Many functions are predefined in VBA and ready to use.
   - When no preexisting function will fit your needs, you have the ability to author calculations directly into procedures; however, a custom function allows cleaner design.

5. **Use DAO to access data.**
   - Data Access Objects refers to an object library specifically created to work with Access databases.
   - To create a recordset in DAO, you must first explicitly connect to a database, usually the database that is currently opened. Next, you create a recordset object based on a table, a query, or an SQL statement. Then, you can loop through the records in the recordset and count the total number of records, count only the records that meet a certain criteria, or modify field data of all records that meet a certain criteria.

6. **Use ADO to access data.**
   - ActiveX Data Objects was designed for connecting to a wide range of external data sources.
   - In ADO (as in DAO), it is important to declare database variables with the object library prefix.
   - Before you can use the ADO object library, you must create a link to the library by clicking Tools on the menu bar, and then selecting References.

7. **Add VBA to forms.**
   - Enhancing the functionality of forms and reports is one of the most common uses of VBA.
   - Almost all of the VBA code added to a form is triggered by an event.
   - Common events include On Open, On Click, On Enter, On Exit, Before Update, and After Update.

8. **Add VBA to reports.**
   - VBA can be used to modify reports.
   - Report events are similar to form events; however, once a report runs, most of the events happen in succession with very little intervention by the user.
   - A report is more versatile if you let the user set one or more parameters before you open it. This can be done using VBA.

9. **Handle errors in VBA.**
   - Two types of errors exist in VBA—handled and unhandled.
   - Error routines can be added to provide user-friendly error messages.
   - If multiple errors occur, a Resume Exit Routine can direct the code to exit a procedure.

Key Terms Matching

Match the key terms with their definitions. Write the key term letter by the appropriate numbered definition.

a. ADO
b. After Update
c. Before Update
d. DAO
e. Edit
f. Error Trapping
g. MoveNext
h. Object Libraries
i. On Current

j. On Dirty
k. On Enter
l. On Error statement
m. Option Compare Database
n. Option Explicit
o. Resume Exit_Routine statement
p. Update
q. VBA debugger

1. _____ Statement is used in a module to declare the default comparison method to use when string data is compared. **p. 141**

2. _____ Statement is used in a module to require that all variables be declared before they are used. **p. 141**

3. _____ Contain the objects that are available in the application that supports VBA. **p. 142**

4. _____ Data Access Object refers to an object library specifically created to work with Access databases. **p. 154**

5. _____ Method is used to advance through the records of a recordset. **p. 155**

6. _____ Method enables you to change the data in a recordset. **p. 156**

7. _____ Method enables you to save the changes in a recordset. **p. 156**

8. _____ ActiveX Data Objects is designed for connecting to a wide range of external data sources. **p. 158**

9. _____ The process of intercepting and handling errors at run time. **p. 167**

10. _____ The event that is triggered by a record being loaded into a form. **p. 168**

11. _____ Refers to the act of placing the insertion point in a text box. **p. 168**

12. _____ Triggered when a record is being edited. **p. 168**

13. _____ Triggered after a record is saved. **p. 167**

14. _____ Triggered before a record is saved. **p. 169**

15. _____ Directs the code to skip to a particular line in the procedure. **p. 172**

16. _____ Directs the code to jump to the exit line. **p. 173**

17. _____ Enables the programmer to momentarily suspend the execution of VBA code. **p. 173**

Multiple Choice

1. All of these types of modules are found in VBA except:

   (a) Debug module.

   (b) Class module.

   (c) Standard module.

   (d) Access object module.

2. Which of the following keystrokes will open the VBA Editor?

   (a) Alt+F12

   (b) F4

   (c) Alt+F11

   (d) Control+Shift+Enter

3. Which statement is incorrect?

   (a) Object libraries are only used by Access and Excel.

   (b) A property is an attribute of an object.

   (c) A method executes an action on an object.

   (d) An event is triggered by a user action.

4. Functions are created in:

   (a) The Object Explorer.

   (b) Procedures.

   (c) Class modules.

   (d) Standard modules.

5. DAO can be used to accomplish all of these except:

   (a) Modify database objects.

   (b) Connect to Excel spreadsheets.

   (c) Create tables and queries.

   (d) Add procedures to form events.

6. ADO is similar to DAO in which way?

   (a) One is simply a newer version of the other.

   (b) Both can easily access external data sources.

   (c) Both can access database objects.

   (d) Both were originally created by IBM.

7. A common reason to add VBA to a form is to:

   (a) Display a different background color for different data entry tasks.

   (b) Remind users which field comes next during data entry.

   (c) Time a user as he or she enters data.

   (d) Validate data as it is entered.

8. Which is not a common reason to add VBA to a report?

   (a) Allow users to change the font size of the data being printed.

   (b) Modify the content of the report.

   (c) Highlight one section to emphasize it.

   (d) Display an error message when no data exists.

9. The On Error GoTo statement is used to:

   (a) Go to the line immediately after an error.

   (b) Redirect the procedure to skip over code and execute the error routine.

   (c) Start the debugger.

   (d) Start over after the user clicks OK.

10. To delete a record in a recordset, you use which VBA statement?

    (a) rst.update.

    (b) rst.delete.

    (c) rst.MoveNext.

    (d) Set rst = Nothing.

1 Wholesale Food Business

T&F Wholesalers exports its food products to customers in Germany, France, Brazil, the United Kingdom, and the United States. The owners of T&F would like to improve the efficiency of their data entry forms by adding a validation process. They would also like to add automatic entry for fields that are calculated based on other fields. This exercise follows the same set of skills as used in Hands-On Exercises 1 and 3 in the chapter. Refer to Figure 3.47 as you complete this exercise.

```
'orm                                    ∨  BeforeUpdate

Option Compare Database
Option Explicit

Private Sub OrderDate_Enter()
    'Set the order date = today
    If IsNull(Me.OrderDate) Then
        Me.OrderDate = Date
    End If
End Sub

Private Sub OrderDate_Exit(Cancel As Integer)
    'Set the expected ship date = order date plus 2 days
    If IsNull(Me.ExpectedShipDate) Then
        Me.ExpectedShipDate = Me.OrderDate + 2
    End If
End Sub

Private Sub Form_BeforeUpdate(Cancel As Integer)
    'Validate freight amount. Must be between 0 and 199.
    If Me.Freight >= 0 And Me.Freight <= 199 Then
        'do nothing
    Else
        MsgBox "Freight must be between $0 and $199", vbOKOnly, _
            "Invalid freight amount"
        Cancel = True
    End If
End Sub
```

FIGURE 3.47 Form Module with Three Procedures ➤

a. Open *v3p1Wholesale*. Save the database as **v3p1Wholesale_LastFirst**, and if necessary enable the content.

b. Open the Orders form in Design view. Click the **Order Date box**.

c. Click the **Event tab**, click **On Enter event** and click **Build**.

d. Type the code from the *Sub OrderDate_Enter* section inside the procedure, as shown in Code Window 3.22.

```
Private Sub OrderDate_Enter()
    'Set the order date = today
    If IsNull(Me.OrderDate) Then
        Me.OrderDate = Date
    End If
End Sub
```

CODE WINDOW 3.22 ➤

e. Minimize the VB Editor and display the Orders form in Form view. Save the form.

f. Test the code using the first record. Press **Tab** until you reach the OrderDate and verify that the code does nothing because an order date already exists. Then, delete the order date and test the code again by tabbing into the field to verify that today's date appears.

g. Switch to Design view. Verify that the OrderDate box is still selected. Click the **On Exit event**. Click **Build** to open the VB Editor. Type the code from the *Private Sub OrderDate_Exit* section inside the procedure, as shown in Code Window 3.23. Save the code.

```
Private Sub OrderDate_Exit(Cancel As Integer)
    'Set the expected ship date = order date plus 2 days
    If IsNull(Me.ExpectedShipDate) Then
        Me.ExpectedShipDate = Me.OrderDate + 2
    End If
End Sub
```

CODE WINDOW 3.23 ➤

h. Save the code, minimize the VB Editor and open the Orders form in Form view. Test the code using the first record. Press **Tab** until you reach the ExpectedShipDate and press **Tab** one more time to verify that the code does nothing because an expected ship date already exists. Then, delete the expected ship date and test the code again by pressing **Tab** until you are past the OrderedShipDate field to verify that today's date plus two appears.

i. Switch to Design view. Select the form using the Selection type box at the top of the Property Sheet. Double-click the **Before Update event** on the Events tab. Click **Build** to open the VB Editor. Type the code from the *Sub Form_BeforeUpdate* section inside the procedure, as shown in Code Window 3.24.

```
Private Sub Form_BeforeUpdate(Cancel As Integer)
    'Validate freight amount. Must be between 0 and 199.
    If Me.Freight >= 0 And Me.Freight <= 199 Then
        'do nothing
    Else
        MsgBox "Freight must be between $0 and $199", vbOKOnly, _
            "Invalid freight amount"
        Cancel = True
    End If
End Sub
```

CODE WINDOW 3.24 ➤

> **TROUBLESHOOTING:** Your procedure may be at the top of the code window or under the other procedures. The order is not important.

j. Save the code and form them switch to Form view. Test the code using the first record. Type **200** into the **Freight field** and click **Next Record** to advance to the next record. Verify that the message *Freight must be between 0 and $199* appears. Press **Esc** to clear the data entry and close the form. Save the changes.

k. Open the Products report in Design view. Open the Property Sheet if necessary and click the **Event tab**. Double-click the **On Open event**.

l. Click **Build** to open the VB Editor. Type the code shown in Code Window 3.25 inside the procedure.

```
Private Sub Report_Open(Cancel As Integer)
    'Declare variables
    Dim intCategory As Integer
    Dim strRS As String


    'Revise the records source -- filter by category
    If MsgBox("Do you want to filter the report by category?", vbYesNo, _
            "Input required") = vbYes Then
        'Filter by Category
        intCategory = InputBox("Enter category (1-8)")

        'Set the record source = the filtered products table
        strRS = "SELECT Products.* FROM Products WHERE CategoryID =" & intCategory
        Me.RecordSource = strRS
    Else
        'Set the record source = the whole products table
        Me.RecordSource = "Products"
    End If

End Sub
```

CODE WINDOW 3.25 ▲

m. Save the code and minimize the VB Editor. Test the code by opening the report in Print Preview. Verify that the messages appear and that there are no typographical errors. Click **Yes** and enter a **1** in the second message to verify that you can filter the report by one category. Close the report.

n. Save and close the database, and submit it based on your instructor's directions.

You have been hired as a financial analyst for EBL Financial. Because of your background with VBA you have been asked to add functionality to their current employee database. You have been asked to use VBA to calculate the monthly retirement contribution per employee. You have also been asked to add the ability to filter the employee report by gender when run. This exercise follows the same set of skills as used in Hands-On Exercises 1 and 3 in the chapter. Refer to Figure 3.48 as you complete this exercise.

a. Open the *v3p2Retirement* database and save it as **v3p2Retirement_LastFirst**.

b. Click the **Database Tools tab**, and then click **Visual Basic** to open the VB Editor.

c. Click **Insert** on the menu bar and select **Module**. Use the code shown in Code window 3.26 and type the entire Public Function ContributionAmount into the Code window.

FIGURE 3.48 Custom Function Calculates Monthly Contribution ➤

```
Private Sub MonthlyContribution_Click()

    'Displays monthly contribution amount
    MsgBox ("Monthly Contribution is " & _
    Format(ContributionAmount(Me.salary, Me.Percentage), "Currency"))

End Sub
```

CODE WINDOW 3.26 ▲

d. Save the module as **Function**. Next, you will call the function from a procedure inside the Employees form.

e. Open the Employees form in Design View. Click the Monthly Contribution button and click the **Event tab** in the property sheet. Choose **Event Procedure** for the On Click property and open the VB Editor. Type the following code inside the procedure:

'Displays Monthly Contribution amount
MsgBox ("Monthly Contribution is " & _
Format (ContributionAmount (Me.Salary, Me.Percentage), "Currency"))

f. Save the code, and then minimize the VB Editor. Open the Employees form in Form view. Click the Monthly Contribution button for the first record. The employee's monthly 401K contribution is displayed in a message box. After reviewing the monthly contribution click OK to close the message box then save and close the form.

g. Open the Employees Report. You will add a procedure to the report that will enable the user to filter employees by gender.

h. Switch to Design view. Open the Property Sheet if necessary and double-click the **On Open event** on the Event tab. Click **Build** to open the VB Editor. Type the procedure shown in Code Window 3.27.

```
Private Sub Report_Open(Cancel As Integer)

    'Declare variables
    Dim strGender As String
    Dim strRS As String

    'Revise the records source -- filter by gender
    If MsgBox("Do you want to filter the report by gender?", vbYesNo, _
            "Input required") = vbYes Then
        'Filter by Category
        strGender = InputBox("Enter gender (F, M.)")

        'Set the record source = the filtered employees table
        strRS = "SELECT Employees.* FROM Employees WHERE Gender = '" & strGender & "'"
        Me.RecordSource = strRS
    Else
        'Set the record source = the whole employees table
        Me.RecordSource = "Employees"
    End If

End Sub
```

CODE WINDOW 3.27 ▲

i. Save the code, and then minimize the VB Editor. Test the code by opening the report in Print Preview. Click **Yes** at the first message to verify that you can filter the report by gender and type **M** to show only males in the report. Close the report, and then save the changes if prompted.

j. Close the database, and submit it based on your instructor's directions.

Mid-Level Exercises

1 HomeOwner Association

You have recently become a member of your community homeowners association. You have been asked by the president to update their current database by removing the inactive members. You have also been asked to create a function to calculate dues unpaid by active members. Dues are $250.00 plus a 10% late fee. Refer to Figure 3.49 as you complete this exercise.

FIGURE 3.49 Custom Function Calculates Total Amount Owed ➤

a. Open *v3m1HomeOwner*. Save the database as **v3m1HomeOwners_LastFirst**. Enable the content.

b. Open the OwnerInformation form in design view, if necessary open the Property Sheet, and select the **Calculate Dues** button.

c. Double-click the **On Click property** and click **Build**. Place your insertion point after the CalculateDues_Click() Private sub and type the code as displayed in Code Window 3.28. Save the code and exit the VB Editor.

CODE WINDOW 3.28 ➤

```vba
Private Sub CalculateDues_Click()

    'Declare Constant
    Const curDues As Currency = 250
    Const sngLateFee As Single = 1.1

    'Declare Variables
    Dim curAmountOwed As Currency

    'Display Homeowners fee

    If Me.HomeOwnerFees = "Unpaid" Then
        curAmountOwed = curDues * sngLateFee

    Else
        curAmountOwed = 0

    End If

    MsgBox "Total amount owed is " & Format(curAmountOwed, "currency")

End Sub
```

d. Open the OwnerInformation form in form view and press the Calculate Dues button. As shown in Figure 3.49, the Total amount owed is $275.00 which is comprised of the $250.00 association fee and penalty. Click **OK** and close the form.

e. Open the VB Editor and insert a new module. Save the Module as DeleteInactive.

f. Type the procedure into the code window as it is shown in Code Window 3.29. Note the **'rst.Delete** line is entered as a comment.

This code will locate all inactive members and returns a count of the records found. In the next step you will remove the ' from the comment **'rst.Delete.** Once removed this will delete the inactive members and return a count on the records found.

CODE WINDOW 3.29 ➤

```
Sub RemoveInactive()

    'Declare variables
    Dim db As DAO.Database
    Dim rst As DAO.Recordset
    Dim intCounter As Integer

    'Set the current database
    Set db = CurrentDb

    'Set the recordset
    Set rst = db.OpenRecordset("OwnerInformation")

    'Cycle through the records
    Do While Not rst.EOF
    If rst!Status = "Inactive" Then
        intCounter = intCounter + 1
        'rst.Delete
    End If
    rst.MoveNext
    Loop
    MsgBox "End of Recordset. " & intCounter & " matches were found."

    'Close the recordset
    rst.Close
    Set rst = Nothing
    Set db = Nothing

End Sub
```

> **TROUBLESHOOTING:** Deleting records from a database cannot be undone. Be sure to make a backup before testing the DeleteInactive procedure.

g. Save the procedure and click Run in the VB Editor. Choose RemoveInactive and click Run.

The code finds five inactive members but will not delete the inactive members until the ' is removed from the 'rst.Delete line.

h. Remove the ' from the **'rst.Delete** line, save the code and run the procedure. Click **OK** to close the message box, save the code, and press Alt+F11 to exit the VB Editor.

i. Open the OwnerInformation table and verify that the five inactive members have been deleted.

j. Submit the database based on your instructor's directions.

Charity Benefit Auction

You are a volunteer for a local charity that is holding a benefit auction. Donations are collected from friends and business partners and the donations are then auctioned off at the annual charity event. The event organizers would like to know the statistics of the donations as they are being collected. You create a form to provide that information. Refer to Figure 3.50 as you complete this exercise.

FIGURE 3.50 Statistics Form Calls Recordset Procedure ➤

a. Open *v3m2Charity*. Save the database as **v3m2Charity_LastFirst**, and then enable the content.

b. Open the Donations table to view the donations to date. Close the table.

c. Create a new form using the Form Design tool. Add a title (label), a rectangle, a button, and three text box controls, as shown in Figure 3.53. Set the Enabled property of the three text box controls on the Data tab to **No**. Set the Format property of the three text box controls to **Currency**. Change the Name of the button to **cmdRefresh**. Rename the text boxes as **txtLowDonation**, **txtHighDonation**, and **txtAverageDonation**.

d. Save the form as **Statistics**.

e. Open the VB Editor, create a new module and type the procedure shown in Code Window 3.30.

```
Public Sub CalculateLowHighAverage()
    'Declare variables
    Dim db As DAO.Database
    Dim rst As DAO.Recordset
    Dim curLowDonation As Currency
    Dim curHighDonation As Currency
    Dim curTotalDonation As Currency
    Dim lngCounter As Long
    Dim curAverageDonation As Currency

    'Set the current database
    Set db = CurrentDb

    'Set the recordset
    Set rst = db.OpenRecordset("Select Donations.* From Donations Where ItemValue Is Not Null")

    'Cycle through the records
    Do While Not rst.EOF
    If lngCounter = 0 Then
        'set the low donation
        curLowDonation = rst!ItemValue
    End If
        If rst!ItemValue < curLowDonation Then
            curLowDonation = rst!ItemValue
        End If
        If rst!ItemValue > curHighDonation Then
            curHighDonation = rst!ItemValue
        End If
        curTotalDonation = curTotalDonation + rst!ItemValue
        lngCounter = lngCounter + 1
    rst.MoveNext
    Loop

    'Update the fields on the statistics form
    Forms![Statistics]![txtLowDonation] = curLowDonation
    Forms![Statistics]![txtHighDonation] = curHighDonation
    Forms![Statistics]![txtAverageDonation] = curTotalDonation / lngCounter

    'Close the recordset
    rst.Close
    Set rst = Nothing
    Set db = Nothing

End Sub
```

CODE WINDOW 3.30 ▲

f. Save the code and minimize the VB Editor.

g. Open the Statistics form in Design view, and then add the following code to the On Click event of the cmdRefresh button:
Call CalculateLowHighAverage

h. Save the form. Switch to Form view and click **Refresh** on the Statistics form. Compare your results to the values in Figure 3.50.

i. Return to the VB Editor and add the code **On Error GoTo Error_Routine** underneath the first line. Then add the error handling code shown in Code Window 3.31.

```
Exit_Routine:
    Exit Sub

Error_Routine:
    MsgBox Err.Number & " " & Err.Description & vbCrLf & _
            "Contact your technical support staff.", vbCritical, "An error has occurred."
    Resume Exit_Routine

End Sub
```

CODE WINDOW 3.31 ▲

j. Save the code. Click **Refresh** on the Statistics form again to test the new code. Close the form if everything is working.

k. Open the Donations List report. Add a procedure that will enable a user to filter the report by category. The procedure should be triggered by the On Open event.

l. Save and close the database, and submit it based on your instructor's directions.

Beyond the Classroom

Create a Late Fee Procedure

The *v3b1loans* file contains data from a local community bank. The database contains information about customers, loans, and loan payments. You will create a procedure that will calculate the late fees of loan payments after they are received. Create a form with a command button that will call the procedure and calculate the late fees. Open the *v3b1loans* file, and then save the database as **v3b1loans_LastFirst**. In the database, open the Payments table, and then review the data in the table. Open the VB Editor, and then create a procedure in a standard module that updates the LateFee field if the payment was received after the due date. The grace period is five days; after five days, assess a percent of payment fee based on the number of days late. For example, a payment eight days late would be charged an 8% late fee. Revise the Payments form and add a new procedure to the Update Late Fees button. Add a statement in the code that will refresh the form; add error handling to the button code. Close the database, and then exit Access. Submit the database based on your instructor's directions.

Create a Recordset Using ADO

All of the recordsets that you have created in this chapter were created using the DAO object library. In this exercise, you will create a recordset using the ADO object library. Open the *v3b2doctors* file, and then save the database as **v3b2doctors_LastFirst**. In the new database, open the Doctors table, and then review the data. Open the VB Editor, click **Tools** on the menu bar, and then click **References**. Add a reference to the Microsoft ActiveX Data Objects 2.8 Library. Search Help and the Internet to find an example of how to create a recordset using ADO. Create a recordset that changes all records with zip code 33070 to 33099. Close the database, and then exit Access. Submit the database based on your instructor's directions.

Debug a Recordset Procedure

 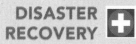

The Mountain Top Lodge would like you to calculate the total guests in each service category. You created a standard module and added a new procedure. The procedure is producing an error. Try to debug the error, run the procedure, and then verify the total in each party. To begin, open the *v3b3lodging* file, and then save the database as **v3b3lodging_LastFirst**. Open the VB Editor, and then run the procedure. Debug the error, and then fix the procedure. Run the procedure again, and then verify the number of total guests in ServiceID 1.

Capstone Exercise

You have been hired as a data analyst for Quantam Property management, a facilities management company that provides full service maintenance to several subdivisions in your city. You have been asked to add several enhancements to the company's current database. You have been asked to create a custom function that will enable the property managers to see the ranking of each property based on value. You have also been asked to add a procedure to a report to allow the user to view all properties over a set price value. Your last step will be to add error handling to your work.

Database File Setup

Open a database, save it with a new name, and then enable content to start this capstone exercise. You will then create a function, modify a form, and then call the function from the form. You will also add a procedure to an existing report.

a. Open the v3c1Condo database.

b. Save the database as **v3c1Condo_LastFirst**, and then enable content.

c. Sort the table by ascending MarketValue. Close the table without saving.

Create a Function

You need to create a function that will rank the properties by the MarketValue as compared to the other properties. The ranking will be displayed as each property is displayed in the Properties form.

a. Open the VB Editor and insert a new module.

b. Enter a new function, as shown in Code Window 3.32.

c. Save the code.

Add an Error Routine

You need to add an error routine that will display a simple, user-friendly message if an error occurs.

a. Return to the VB Editor, add the code **On Error GoTo Error_Routine** underneath the first line

b. Add the following code, as shown in Code Window 3.33.

```
Public Function MarketValueRanking(sMarkVal) As Integer

    'Declare variables
    Dim db As DAO.Database
    Dim rst As DAO.Recordset
    Dim intCounter As Integer

    'Set the current database
    Set db = CurrentDb

    'Set the recordset
    Set rst = db.OpenRecordset("Select Properties.* From Properties Where " & _
        "MarketValue Is Not Null Order By MarketValue")

    'Cycle through the records
    Do While Not rst.EOF
    intCounter = intCounter + 1
        If rst!MarketValue = sMarkVal Then
            Exit Do
        End If
    rst.MoveNext
    Loop

    'Return the value to the calling procedure
    MarketValueRanking = intCounter

    'Close the recordset
    rst.Close
    Set rst = Nothing
    Set db = Nothing

End Function
```

CODE WINDOW 3.32 ▲

```
Exit_Routine:
    Exit Function

Error_Routine:
    MsgBox Err.Number & " " & Err.Description & vbCrLf & _
        "Contact your technical support staff.", vbCritical, "An error has occured."
    Resume Exit_Routine
End Function
```

CODE WINDOW 3.33 ▲

c. Save the code.

d. Minimize the VB Editor.

Modify the Properties Form

First, you will modify the Properties form, and then you will call the new function from the On_Current event of the Properties form.

a. Open the PropertiesForm form in Design View.

b. Reduce the width of all fields on the form by one-half.

c. Add a new text box to the space to the right of the MarketValue box.

d. Name the new text box **txtPropertyRank**. Name its label **Rank:**

e. Change the BackColor property of the text box to **Blue-Gray, Text 2, Lighter 80%.**

f. Change the Enabled property to No.

g. Save the form.

Call the Function from the On Current Event of the Form

Now that the form modifications are complete, you will call the new function from the On Current event of the PropertiesForm form.

a. Open the Property Sheet and verify form is selected.

b. Create an Event Procedure in the **On Current event** of the form.

c. Type the following line of code in the VB Editor: **txtPropertyRank=MarketValueRanking(MarketValue)**

d. Save the procedure.

e. Minimize the VB Editor.

f. Switch to Form view.

g. Advance to the next record, and then verify the rank is being updated. Note the rank.

h. Open the Properties table, sort by MarketValue and compare the table rank to the form's rank to verify the rank.

i. Verify the rank of several additional properties, then close the table and form.

Add a Filter Procedure to the Properties Report

Your superiors are interested in viewing only higher valued properties. Your next task will be to add a procedure to the On Open event of the Properties Report that will enable you to filter for properties greater then a certain value.

a. Open the PropertiesReport report in Design view.

b. Add an Event Procedure to the On Open event of the report.

c. Type the procedure shown in Code Window 3.34 in the VB Editor

```
Private Sub Report_Open(Cancel As Integer)

    'Declare variables
    Dim lngMarketValueFloor As Long
    Dim strRS As String

    'Revise the records source -- show properties with value > X
    If MsgBox("Do you want to see only properties with value > X ?", vbYesNo, _
            "Input required") = vbYes Then
        'Filter by Category
        lngMarketValueFloor = InputBox("Enter the minimum property value (ex. 550000)")

        'Set the record source = the filtered properties table
        strRS = "SELECT Properties.* FROM Properties WHERE MarketValue > " & _
        lngMarketValueFloor
        Me.RecordSource = strRS
    Else
        'Set the record source = the whole products table
        Me.RecordSource = "SELECT Properties.* FROM Properties WHERE MarketValue Is Not Null"
    End If

End Sub
```

CODE WINDOW 3.34 ▲

d. Save the procedure

e. Minimize the VB Editor.

f. Open the report in Print Preview.

g. Click **No** in response to the message box. Close the report.

h. Rerun the report and click **Yes** in response to the first message box.

i. Enter **200000** in the next message box.

j. Verify that the records displayed are for all properties over $200,000.

k. Close the report.

l. Save and close the database, and submit it based on your instructor's directions.

Glossary

ADO (ActiveX Data Objects) An object library designed for connecting to a wide range of external data sources.

After Update An event that is triggered after a record is saved.

And operator A logical operator that requires that two or more conditions be met to evaluate to True.

Argument A value that provides necessary information to a procedure or a function.

Before Update An event that is triggered before a record is saved.

Bound control A control that is connected to a data source in the host application.

Calling procedure A statement within a procedure that calls or executes a function.

Caption property An object or controls' attribute that displays onscreen.

CheckBox control A control that enables the user to select one or more options at the same time.

Class module A module that stores public code definitions of a class, such as properties and methods.

Code window A text editor for writing and editing VBA procedures.

Collection A group of objects with similar characteristics.

CommandButton control An object that enables the user to click it; usually triggers VBA code to complete an algorithm of steps.

Comment A textual description that explains a section of programming code. In VBA, comment lines start with the prime character (') and appear in green in the Code window.

Concatenate The process of joining two or more text strings.

Condition An expression that determines if a situation is true.

Constant A programmer-defined name that stores values that remain the same (or constant) during run time.

Control An object, such as a text box, that enables interaction with the user.

ControlSource property An attribute that defines the cell to which a control is bound.

Counter variable A variable used to count the number of times a loop repeats.

DAO (Data Access Objects) An object library specifically created to work with Access databases.

Data type An indicator that specifies what type of data (such as text or number) can be stored in the variable or constant.

Data validation The process of checking data entered to ensure it meets certain requirements, such as a numeric value or a value within a specified range.

Decision structure A block of code that uses relational operators to make comparisons and then executes alternative statements based on the outcome.

Declaration A statement that creates a variable or constant and specifies its data type and name.

Design time The mode for designing, writing, and editing programming statements.

Do...Loop structure A repetition structure that repeats designated statements as long as a condition is true or until a condition is satisfied.

Edit A method that enables you to change the data in a recordset.

Enabled property An attribute of True or False that determines whether a control can receive focus and respond to the user.

Error Trapping The process of intercepting and handling errors at run time.

Event An event is what happens when a user takes an action; an event can also trigger the execution of code.

Focus A property that shows the control is active.

For...Next structure A repetition structure that repeats statements a specific number of times.

Format function A function that formats the first argument (such as a number) into a particular appearance, such as a currency format or date format.

Frame control An object that displays a frame or border around selected controls on a form.

Function procedure A procedure that performs an action and returns a value.

If...Then structure A statement that performs a logical test and executes one or more statements if the test is True.

If...Then...Else structure A statement that performs a logical test and executes different statements based on whether the test is true or false.

Input box A dialog box that prompts the user to enter data.

InputBox function A function that displays a prompt dialog box to the user to enter a value.

Integral data type A data type that can store only whole numbers.

IsNumeric function A function that checks a string and returns True if the string can evaluate to a number or False if the string cannot evaluate to a number.

Iteration One execution of a loop statement.

Keyword Text or a symbol used for a specific purpose in a programming language.

Label control An object that displays text onscreen, usually to describe other controls that do not have captions.

Line-continuation character A space followed by an underscore that programmers manually insert to display one statement on two or more lines in the Code window.

ListBox control An object that displays a list of items from which the user may select.

Logical operator An operator that uses Boolean logic to perform a logical test.

Logical test A decision structure that uses a logical operator to evaluate a condition or relationship between two statements and returns a value of True or False.

Loop A set of statements that repeats for a repetition structure.

Message box A dialog box that displays a message or information and contains one or more options for the user to respond.

Method An action that can be taken by an object.

Module A container used to organize programming procedures within a project.

MoveNext A method used to advance through the records of a recordset.

MsgBox function A function that displays a message box onscreen and returns an integer to indicate which button the user clicked.

MsgBox statement A statement that displays a message box onscreen with optional buttons, icons, and title bar text.

Name property An object or control's attribute in which you reference that object in code.

Object Libraries Structures that contain the objects available in the applications that support VBA.

Object model A framework that organizes objects into a hierarchy.

Object An element, such as a worksheet cell, within a host application.

Object-oriented programming language A language that uses methods to manipulate objects.

On Current The event that is triggered by a record being loaded into a form.

On Dirty An event that is triggered when a record is being edited.

On Enter The act of placing the insertion point in a text box.

On Error Statement A statement that directs the code to skip to a particular line in the procedure when there is an error.

Operator One or more characters that performs a calculation.

Option Compare Database A statement used in a module to declare the default comparison method to use when string data is compared.

Option Explicit A statement used in a module to require that all variables be declared before they are used.

Or operator A logical operator that requires that only one condition be met to evaluate to True.

Order of precedence A rule that controls the sequence in which arithmetic operations are performed.

Posttest A test that executes the code within the loop one time and then performs the logical test to determine if the loop iterates again.

Pretest A test that performs the logical test first and then executes the code within the loop if the test is true.

Private procedure A procedure available only to a specific object or module.

Procedure A named sequence of programming statements that performs a set of actions.

Programming structure The sequence in which the program statements execute at runtime.

Project A collection of modules and objects in an Office file, such as an Excel workbook or an Access database.

Property procedure A procedure that creates or manipulates a custom property.

Property An attribute of an object that defines a characteristic. For example, a VBA form has a Height property for which the user can specify the value of the height.

Public procedure A procedure that is available to any object in the application.

Recordset A set of records in memory selected from a table or query.

Relational operator An operator that is a symbol or word that determines the relationship between two statements.

Repetition structure A structure that repeats the execution of a series of statements at runtime.

Resume Exit_Routine statement A statement that directs the code to jump to the exit line.

RowSource property A property that specifies items through an Excel worksheet range that will appear in a list box or combo box at run time.

Runtime The mode for executing a program.

Scope A designation that specifies which statements can access a variable or constant.

Select Case structure A statement that compares an expression and then executes the code for the matching case.

Sequence structure A structure that executes the statements in the sequence they are listed in the procedure.

Standard module A module that stores procedures available to an object or used by any event in the application.

Step value The number by which the counter is incremented or decremented during each iteration of the loop.

Sub procedure A procedure that performs an action but does not return a specific value.

Syntax error An error that occurs when code contains a misspelled or misused keyword, incorrect punctuation, or undefined elements.

TabIndex property A property that determines the order in which a control receives the focus.

TabStop property A property that has an attribute of True or False that determines whether a control receives focus when the Tab key is pressed.

TextAlign property A property that specifies the horizontal alignment of a caption appearing in a label.

TextBox control An object that enables the user to type data on a form.

Toolbox A palette that contains the standard controls that can be added to a form.

Unbound control A control that is not connected to a data source in the host application.

Update A method that enables you to save the changes in a recordset.

Val function A function that converts a text argument into a numeric value and returns that numeric value for display, use in calculations, or to store in a variable.

Variable A programmer-defined name that stores values that can change or vary during runtime.

VBA debugger A tool that enables the programmer to momentarily suspend the execution of VBA code.

Visual Basic for Applications (VBA) A programming language that enhances the functionality of Microsoft Office applications.

Index

+ (addition, concatenation, string
    concatenation), 26, 28
/ (division), 28
\ (integer division), 28
= (equal operator), 37
* (multiplication), 28
& (ampersand, concatenation, string
    concatenation), 26, 28
– (subtraction, negation), 28
! delimiter, 156
^ (exponentiation), 28
> (greater than), 37
>=(greater than or equal to), 37
<(less than), 37
<=(less than or equal to), 37
<> (not equal to), 37
.xlsm (Macro-Enabled Workbook file
    format), 4
.xlsx, 4

A

Access. *See also* code
    message box in, 9
    object modules, 138, 140
    objects, 7, 142–145
    VBA and, 2, 137–174
    VB Editor and, 3, 138
Activate method, 95, 96
ActiveX Data Objects (ADO), 158–159
    DAO *v.,* 158, 159
    defined, 158
    recordset, 159
AddItem method, 96
addition (+), 26, 28
AddNew method, 158
ADO (ActiveX Data Objects), 158–159
    DAO *v.,* 158, 159
    defined, 158
    recordset, 159
After Update, 167
Alt + F11, 2, 140
ampersand (&), 26, 28
And logical operator, 43–44
application, for distribution, 108–109
Application object, 94
argument, defined, 10
arithmetic operators, 28
assignment statement, 24
Auto List Members feature, 7
Auto Syntax Check, 24

B

Before Update, 144–145, 167, 169–170
black color-coding, 6
bln, 23

blue color-coding, 6
Boolean, 21, 22
Borrower Information frame, 82–83
bound controls, 81–82
breakpoints, 173
buttons, 10–12
    CommandButton control, 77
    integers returned by, 11
    OptionButton control, 77
    SpinButton control, 77
    syntax, 10
    ToggleButton control, 77
Byte, 21

C

calling procedure, 97–99
calling statement, 98–99
    returned value, 99
Call keyword, 6
CamelCase, 8, 23, 77
Caption property, 75–76
Categorized tab, 75
cbo, 78
changing references, 159
CheckBox control, 80
checking, for numeric values, 42–43
chk, 78
chkAccount, 84
Choose Builder dialog box, 141, 169
Chr function, 30
class modules
    code in, 139–140
    defined, 7, 138
Clear method, 95
Close method, 97
cmd, 78
code
    with Access object module, 140
    to activate the instructions
        worksheet, 109
    with class modules (in Access),
        139–140
    color-coding, 6, 7
    to create list, 107–108
    elements, in Code window, 5–6
    for forms (Access), 140–142,
        167–170
    for reports (Access), 140–142,
        170–174
    with standard modules (in Access),
        138–139
    syntax, 5
Code Builder, 141, 149, 169
Code window, 3
    black, 6
    blue, 6

code elements in, 5–6
    color-coding, 6
    defined, 4
    green, 6
    red, 6
collection, 74
color-coding
    black, 6
    blue, 6
    green, 6
    red, 6
ComboBox control
    description, 76
    ranges in, 82
    RowSource property and, 82
CommandButton control, 80
comments
    defined, 6
    green color-coding, 6
concatenate (+), 26, 28
conditional compiler constants, 20
conditions, 37
constants
    conditional compiler, 20
    defined, 20
    intrinsic, 20
    naming, 22–23
    symbolic, 20, 23, 24
    user-defined, 20, 23, 24
    variables *v.,* 20
Const keyword, 24
controls, 76–77. *See also specific controls*
    adding procedure to, 94–97
    adding, to forms, 76–81
    adjusting, 76–77
    bound, 81–82
    list of, 76–77
    naming, 77–78
    Toolbox and, 76, 77
    unbound, 81–82
    on worksheet, 84–85
ControlSource property, 82
conventions
    CamelCase, 23, 77
    Modified Hungarian Notation, 77
    naming constants, 23
    naming variables, 22
    programming, 6, 7
converting strings to numeric values, 26–27
counter variable, 51
cur, 23
Currency data type, 21, 22
Currency format, 29
CurrentDb statement, 158
CurrentProject.Connection, 158, 159
Customer Information worksheet, 97
custom functions, 145–146

values, assigned to variables, 24–25
variables
    constants *v.*, 20
    counter, 51
    defined, 20
    naming, 22
    Require Variable Declaration check
      box, 142
    values assigned to, 24–25
Variant data type, 21
VBA (Visual Basic for Applications). *See
    also* Help
    Access and, 2, 137–174
    defined, 2
    Excel and, 2, 73–115
    introduction to, 2–12
    launching, 2
    macros and, 1, 2, 4, 7
    as object-oriented programming
      language, 7
    uses of, 3, 138, 167
    Visual Basic *v.*, 2
vbAbortRetryIgnore, 10
VBA code
    with Access object module, 140
    with class modules (in Access), 139–140
    color-coding, 6
    elements, in Code window, 5–6
    for forms (Access), 140–142, 167–170
    for reports (Access), 140–142, 170–174
    with standard modules (in Access), 138–139
    syntax, 5

VBA debugger, 173
vbCritical, 10
VB Editor (Visual Basic Editor)
    Access and, 3, 138
    Access object module and, 140
    class module and, 139–140
    Excel and, 3
    forms/reports (Access) and, 140–142
    shortcuts to, 140
    standard module and, 138–139
vbExclamation, 10
vbInformation, 10
vbOKCancel, 10
vbOKOnly, 10
vbQuestion, 10
vbRetryCancel, 10
vbYesNo, 10
vbYesNoCancel, 10
Visual Basic, 2
Visual Basic Editor (VB Editor)
    Access and, 3, 138
    Access object module and, 140
    class module and, 139–140
    Excel and, 3
    forms/reports (Access) and, 140–142
    shortcuts to, 140
    standard module and, 138–139
Visual Basic for Applications (VBA).
    See also Help
    Access and, 2, 137–174
    defined, 2
    Excel and, 2, 73–115

    getting help and, 2–4
    introduction to, 2–12
    launching, 2
    macros and, 1, 2, 4, 7
    as object-oriented programming
      language, 7
    uses of, 3, 138, 167
    Visual Basic *v.*, 2

While keyword, 52, 53
Width property, 76
Windows Explorer, 4
With keyword, 5
worksheets
    controls inserted on, 84–85
    Customer Information, 97
    disclosure, 106–109
    Instructions, 84, 97, 108, 109
    lists in, 106–108
    loan payment schedule, 106–109
    macro-enabled, 74
    Payment, 94
    preparing, 106–107

Y

Yes/No format, 29